FRANZ KAFKA

A Biography

MAX BROD

THE BIOGRAPHY OF
FRANZ KAFKA

Translated from the German by
G. HUMPHREYS ROBERTS

" Don't despair, not even over the fact that you don't despair. Just when it seems that all is over, new forces come to your assistance after all, and just that means that you are alive."

" Passing satisfaction I can still have from works like *The Country Doctor*. But happiness only if I can raise the world into the pure, the true, the unchangeable."

" A heavy downpour of rain. Stand and face the rain, let its steel rays pierce you, float in the water that wants to carry you with it, but hold fast all the same, just stand up straight and wait for the sudden and endless shining of the sun."

From Franz Kafka's diaries.

LONDON
SECKER & WARBURG
1948

Martin Secker & Warburg Ltd.
7 John Street, Bloomsbury, W.C.1

First published 1947
Reprinted 1948

The true path passes over a tight-rope that is not stretched high in the air, but just above the ground. It seems to be intended rather to make one stumble over it, than to be walked along.

All human mistakes are impatience, premature breaking off of methodical procedure, an apparent staking off of an apparent thing.

Original Copyright 1937
by Heinrich Mercy Sohn, Prague
Copyright 1946 by Max Brod

CONTENTS

ILLUSTRATIONS

*These Plates will be found in
one section following
page 96*

FRANZ KAFKA, son of Hermann and Julie Kafka, was born in Prague, 3 July 1883. The name Kafka is Czech by origin and—in its correct spelling of "Kavka"—literally means "Jackdaw". This bird, with its big head and beautiful tail, was embossed on the business envelopes of Messrs. Hermann Kafka in which Franz in the old days often used to enclose his letters to me.

Kafka is not an uncommon surname among Jews whose families came from Czech districts, that is to say, Jews whose families lived in Czech districts at the time that the Emperor Joseph II ordered a census of all Jews. It provides no clue to the bearer's political or national sympathies. Franz's father, it is true, seems to have had a certain sympathy—though one could hardly call it a marked one—with the fighting Czech parties of Old Austria, and memories of his Czech home town may well have contributed to it. But Franz went to German schools only, was brought up as a German, and only later, led by his own inclinations, acquired a thorough knowledge of Czech and a deep understanding for its literature —without, of course, neglecting his close connection with German culture. The importance of his Jewish background, of which he later became conscious, will be discussed when the time comes. A second cousin of Franz's, very like him in appearance, in fact a sort of sturdier, stronger edition of Franz, whom Franz much admired for his systematic energy and organising ability, was a leading figure in German liberal circles when he was still a student, as well as later as a university don and member of the Czech parliament. This was Professor Bruno Kafka, who, although he died young, could point to ample evidence of a fruitful life as a critic and creative collaborator in drawing up bills of parliament, as a politician, as the editor of the posthumous scientific writings of Krasnopolski, and by his own work in jurisprudence. Franz's and Bruno's fathers were first cousins.

This is what Kafka writes about his parentage in his diary :
"In Hebrew my name is Amschel, the same as my own grandfather's on my mother's side, whom my mother, who was six years old when he died, can just remember as a very pious and learned man, with a long white beard. She remembers she had to take hold of the corpse by the toes and beg her grandfather's forgiveness for any wrong she might possibly have done him. She remembers, too, what a quantity of books

[7]

her grandfather had, and how they filled all the wall space. He used to bathe in the river every day, even in winter, when he would cut a hole in the ice to bathe in. My mother's mother died at an early age of typhoid fever. After her death her grandmother succumbed to low spirits, refused to eat, and would not speak to anyone. One day, a year after her daughter's death, she went for a walk and never came back. They dragged her body out of the Elbe. My mother's great-grandfather was an even greater scholar than her grandfather, and enjoyed the same respect among Christians and Jews. His piety was such that a miracle took place during a big fire, when the fire passed over his house, and spared it, though all the other houses round about were burnt down. He had four sons ; one turned Christian and became a doctor. All of them except my mother's grandfather died young. He had a son whom my mother knew as mad Uncle Nathan, and a daughter who was, of course, my mother's mother."

From Franz's mother, whom I often used to talk to until her death in 1934—she outlived her son by ten years—and who was a quiet, pleasant, extremely clever, not to say wise, woman, I was able to get details to complete the picture. According to her, the Kafkas, on the father's side, came from Wossek near Strakonic (South Bohemia). Hermann Kafka's father was a butcher. Hermann's youth was hard and full of hard work; obviously his capacity for work and endurance was boundless. The rest of the family, too—three brothers and two sisters—were, in the words of Mrs. Julie Kafka, Franz's mother, " giants ". All his life Franz was over-shadowed by the figure of his powerful and extraordinarily imposing father—tall, broad-shouldered—who, at the end of a life full of work and success in business, but also full of worries and illness, succeeded in leaving a large family, children and nephews, in whom he took a patriarchal pride and, after selling a wholesale business in the Old Town Square, which still exists (ED. note 1937), a block of flats in the centre of Prague. The way this family with all its ramifications was founded and kept with great sacrifice and effort in good middle-class style by nothing but its founder's own hard, thorough, careful work, always remained a shining example for Franz's imagination and creative genius. His admiration for his father in this respect was endless—it had a touch of the heroic in it ; in fact, an impartial onlooker who was not under the spell of the family circle could not but feel that it contained, alongside right and proper elements, some-thing of exaggeration too. Anyhow, it was fundamental in Franz's emotional development. How much so can be seen from the following —critical—entries in the diary which I quote because they give a good picture of how his father began life.

Franz writes :

" It's unpleasant to listen to father talking about what he had to go through as a child, with his constant digs at how lucky people are nowadays, especially his own children. Nobody denies that for years he had sores on his legs because his winter clothes were too light ; that he was often hungry ; that when he was only ten he had to push a handcart round the villages, in winter too, and very early in the morning—but, a thing he will never understand, from these undeniable facts, together with the equally undeniable fact that I have not been through all this, it doesn't in the least follow that I have been luckier than he ; that he can preen himself on these sores on his legs ; that he should take it absolutely for granted, and insist on it ; that I can't appreciate what he went through then ; and that finally I must be unboundedly grateful to him just because I never went through the same. How I should like to hear him talking on for ever about his childhood and his parents, but to hear all this in a boastful and quarrelsome tone is distressing. He is for ever beating his hands together : ' Who nowadays knows anything about it ! What do the children know about it ! Nobody else has been through it ! Is there one of you children knows anything about it ? ' To-day Aunt Julie was here, and there was the same kind of talk. She has that enormous face that all our relations on father's side have. There's just a tiny upsetting something about either the set or the colour of her eyes. When she was ten she had to go into service as a kitchenmaid. When it was freezing cold she had to run about in a wet skirt ; the skin on her legs used to chap ; the skirt used to freeze, and didn't get dry until she got to bed in the evening."

I am now going back to what Franz's mother told me. His grandmother on his father's side, a Platovsky, was described as very kindhearted ; she had a great reputation among the people of the village for her medical knowledge. In general, on the father's side the predominant hereditary characteristics would seem to be a fighting capacity for living and getting the better of life, even physical strength, too. Hermann did three years' military service, and liked to talk about his soldiering even when he was an old man—used to sing soldiers' songs when he was in a good mood—which was not very often, admittedly. His father, Franz's grandfather that is, could lift a sack of flour from the ground with his teeth. Once when some gipsies went into a lonely little inn, the terrified landlord sent for Kafka's grandfather. It was not long before he had beaten the unwelcome guests out of the place.

When we turn to the mother's family we are presented with quite a different picture. Here we find scholars, dreamers, inclined to eccentricity, and others driven by this inclination to the adventurous, the exotic, or the freakish and reclusive.

The passage from Franz's diary quoted above hints at the piety and scholarly reputation—in rabbinical lore—of his mother's grandfather and great-grandfather. Bathing in the icy river is to be regarded, too, as a rite practised by an exceptionally pious man, and not as part of a " back-to-Nature " health cult which did not exist at that time, or at any rate was unknown among the Jews. These two men belonged to the Porias family and lived at Poděbrad. The great-grandfather always wore the phylacteries, which his religion ordained, over his clothes, not under them. Children used to run after him and mock him, but were later spoken to in the—Christian—school, and told they mustn't make fun of such a pious man. The grandfather's only child, who died so young and thus probably caused her mother's suicide, was Esther Porias, and she married a Jakob Löwy. There were six children, the second eldest (Julie Löwy) became Franz Kafka's mother. The eldest brother (Alfred) went abroad as a young man, and rose, covered with decorations, to be general manager of the Spanish railways. He stayed a bachelor, often came to Prague, and had a certain influence on Franz's boyhood, chiefly because Franz hoped he would give him his start in practical life. Franz longed for far-off lands, to which in fact another of his mother's brothers had been led by his career—Joseph—who was in charge of a trading-station in the Congo, and had fitted out caravans sometimes as many as a hundred and fifty strong. He lived later in Paris, married to a Frenchwoman. What was life in their case became literature in Kafka's work, became all the exotic countries which formed the scenes of Kafka's completed works and drafts. Uncle Alfred in Madrid was reputed to be reserved, but kindly, and to have a strong feeling for the family. (I met him but retain no clear-cut impression.) How disappointed Kafka was in him can be seen in a letter to a friend of his boyhood, Oskar Pollak. Franz had asked him " If he couldn't somehow help me to get out of all this, and if he couldn't take me somewhere where I could at last set my hand to something fresh ". Franz had always looked on his legal profession solely as a makeshift, and dreamt of other activities. His relations with his uncle, to whom, we may be sure, he had only shyly hinted his youthful desires, nevertheless remained not unfriendly, within the general family coolness.

Another of his mother's brothers (Rudolf), lived a lonely crank in a little book-keeper's office in the Košiř brewery, and went over to Catholicism out of conviction. The youngest brother (Siegfried) was a country doctor in Triesch, also a bachelor, came later to Prague and settled in the house that belonged to the Kafka family, and played an active part in Franz's fate in the last stage of his life through his medical treatment of him.

Franz was born, according to his mother, in the house on the corner of Maislgasse and Karpfengasse (now Kaprová). Other childhood scenes were the Lämel Institute in the Geistgasse (Dušní), the house called " Minuta ", and the house on the corner of Wenzelsplatz and Smečky. When I went to see him first, the Kafkas lived in the narrow, twisty, ancient, but friendly building next to the Thein Church, in the Zeltner-gasse (No. 3 Celetna). His father's warehouse was also in the Zeltnergasse before it was transferred to premises in the Kinsky Palace in the Old Town Square. In Kafka's *Betrachtung* and other works of his early period, and of course in the diary, you can see the manifold impressions left by the sights and situation of this warehouse. You have only to read the sketch *Der Kaufmann*. Who are these " unapproachable people from the country " whose fashions the "Merchant" must cater for—" different from those that reign among the people in my circle " ? Hermann Kafka's wholesale warehouse stocked haberdashery for sale to retailers in villages and country towns. I remember with particular distinctness the quantities of warm slippers I saw in the warehouse when Franz, accompanied by me, made yet another vain attempt somehow to help his father, groaning under the amount of work he had, or at least to show his goodwill, to win without making a great fuss a friendly glance or a word of recognition from him. His mother herself was untiringly busy helping his father in the business, and most probably irreplaceable. I even saw one of Franz's sisters there for some time. But that was not nearly enough for his father, whose domineering character would best have liked to have his family round him all the time. How far back, and how dimly these recollections stretch! But two other homes where I often went to see Franz are quite clear in my memory—Niklasstrasse 36 (now Pařiška), overlooking the Quay, the Moldava, the baths, the bridges, and the green slope of the Belvedere ; and the Oppelt house on the corner of Niklasstrasse and the Old Town Square. Kafka's study was on the Niklas Street side, with its window right on the left of the top floor. You looked down on a more-than-lifesize baroque figure on the Russian church.

Franz was the eldest. Two brothers (Heinrich and George) died in infancy (one was two, the other a year and a half old). Six years later came the series of three sisters, who always held together and were conscious of the gap between them and their brother. Later, after Franz's illness, the youngest sister closed up this distance with the greatest firmness. She was and remained for Franz one of the most trusted and intimate of human beings—but Franz's childhood, by all accounts, must have been indescribably lonely. As his mother was busy all day in the warehouse, and his father couldn't do without her company—particularly for a game of cards—in the evenings either, Franz's education was

entrusted chiefly to governesses and soulless school. His first memories
of erotic awakening are connected with a French governess or some
Frenchwoman.

The sadness and awkwardness of his early years—"earthweight" Kafka
calls this characteristic in another connection—are described in pages in
the diary like the following from 1911, a long way back, that is to say:

"While I sometimes believe that, all through my secondary schooldays
and even earlier, I could think unusually clearly, and that it is only
because my memory later became weaker that this cannot be appraised
correctly, at other times I admit that my bad memory only wants to
flatter me and that I was mentally extremely lazy in things which are
unimportant in themselves but fraught with consequences. Thus I can
remember, anyhow, that when I was at my secondary school I often
debated, even if not very thoroughly—I got tired easily even then,
probably—with Bergmann in some fashion either following my own
inward reasoning or following the Talmud, in a way I copied from him,
about God and the possibility of His existence. At that time I used to
like tacking the debate on to an article I had found in some Christian
paper—I think *The Christian World*—in which a clock and the world
were compared to a watchmaker and God, and the existence of the
watchmaker was supposed to prove that of God. I thought I could
refute this very well as far as Bergmann was concerned, although the
refutation was not firmly founded in me myself, and I had first, before I
could produce it, to fit it together like a jigsaw puzzle. But the refutation did once take place as we were walking round the Town Hall clock.
I remember it so exactly because we reminded one another of it a few
years ago. But while I believed I excelled in that—it was only through
the urge to excel, and the pleasure in producing an effect, and in the effect
itself, that I could bring myself to do it—it was through not thinking
deeply enough that I always walked about in bad clothes which my
parents had made for me first by one customer then by another, but
longest of all by a tailor in Nusle. I noticed, of course, as it was only too
easy to do, that I was particularly badly dressed, and even had an eye for
others who were well dressed, but my brain didn't discover for years that
my clothes were responsible for my miserable appearance. As I was
already on the way, more in apprehension that in reality, to under-
estimate myself, I was convinced that it was only on me that clothes
looked either as stiff as boards or hung in creases. I didn't want any new
clothes at all; because if I had to look ugly any way, I wanted at least
to be comfortable, and further, since people were accustomed to my old
clothes, to avoid demonstrating to the world the ugliness of new ones.
These constant refusals when my mother wanted to have these new

clothes made for me, because she, with the eye of a grown-up, could after all see the difference between the old and the new clothes, also had their effect on me, as, with my parents confirming it, I couldn't help telling myself I didn't care about my appearance. In consequence, I let my badly cut clothes govern my carriage, walked about with my back bent, my shoulders crooked, and my arms and hands all over the place ; I was afraid of mirrors because, according to one of my ways of looking at it, they showed an inescapable ugliness, which moreover could not be absolutely faithfully mirrored, because if I had really looked like that I must have excited even greater attention. I put up with gentle pokes in the back from my mother on our Sunday walks, and with warnings and prophecies which were much too remote for me to be able to connect them with the sufferings I was then enduring. In general, my worst defect was an incapacity for taking the least thought for the actual future. I stayed with my thoughts firmly on the present circumstances, not out of thoroughness or from any too firmly held interest in them, but from sadness and fear—from sadness because, since the present was so sad I believed I dare not leave it until it turned into happiness ; from fear, because, afraid as I' was of the smallest present step, I considered myself unworthy, with my contemptible childish behaviour, seriously and responsibly to form an opinion about the great adult future, which, in any case, generally appeared to me so impossible that every tiny advance seemed a fraud, and the next impossible of achievement. Miracles I could admit more easily than any real progress, but was too unconcerned not to leave miracles in their sphere and real progress in its. As a result I could spend a long time before going to sleep, imagining myself one day driving into the ghetto as a rich man in a coach-and-four, and with one word rescuing a beautiful girl who was being unjustly beaten, and taking her away with me in my carriage, but undisturbed by all this make-believe which probably fed on nothing more than a sexuality which was already unhealthy, the conviction remained that I should not get through the end-of-year exam, and even if I did I should make no headway in the next class ; and even if by some swindle that could be avoided, I was bound to fail matriculation completely, and anyhow, it was quite certain, no matter at what particular moment it might happen, my parents, so far lulled by my, to all appearances, regular progress, and the rest of the world with them, would suddenly be surprised by the revelation of some unheard-of incapacity. But seeing that the only fingerpost to the future I ever looked at was my incapacity—only very seldom my feeble literary work—thinking over the future brought me no profit ; it was merely a drawing-out of my present sadness. If I wanted to, I could hold myself straight enough, but it made me tired, and I couldn't see what difference round shoulders could make to my future. If I am to have a future, my feeling was, everything will come right of itself. Such a principle I didn't choose because it gave me any confidence in the future, in the existence of which I didn't believe anyway, but rather for the purpose of making life easier. My principle was to walk, to dress, to wash, to read, above all to shut myself up in my room in the way that caused me the least trouble, and that demanded the least courage. If I departed from this principle, I only landed in some ridiculous evasion. There was a time when it seemed it was impossible for me to manage any longer without some kind of evening clothes, particularly as I had to make up my mind whether I should join a dancing-class or not. The tailor from Nusle was summoned and the style of the suit was discussed. As always in such cases I couldn't make up my mind, because I was always afraid that if I made a definite statement I might be rushed not only into some unpleasant next step but even further along into something still more frightful. So first of all I decided I wouldn't have a black suit ; but when I was put to shame in front of the stranger by its being pointed out to me that I had no evening wear at all, I allowed the question of an evening-dress suit to be brought up ; but as I felt that evening-dress was a revolution of my habits that one could just bear to hear mentioned, but could never allow to be realised, we decided on a dinner-jacket, which I thought I might at least be able to wear, because it was so like an ordinary jacket. But when I heard that the jacket had to be low-cut, which meant I should have to wear a boiled shirt, I almost overstrained myself to decide against it, knowing that this kind of thing could be warded off. I didn't want that kind of dinner-jacket ; I was prepared to have one lined with silk and with silk facings, if that had to be, but the jacket must button high. Such a dinner-jacket the tailor had never heard of, but he remarked that whatever kind of suit I was thinking of, it certainly couldn't be for going to dances in. Very well, then it wasn't for going to dances I wanted it, I didn't want to dance at all in fact ; that was a question which was far from being settled, but I did want to have a suit made like the one I described. What made the tailor even less capable of grasping my meaning was that hitherto I had had myself measured and fitted for new clothes in a kind of ashamed haste, without expressing any comments or desires. So the only thing left for me to do, particularly as my mother was insistent, was, embarrassing as it might be, to go with him across the Old Town Square to a shop window where I had seen a harmless dinner-jacket of this kind displayed for quite a long time, and had recognised it as the right thing for me. But unluckily it had already been taken out of the window, I couldn't see it anywhere inside, even after trying my hardest to peer into the shop ; to walk into the shop solely to look at the dinner-jacket I didn't dare, so we had to go back in the same state of indecision. But I had the feeling that the futility of this journey had already cast a curse on the future dinner-jacket; at least I used the annoyance of all this humming and hahing as an excuse for sending the tailor away with some small order or other, and a few words of comfort about the dinner-jacket, and stayed behind, tired, to listen to my mother's reproaches, shut out for ever—everything that happened to me was for ever—from girls, making an elegant appearance, and balls. The happiness which I felt about it at the same time made me feel miserable, and besides I was afraid I had made a bigger fool of myself in front of my tailor than any of his customers had ever done."

Franz attended the German elementary school in the Fleischmarkt, and then the German Grammar School in the Old Town Square. The latter was considered the most severe in Prague. The attendance was small. In its roomy classrooms, as there were not many pupils, naturally each one's turn came quicker and each one was asked more questions than in other luckier, lazier secondary schools. The masters were feared. I went to St. Stephen's Grammar School, and didn't know Kafka at that time, but dark rumours reached me by other routes. I saw the chillingly elegant rooms when I went to the optional French lessons, which were given for us pupils from St. Stephen's Grammar School also in the Kinsky Palace, where the premises of the Old Town Grammar School were. Years afterwards Franz sometimes told me he passed in mathematics only "by crying during the examination", and thanks to the Hugo Bergmann mentioned above in the excerpt from the diary, who let him copy his homework. Otherwise he seems to have been a really good pupil. At the Old Town Grammar School there were only good pupils, the others were mercilessly weeded out in the lower classes.

According to his mother, he was a weak, delicate child, generally serious, but nevertheless ready for an occasional prank—a child who read a lot, and didn't want to take any exercise—this last is in contrast with the older Kafka's strong interest in games and physical training.

A photograph of him as a child shows a little boy of about five, slender, with big, questioning eyes, and a dour, tight-lipped, self-willed mouth. His black hair combed straight down nearly to his eyebrows strengthens the impression of an almost threatening peevishness, with which the limp way he lets his hands droop is in keeping, but not the carefully chosen sailor-suit, the big hat, and the walking-stick.

Franz played very little with his sisters, the difference in their ages was too great and seems rather to have led to occasional quarrels. Only for his parents' birthdays little Franz wrote plays for his sisters. They were acted in the family circle, the custom lasted until they were adolescent, the sisters remember some of the plays and some of the lines to this day. One of the plays was called *The Equilibrist*, another one *George of Podie-brad*, another *The Photographs Speak*—of which the family photographs standing on the console-table form the subject. Franz never acted in them, he was only the author and stage manager. Later he suggested to his sisters that instead of his things they should do short plays of Hans Sachs which he arranged for them.

It is among the boys he went to school with that we must look for young Franz's real associates. The small class contained a few figures whose importance will appear later. There was besides Kafka, Hugo Bergmann, of whom we have already spoken, who in years to come became a famous philosopher; at present he is Professor and Rector of the Hebrew University at Jerusalem. While they were at school together, although they were in close relationship with each other, Kafka and Bergmann seem never to have recognised each other's true worth. The same is true of Emil Utitz, later Professor of Philosophy at Halle and Prague, and of Paul Kisch, literary historian, and editor of the *Neue Freie Presse*. Oskar Pollak was the only one with whom he developed a more intimate friendship, which we shall have to go into later.

Of all the impressions of Kafka's childhood the one that is of out-standing importance is the grand image of his father—exaggerated in its grandeur as it undoubtedly is by Kafka's natural genius. One of Kafka's last writings deals with this. In November 1919, when we were living together in Schelesen near Liboch—that is why I can reconstruct the mood of those days fairly exactly—he wrote a very circumstantial " Letter to My Father ". It is hardly a work that one can call a letter any more, it is a short book, but one that cannot yet be published—at the same time it is certainly one of the most remarkable and, for all its simplicity of style, one of the most difficult of documents dealing with a life-struggle. It is not easy to get to the bottom of the whole affair ; in some passages it is easy, naturally, to find some correspondence with the theses of psycho-analysis, but they are confined rather to the surface of the facts and do not go down to their deeper implications. For reasons of a personal nature this " Letter to My Father " cannot yet be given wide publicity. But the few excerpts and quotations I am able to produce already contribute something indispensable to the understanding of Kafka's development.

Although it is more than a hundred pages long, the letter, as I can testify from my conversations with Kafka, was intended actually to be handed to his father, through his mother, and Kafka was for some time of the opinion that by this letter he was doing something towards clearing up his relationship with his father which had become distressingly stagnant and painfully scabbed over. In reality the opposite would probably have happened. The explanation of himself to his father that the letter aimed at would never have been achieved. And Franz's mother did not pass on the letter but gave it back to him, probably with a few comforting words. Afterwards we never mentioned the whole affair again.

"Dear Father," the letter begins, " you once asked me why I maintain I am afraid of you. As usual, I didn't know how to answer you, partly because of this very fear I have of you, and partly because the explanation of this fear involves so many details that when I am talking I can't keep half of them together." After this there follows a most detailed analysis of the relations of this peculiar father to this peculiar child, and vice versa ; then comes a most severe self-analysis which grows, episode by episode, into a short autobiography, with special reference, arising naturally from his theme, to the years of his childhood. That is why this is just the place to quote some passages from the letter.

Kafka always set very great store by autobiographical sketches, as one can see not only from the fact that he kept a diary over long periods of his life, but also from remarks such as the following : " My urge to write my autobiography would be the first thing I should set to work and obey the moment I managed to get free of office work. Some such drastic change I should have to have in view as a temporary goal, when I begin to write, to be able to give some direction to the mass of events. Any other change than this, which is itself so terribly unlikely, that would lift me out of the rut, I cannot foresee. But after that the writing of my autobiography would be sheer pleasure, because it would go so easily, just like writing down one's dreams, and yet would have an entirely different result, a great result that would influence me for ever, and that would at the same time be accessible to the understanding and feeling of everyone else." A letter to me, in which the idea of " tracing the outline of my (i.e. Kafka's) life with complete decisiveness " was very favourably considered, points in the same direction : " The next step would be that I would hold myself together, not fritter myself away in meaningless speculation, keep a clear vision ". Thus in the case of Kafka, the desire to set his extremely complex soul in order far outweighed the ordinary pleasure a writer feels in revealing his most intimate feelings, which Thomas Mann, in his essay " Goethe and Tolstoy " once so beautifully described as a writer's inevitable failing and unconditional claim on the world, to be loved with his weaknesses as well as with his qualities. " The remarkable thing is that the world acknowledges and admits his claim." The fight that Kafka himself fought for his own perfection (he would have said against his egregious imperfection) was so hard, that he could not dream of dramatising or " arranging " things for the outside world.

True as it is that the " Letter to My Father " was written solely for the sake of the matter in hand, just as true is it that its contents, its subjective truth when confronted with the sober facts, remains in spite of everything ambiguous and ambuscaded. Here and there I feel the perspective is distorted, unsupported assumptions are occasionally dragged in and made to fit the facts ; on what appear to be negligible, immediate reactions, a whole edifice is built up, the ramifications of which it is impossible to grasp as a whole, which in fact in the end definitely turns on its own axis and contradicts itself, and yet manages to stand erect on its own foundation. At the end, indeed, the letter pretends the father himself is speaking and answering the letter in these words : " While I put the whole blame on you as frankly as I mean it, you on the other hand insist you are ' over-clever ' and ' over-sensitive ' and want to declare me, too, free from any blame. Naturally you are only partially successful in the latter—which is all you want—and reading between the lines, despite all your fine words about being, and nature, and opposition, and helplessness, it appears that I am really the aggressor and everything you did was only in self-defence. So now by your dishonesty you have already achieved enough, for you have proved three things ; firstly, that you are innocent ; secondly, that I am guilty ; and thirdly, that out of sheer greatness of heart you are prepared not only to forgive me, but, what is much more, and much less, even to go further and prove, and try and convince yourself, that I—contrary to the truth of course—am also innocent. That ought to be enough for you, but it isn't. You have in fact made up your mind that you want to live on me altogether. I admit we fight each other, but there are two kinds of fight. There is the chivalrous fight, where two independent opponents test their strength against each other, each stands on his own, loses for himself, wins for himself. And there is the fight of the vermin, which not only bite, but at the same time suck the blood on which they live. They are really the professional soldier, and that is what you are. You cannot stand up to life, but in order to set yourself up in it comfortably, free from care, and without self-reproach, you prove that I robbed you of your capacity to stand up to life, and shoved it in my pocket." (This, by the way, is an exposition in the light of which genesis of Franz Kafka's " vermin story "—The Metamorphosis (Die Verwandlung)—becomes clearer, as also that of the short story " The Verdict " (Das Urteil), etc.)

Just as in these lines of the last paragraph, the main theme of the whole letter remains unchangedly the same—it is only the question of who is guilty that takes on a different aspect in the last paragraph—and might be formulated thus : the weakness of the son is opposed to the strength of the father, who made himself entirely, and who in the consciousness of his achievement and of his strong, unbroken self through which this achievement was made, regards himself as the standard measure of the world, and that with the right of a naïve man who has never thought things out, and followed only his own instincts as far as principles are concerned—in fact to some extent a man of instinct. But a constant awareness that the opposites are not so glaring and clear cut as the "Letter", for all its efforts to do justice to the complexities of life, cannot help but portray them—this awareness which is something one takes for granted in any work of Kafka's—pervades the whole text, and stands out clearest in the words of the last sentence, which are the most reconciliatory in the discussion : "Naturally, in reality things cannot fit together so neatly as the examples in my letter, life is more than a game of patience ; but were the proofs to be corrected on the lines suggested in my objection, a proof-reading which I am unable and unwilling myself to carry out in detail, something so near the truth would be arrived at that it might comfort us both a little, and make our lives and our deaths easier ".

Apart from this reservation, the contrast between the two characters is sharply drawn. The characteristics Franz Kafka inherited from the two families he was born into, the odd, shy, quiet people of his mother's side (Löwy) and the realistic father's family, he himself describes as follows : "Just compare us ! Myself, to put it as briefly as possible, a Löwy with a certain amount of Kafka at the bottom, which however can just not be got going by the Kafka will-to-live, to do business, to conquer. . . . You, on the other hand, a real Kafka with your strength, health, appetite, decision, eloquence, self-satisfaction, superiority over the world, endurance, presence of mind, knowledge of the world, a certain largeness, and naturally with all the weaknesses and failings that go with these qualities, and in which your temperament and sometimes your temper encourage you." Compare with this the characteristics listed in another passage of what Franz considered he inherited from his mother's family : "Obstinacy, sensitivity, a sense of justice, restlessness ". What a gamut of contrasts, that can only be described as tragic, from this point to the vital portrait of the father that appears once more towards the end of the "Letter", in the passage where Kafka speaks of the failure of his attempts to get married. A comparison is made between the father and the son, according to which the father has everything he wants and the son nothing : "The chief obstacle to my marriage is the conviction, which I can no longer eradicate, that to keep a family, particularly to be the head of one, what is necessary is just what I recognise you have— just everything together, good and bad, just as it is organically united in you, viz. strength and contempt for others, health and a certain excess, eloquence and standoffishness, self-confidence and dissatisfaction with everybody else, superiority to the world and tyranny, knowledge of the world and distrust of most people in it, and then advantages with no disadvantage attached, such as industry, endurance, presence of mind, fearlessness. Of all these qualities I had comparatively almost nothing, or only very little, so how should I dare to marry under such conditions when I saw that even you had a hard struggle in your married life, and even failed, as far as your children were concerned ? Of course I didn't put this question to myself in so many words, nor answer it in so many words, otherwise I should have fallen into the ordinary way of thinking on the subject, and discovered other men who are different from you— Uncle R., to mention one in your own circle—and who have married all the same, and at least not collapsed under the strain, which is already a great deal, and would have been enough for me. But I just didn't ask myself this question, but lived it ever since my childhood. I didn't, in fact, examine myself from the standpoint of marriage, but from the standpoint of every little thing ; from the standpoint of every little thing you convinced me, as I have tried to explain, both by your example and by the way you brought me up, of my incapacity, and what turned out to be true for every little thing, and proved you were right, was bound of course, to be monstrously true for the greatest thing—marriage."

Here it seems impossible any longer to reject the connection with Freud's theories, particularly with his explanation of the " subconscious ".

And yet I hesitate and must utter my protests against finding connections in this facile way, not least of all because Franz Kafka knew these theories very well and considered them always as a very rough and ready explanation which didn't do justice to detail, or rather to the real heart-beat of the conflict. In the following lines I shall therefore try to give a different slant on the facts, and refer to the example of Kleist. First of all it must be admitted that Kafka's own remark that he had never put into so many words or into the " ordinary way of thinking ", but rather " lived ever since childhood " the question that was bound up with the superiority of the father which the son so tremendously felt, seems to confirm the psycho-analyst in his usual method of approach. The same thing applies to the picture he gives of his father's " Method of bringing up children " and the many entries in Franz Kafka's diary on the subject of how badly he was brought up, and the letters in the appendix on the bringing up of children written with reference to an essay of Swift's (" children should be brought up only away from their families, not by their parents ") represent the further thematic development of this subject.

Almost the whole of the letter is devoted to the way his father brought him up. " I was a nervous child," said Kafka, " but I was certainly sulky, too, as children are ; it is also true that my mother spoiled me, but I can't believe that I was a particularly difficult child, I can't believe that a friendly word, taking me quietly by the hand, a friendly glance, would not have got me to do anything that was wanted. Now at bottom you are a kind and gentle man (what I am about to say doesn't contradict this ; I am talking only of the appearance you presented to the child), but not every child has the patience and the courage to go on looking until it has found the good side. You can only handle a child in the way you were created yourself, with violence, noise, and temper, and in this case moreover you thought this was the most suitable way, because you wanted to bring me up to be a strong, brave boy."

The "Letter" recalls with uncanny penetration an insignificant punishment in earliest childhood, which was concerned anyhow with the child's moral rather than bodily welfare, and yet made an ineradicable impression on the son because he recognised " that I was such a mere nothing to him ". The slighting criticisms that the father let drop of the child's little pleasures, of the friends he went about with, of his whole way of living and behaviour, came to be felt as an enormous burden, and led finally to the child's despising himself. The father himself didn't follow his own criticisms and rules too strictly, and this very lack of logic appears to the son, on looking back, as a sign of unruly zest for life and unbreakable will-power. " You had worked yourself up to such a position by your own strength, that you had unlimited confidence in your own opinion. . . . From your armchair you ruled the world. Your opinion was right, everybody else's was mad, eccentric, crazy, not normal. At the same time your self-confidence was so great that there was no need for you to be consistent, and yet you were always right. You often even happened to have no opinion whatever on a subject, in which case any possible opinion on the subject must, without exception, be wrong. You could swear at the Czechs, for example, and then at the Germans, and then at the Jews, not for any particular reason but for every reason, and in the end there was nobody left but yourself. For me you developed the bewildering effect that all tyrants have whose might is founded not on reason, but on their own person."

It must be pointed out here how great a role for Kafka the principle of authority played, alongside elements of the dignity of man, that is to say Democracy, in *The Trial*, in *The Castle*, in all the short stories and fragments that belong to *The Chinese Wall*. You may well know from personal experience what a spell can be exerted by self-confident and irrational personalities, who aren't troubled about their principles or their self-contradictions, so long as one doesn't either (*a*) see through these contradictions, or (*b*) need the person as he or she is—as for example a woman one is in love with—and therefore have to put up with him

[21]

under all circumstances. The question arises, posed in sober arrogance, "What did Kafka need his father for?" Or, better put, "Why was he not able to break away from him, although he adopted a critical attitude towards him in so far as (a) of the above reasons for feeling dependent on a person doesn't apply—why didn't he seek refuge in that distance which so many children feel obliged to put between themselves and their parents ; or rather, since he did manage to put that distance between himself and his father, and in later years hardly spoke to him, why did he suffer so from this distance and coldness? Must he not have said to himself that between two such entirely different characters as his and his father's an intimate union was just impossible?" It is true Franz could understand his father, and not only value him according to his deserts, but also look on him with loving admiration. But his father was by his very nature, and of course through no fault of his own, as Kafka emphasises again and again in the "Letter", but just because of his nature, that is to say, unconditionally and finally, barred from any understanding attempt to probe his son's peculiar character. In how many talks did I not try and make clear to my friend—whose deepest wound, I knew, without yet having seen the diary, was just this—how he overestimated his father, and how stupid it is to despise oneself. It was all useless, the torrent of arguments that Kafka produced (when he didn't prefer, as he frequently did, to keep quiet) could really shatter and repel me for a moment.

Still to-day I feel that the fundamental question, "What difference could his father's approval make to Kafka?" is put not from Kafka's point of view but from an outsider's. That fact that he did need it existed once and for all as an innate, irrefutable feeling, and its effects lasted to the end of his life as "a general load of fear, weakness, and self-contempt". In the "Letter" his father's verdict is given a wholly disproportionate power of deciding the life or death of all Kafka's efforts (cf. the short story Das Urteil). The "Letter" says, "Courage, decision, confidence, pleasure in this or that could not hold out to the end, if you were opposed to it, or even if your opposition were only presumed—and presumed it might well be almost whatever I did. . . . In your presence—you are an excellent orator, the moment it is a question of anything that concerns you—I began to stammer and stutter, even that was too much for you, so finally I shut up, at first probably out of pig-headedness, later because I could neither think nor speak in front of you. And as it was you who really brought me up, it affected my whole life in all its aspects." At this point a remarkable parallel forces itself on one's attention which one might do well to consider before going on to the next stage—"Infantile-complex": it seems that Kleist, too, suffered from the same affliction of stuttering. Kafka's remark that he stuttered, can, in any case, *only* refer to his dealings with his father. When talking to anyone else, when he did bring himself to talk, that is, and broke his usual silence, he talked absolutely freely, easily, elegantly, and with a winning wealth and flow of ideas that was often playful, always astoundingly natural, and anything but " stammering ".

The result of his father's upbringing, was, according to the " Letter " (and in this passage Kafka provides his own commentary to the conclusion of his novel *The Trial*) : " In front of you I lost my self-confidence and exchanged it for an infinite sense of guilt. In the recollection of this infinity I once wrote about someone, quite truly, ' He is afraid the shame will even live on after him ' ". Kafka goes on to construe his life after this as a series of efforts to break loose from his father's sphere, to reach fields where he would be safe from his father's influence. It is worth noting that Kafka, who when passing judgement on literary work condemned nothing so severely as " constructions placed on things " which, lacking any breath of organic life that blossoms forth in ever unexpected directions, cling desperately to arbitrarily rigid and abstract combinations, himself falls into placing " constructions " on things, and dovetails into them, alongside what is genuine, also things that are half-true or exaggerated. That is why he wants to lump all his literary work together as an " attempt to get away from my father ", as though his pleasure in art and his joy in creating would not have grown of their own accord out of his own powers. To those who knew him closely, at least, he presented quite a different picture from that of a man haunted by the " father-image " ; they had the picture of a man glowingly under the impulsion of form, the desire and power to mould things, the urge to know, interest in observing life and the love of humanity. One must admit, of course, that part of the picture was what he thus describes, in deeply moving terms, in the " Letter to My Father " : " My writings were about you, in them I merely poured out the lamentations I could not pour out on your breast. It was a farewell deliberately drawn out, save that, although you, it is true, imposed it, the direction it was given *I* determined."

It is under this same aspect, of an attempt at escape, that Kafka, in the " Letter " looks at other spheres of his life—the family, friendship, Judaism, profession, finally the two attempts he made at getting married. " My opinion of myself depended more on you than on anything else, such as, for example, on any outward success. . . . Where I lived I was an outcast, condemned, defeated, and although I struggled my utmost to flee elsewhere, it was labour in vain, because I was trying to do something that was impossible, that was beyond my strength except for a few insignificant exceptions." After a general survey of the conditions of his boyhood, Kafka arrived at the following depressing characteristic of himself, a characteristic described probably much too pessimistically through retrospection, and under the influence of the " father-construction " he so stubbornly clings to in the " Letter ". He asserts he learnt little or nothing while at his secondary school—an assertion I cannot but dispute from my own private knowledge, for example of his knowledge of Greek, for we read Plato together at the university—and then continues, " Ever since I can remember I was so concerned about the problem of spiritual existence that everything else was indifferent to me. Jewish schoolboys in our country are often peculiar, you can find the most improbable things among them, but my cool, hardly hidden, imperturbable, childishly helpless, at times almost ridiculous, self-satisfied animal indifference of a child ' sufficient unto himself ', and yet coolly fantastic, I have never seen anywhere else, but all the same it was my only protection against my nerves collapsing through fear and my sense of guilt."

The " attempts to escape " will be dealt with in their proper place, though not altogether from the standpoint of the " Letter to My Father ". Only his accounts of how he tried Judaism as a way of escape from his father's domination might find room here, because they are of vital importance for his youth, and have a further general significance both for Kafka's recognition of Judaism during that period of transition, and for his later religious development. " I found just as little escape from you in the Jewish faith. Here, in itself, was a possible escape, nay more, it would have been possible for us to have found each other in Judaism, or at least for us to have found in it a point from which we could have travelled the same road. But what kind of Judaism did I get from you ! In the course of the years, I have reached to it in three different ways.

" When I was a child I agreed with you, and reproached myself for not going often enough to the synagogue, not keeping the fasts, etc. . . . I thought I was doing you an injustice, not myself, and the feeling of guilt, which was always ready to hand, overwhelmed me.

" Later, when I was a young man, I couldn't understand how you, with the insignificant fragments of Judaism you possessed, could reproach me—out of godliness, as you put it—with not making an effort to put the same insignificant fragments into practice. It was really, as far as I could see, nothing, a joke, not even a joke. On four days in the year you went to the synagogue, where you were at least nearer in spirit to the indifferent than to those who took it all seriously, went through the prayers patiently as a formality, sometimes astonished me by being able to show me in the prayer book the place which was just being chanted, otherwise, provided —that was the chief thing—I was only in the synagogue, I could twist and turn about as much as I liked. So I used to yawn and fiddle the long hours away—the only place where I have been as bored later on was, I believe, when I went to dancing-lessons—and tried my best to enjoy the few little distractions there were, such as, for example, the opening of the Ark of the Covenant, which always reminded me of a shooting-range at a fair, where there was also a box with a door which opened if you hit the bulls-eye, except that there something interesting came out, whereas here there were always just the same old dolls with no heads. Apart from everything else I was also always terrified there, not only, as you can understand, of the crowds of people one had to come into close contact with, but also because you once casually mentioned that I myself might be called on to read the lessons. For years I trembled at the thought of it. Otherwise I was not essentially disturbed in my boredom, except perhaps by the Barmizwe (Celebration of the 13th Coming of Age), which anyhow only meant a lot of silly learning by heart, in other words led only to a ridiculous kind of examination ; and again, as far as you were concerned, when you were called on to read the lessons, which as far as I could feel was a purely business affair, and got through it well, or when you stayed on in the synagogue for the All Souls Remembrance, and I was sent away, which for a long time, obviously owing to my being sent away, and a complete lack of any deeper interest in it, left one with the feeling, of which I was hardly conscious even, that there was something indecent about it. That is how it was in the synagogue. At home it was even more miserable, and confined itself to the first Eve of the Passover, which always turned rather into a comedy with fits of laughter, brought about it is true by the influence of the elder children. (Why did you have to give in to this influence ? Because you yourself had produced it, of course.) So that was the stuff that was handed on to me to build my faith out of, except perhaps your hand pointing to ' the sons of F. the millionaire ', who were in the synagogue with their father on the high festivals. What better there was to do with such material than get rid of it as quickly as possible I couldn't imagine ; in fact, just getting rid of it seemed to me the most godly thing to do with it.

" But still later in my life I saw things differently again, and understood how you could believe I was wickedly betraying you in this matter too. You really did bring something of Judaism with you out of your tiny little ghetto-like country parish ; it wasn't much, and a little of that got lost in the city and in the army, but all the same there was just enough left of impressions and memories of youth to satisfy your kind of Judaism, particularly as you didn't need much help of that kind, seeing that you came of a very sturdy stock, and, as far as you were concerned, could hardly be shaken by religious doubts unless they got mixed up too much with business doubts. Fundamentally the faith that guided your life was that you believed in the absolute rightness of the opinions of a certain class of Jewish business-men, and really, since these opinions were part of your origin, it was but belief in yourself. There was enough Judaism in that, too, but as far as your child was concerned, it was not enough to be passed on, it trickled away drop by drop as you tried to hand it on. Partly they were impressions of childhood, which are incommunicable, partly it was your dreaded person. It was impossible, too, to make a child driven to over-critical observation by sheer fear understand that the few insignificant details you performed in the name of Judaism, with an indifference which matched their insignificance, could have a higher meaning. For you they had a meaning, as little memories of old times, and that is why you wanted to hand them on to me, but could do so, since they had no more intrinsic value for you yourself, only by persuasion or threats ; that could not succeed, on the one hand, and on the other hand, couldn't fail, since you didn't realise the weakness of your position in this matter, to make you furious with me for what you thought was my intransigence.

"Anyway, the whole business is no isolated phenomenon, it's the same with most of this Jewish generation of the transition period, that has migrated from the country, which is still comparatively religious, into the towns ; it was a natural result, only that just in our case, where there is certainly no lack of bitternesses, just this one more, which is painful enough, had to be added. On the other hand, you must believe, just as I do, in your innocence in this point, too, but you must explain your innocence by your nature and the state of the times, but not simply by outward circumstances, and say for example that you had too much other work and too many other worries to have been able to bother your head about such things. In this way you always manage to twist your undoubted innocence into an undeserved reproach against other people. The argument can in this case, as in all the others, very easily be refuted. It wouldn't have been a question of giving your children any particular lessons, but of the example of your own life. Had your Judaism been stronger, your example would have been more compelling, that is obvious, and this again is not at all a reproach but only a warding off of your reproaches. You have lately been reading Franklin's memoirs of his youth. I really gave it you to read on purpose, not, as you ironically remarked, for the sake of a short passage on vegetarianism, but because of the description it contains of the relationship between the author and his father, and the relationship between the author and his son, as it finds expression precisely in these memoirs written for the son. I don't want to call particular attention to any details here.

"I got a certain delayed confirmation of this conception of your

Judaism from your attitude in the last few years, when it seemed to you that I was taking more interest in Jewish questions. Since you have as a matter of course a dislike for any of my occupations, and particularly for the nature of my interest in anything, you developed a dislike in this case too. And yet for all that one might have expected you would make a little exception in this case. It was, after all, the Judaism of your Jewish faith that was occupying my attention, and therefore there was a chance of establishing new points of contact between us. I don't deny that if you had shown any interest in them, these things would immediately have become suspect in my eyes for that reason. I haven't the slightest intention of affirming that I am any better than you in this respect. But it never came to the test. Through my agency Judaism became revolting to you, Jewish writings unreadable, they ' disgusted ' you—that might have meant that you were insisting that that form of Judaism which you revealed to me in my childhood was the only right one, one must go no further. But that you should insist on this point was hardly imaginable. In that case your ' disgust '—apart from the fact that it was felt not against Judaism, but against my own person—could only mean that you unconsciously realised the weakness of your Judaism and my Jewish upbringing, did not wish to be reminded of it in any shape or form, and reacted to all reminders with frank hatred. In any case, your negatively high opinion of my new interest in things Jewish was very exaggerated ; in the first place, it brought your curse with it ; and secondly, what was vital to its growth was the fundamental relationship with my fellow-men, in my case, in fact, it was fatal."

Alongside the father, the mother appears "in the turmoil of childhood [7] as the emblem of reason". Her un-selfassertive attitude towards the father the son complains of, but also fully understands, just as much from the point of view of love for her husband as from the point of view of the common sense of giving way to a man who anyhow cannot stand being gainsaid. But the idea that by doing this the parents formed a unity, a common front against their son, which the mother could leave only secretly even to show her love for him, that idea has left a deep mark on all Kafka's work. You can find it everywhere, look at the short story " The Married Couple " (*Das Ehepaar*) ; if you look at it from this angle, it becomes one of Kafka's most inspiring and personal works. Every word in it, rightly understood, is full of clues, from the complaints about business in the beginning to the words towards the end in which Mr. N.'s wife reminds the visitor, or rather intruder, of his own mother, and causes him to utter these words ; " Whatever you may say, a mother can do wonders. She puts together again what we have wrecked. I lost her when I was a child." And the final note, "Oh, how many steps towards failure have to be taken in business, and yet we must continue to shoulder the burden."

The odd thing is not that Kafka very early in life felt his father's character was something foreign to his own, although at the same time something highly worthy of admiration for its vitality and strength. The odd thing is that even as he was growing older he still wished above all for his father's approval, which *could* never be granted. " You have an unusually beautiful kind of quiet, satisfied smile, such as one seldom sees, which can make the recipient quite happy," says Kafka in the " Letter ". He reckons up the moments when he felt close to his father : " It was not often, of course, but it was wonderful. For example, when I used to see you on a hot summer afternoon tired after lunch, sleeping a little in the shop, with your elbow on the desk, or when you came on a Sunday, worn out, to have a little fresh air with us in the country ; or when mother was dangerously ill and you clung to the bookcase, shaken with sobs ; or when, during my last illness, you came softly to my room to see me, stopped at the door, just stuck your head in, and out of consideration for me, only waved a hand to me. On occasions like this one lay down and cried for joy, and is crying now as one writes about it." . . . He dedicated one of his books, *The Country Doctor (Der Landartz)*, to his father. Franz often recounted the reply with which his father received the book—he certainly meant no harm by it—his father said nothing but, " Put it on the table by my bed."

And what a melancholy ring the sentence in the diary has, with which Franz closes a description of an evening, of an act with which he was for once completely satisfied : after a great deal of trouble he had arranged, he thought with a great deal of prudence and success, a recitation evening in the Jewish town hall for a poor Polish Jew actor, himself made the introductory—and significant—speech. (It was the only lecture he ever gave—otherwise one can only record a reading from his own works at Munich, and a reading from Kleist's *Michael Kohlhaas* in the Toynbee Hall in Prague.) But he ends the description sadly with the words in brackets, as though spoken from the depth of his soul, " My parents were not there."

K + Proust

Life in Kafka's parents' house has many resemblances to that in Proust's house (Léon Pierre-Quint : *Marcel Proust, Sa Vie, Son Œuvre*). " Son père, parti tôt le matin, ne voyait presque pas son fils." On the other hand the mother " une femme douce . . . elle veillait avec soin sur lui, lui pardonnait d'avance ses fantaisies, les habitudes de nonchalance auxquelles il s'abandonnait." If one were to investigate what they had in common in the way their parents brought them up, one might perhaps also come upon the common roots of the similarity of outlook and style of two authors who were contemporaries, and yet never heard of one another—a fact that refers an investigator trying to co-ordinate his facts back to the darkness of the general world chaos. The unusual precise-ness of the descriptions, the love of detail, a peculiarity I might describe as " copy fever " (*Akribismus*)—the feeling of being outcasts in the family circle, even certain analogies of race (Proust's mother was a Jewess) and even of outward fate—all this challenges one again and again to make the comparison, although of course Proust's metropolitan surroundings and Kafka's bourgeois Prague led to important differences in their development.

For cases such as those of Proust, Kleist, and Kafka, who all their life long never grew out of the impressions of their childhood, and the dominating factor of their family and the family tradition, the psycho-analysts have their scheme of a subconscious erotic mother-complex, and a subconscious hate of the father. But for the infantile complex there is surely—not that I wish to exclude the co-responsibility of motives which are relevant from the psycho-analytical side—the simpler explana-tion that the parents are the *first* problem a child comes up against, the first resistance he has to assert himself against ; his arguments with them are the model for all his later fights in life. A man begins his duel with life and the world. First round : his parents. Then life sends other opponents for him to stand up to ; school-fellows, teachers, fellow-citizens, the public, the unfathomable world of women. Nothing but enemies—or at least nothing but opponents, among whom it is hard to find those who mean well ; and finding them is already itself a battle, an activity, a task, a life-test imposed upon men. The way in which the man and fighter is able to get through his first round is an indication of his future, and can be considered as a symbol of the future. By the researcher the beginnings will rightly be regarded as the real roughcasts or representations of further phases of his life, and in fact of his life as a whole altogether. While the psycho-analyst supposes that a man draws the picture he has of God involuntarily after his own father, the opposite possibility (which Heinz Politzer was the first to point out) cannot be excluded that it is just sensitive people like Kafka who have their idea of " father " enriched, enlarged, and their horizon filled by their experience of God (or rather, as I have tried to show here, by the experience of the universe which opposes and fights against them as they grow older).

" Oh, that I knew the way, the dear way back to the land of child-hood ", sings Klaus Groth set by Brahms. This longing occurs only as an occasional episode in the case of the average man, perhaps as a sign of weariness at the end of a hard day—which raises the question as to whether

[29]

a man who is tired doesn't perhaps show his character more truly than an ambitious man, or a man keyed up by the necessity of earning his living. But alongside this episodic " Back to the land of childhood ", there exists too the true infantile complex, the deciding of a man's fate by the events of his young days, from which a certain type of man never breaks loose for the whole of his life.

The child trusts his parents and wants his parents to trust him too. This is the point out of which arises one of the first great conflicts to which the soul of man is exposed. Instead of mutual trust, the world offers something entirely different—struggle, war—of how deep and glowing an emotional experience this first collision with parents and the family may be, the life of a typical infantile poet, Kleist, is an example in the grand manner. All Kleist's days the thought hung over him, " What will the family—the extension of the parent-milieu—say about my way of life ? Will they trust me ? " Of course, the discrepancy between Kleist's old Prussian family, which considered fame could be won only on the field of battle or in the seats of government, and the delicate, emotional, unstable poet who was at the same time, one can only say, tyrannised by the highest ethic principles, was enormous. He knew that in the eyes of his family his verses and dramas meant not much more than an immoral excess, the work of a ne'er-do-well. Kafka read Kleist's letters with special interest, and made note of the passages which show that Kleist's family looked on the poet as " a completely useless member of the human community, who deserved no further consideration," and remarked with silent irony that on the centenary of his death, the family laid on Kleist's grave a wreath with the inscription, " To the best of his breed."

The hearty man is inclined, shrugging his shoulders and rather disdainfully, to gloss over how intensely the sensitive man looks for confirmation of himself, and of his innermost being, for faith and acceptance, to his own family and breaks down when he feels that he isn't understood in his own home. The hearty man, you see, soon reaches a point in his development when he says to himself—rightly or wrongly—" Oh, what do I care ; my family is unteachable, incorrigible. But the world is wide. There are other courts of appeal after all. I shall show them what I am worth, and not give a damn what that lot at home think of me. . . ." Here again, though, we have a glimpse of the tragi-comedy of life. For in fact your hearty man, who gives up trying to win the trust of his family, has not gained anything very much over the sensitive man. The conflicts that the " wide world "—alas, it soon becomes so narrow—holds in store for him, are the same, almost to a T, as the first one, in which one begs for trust and doesn't get it. Whether it is your friend or your boss, the one you love above everything else, or simply your neighbour that has just one little matter to settle with you ; over and over, you would like to be recognised according to your own self, your own person, your own heart's inclination—but they always ask only what you have done, and really, if you look at it rationally, they have nothing else by which they can judge your state of mind except the manifestations of that state of mind. But you don't want to be judged, you want people to have faith in you. For every man—just like every god—demands faith on every side of him. The soul can only blossom forth to its sublime and rare capacities when it feels it is being met with faith.

This question of faith is so much the hub of things, that one philosopher —Felix Weltsch—has described the " decision of faith " as the foundation of all ethics. One cannot prove that the world as a whole has any meaning, or that it is the work of a good spirit, or that it is meaningless and wicked. This is a thing that one has only to believe or reject, with no proof whatsoever. In exactly the same way, essentially, the being, the virtue of every man is either believed or rejected, without any proof. For just in this field exact proof cannot be produced : what a man had done is subject to conflicting judgements, and often what is most useful comes from the most corrupt soul. Thus the first conflict—the vain striving to win the faith of the family—is the preformation of all the conflicts of life that follow it and at the same time includes them all. This shrugging of shoulders over the infantiles who are caught up in this very first conflict, in the van of the battle as one might say, is nevertheless not so entirely justified, as it appears to be at first sight. These " unpractical " people perhaps curtail many a long chain of doubt and distress which would only lead into the void ; they are, as it turns out in the end, not only more delicately sensitive, but also nearer truth and the deepest understanding. That is why the picture of the world given by an " infantile " poet such as Kleist was, moves us so : infantilism is no weakness in his case ; it is only a more honest, a more serious comprehension of the fatal fundamental constellation of existence, in which we all stand opposed to one another, all mistrusting one another, each one with the secret plea in his heart that one should after all have faith in him, even though he can give no proof of himself. What a number of moving situations Kleist[1] found to work up this one eternal situation, in which someone has fallen into the most shameful disgrace, in which every outward circumstance tells against him, and in which nevertheless with the utter self-surrender of a clear conscience he demands that we do not condemn him. I even have the feeling that all Kleist's work is centred round this *one* point. The ideal image of his faith is Kätchen von Heilbrunn. But just as Kätchen has faith in her

[1] And Kafka also : cf. *America*.

knight, Penthesiles wants Achilles to sense her love though all the appearances condemn her. " If only you had not mistrusted me " are her last words. And Alkmene before the husband who spurns her, Eve (in *The Broken Jug*) before her fiancé, the apparently so cruel elector before the Prince of Homburg—they all stand there burdened with acts difficult to explain away ; dark, guilty, at the very least not good acts, and yet they are innocent and have no more heartfelt wish than that their lover should recognise their enormous love. It is the fundamental situation of humanity with which, in Kleist's case, the situation of his own purely personal life grew commensurate. He had the wickedness to write verse instead of legal documents—but underneath this naughtiness and levity his family should recognise that he was a proper fellow after all. The most moving symbol he created is this : the Marchioness von O. becomes pregnant (just as genius inspires a work in the soul of the artist), she doesn't know how it happened, medical evidence is to the most positive degree against her, and yet she is innocent. Kleist is extremely inventive in piling up the evidence of guilt around his heroine with every possible argument, like the faggots round the stake of a martyr. The lightning that tears the clouds to rags and reveals blinding, snow-white innocence is all the brighter. Hence the overpowering pathos of the scene in which the father of the Marchioness of O. realises the full purity of her soul, and begs her forgiveness. What boldness guided the writer's pen, and made him—long before Freud—set down these words which one cannot read without being shaken to the core of one's being :

" The daughter motionless, her head leaned back, her eyes shut fast, in her father's arms . . . while the latter, sitting in his armchair, his wide eyes full of shining tears, pressed long, hot, and hungry kisses on her mouth, just like a lover ! The daughter said nothing ; he said nothing ; but he sat with his face bent over her, as over the face of the first girl he ever loved, and set her mouth right and kissed her. . . ."

How often may Kleist have had visions of such a scene with all the magic of wishes come true. How often has every " infantile " shared such or similar dreams with him ! That Franz Kafka's writing has several important features in common with Kleist's work, particularly as far as his prose style is concerned, which cannot at all be explained as a mere emotional echo, has often been pointed out before. But so far as I know no one has ever pointed to the spiritual nearness of their fundamental outlook. This fundamental standpoint is in the truest sense of the word so much a part of them both that even in their portraits they resemble each other, at least in so far as boyishness and purity of features are concerned. In Kafka's work, too, one finds the centre-point is " responsibility towards the family " ! This is the key to short stories like *The Metamorphosis*, "The Verdict", "The Stoker" (*Der Heizer*), and to many a detail in other works. Also the peculiar trick of setting up symbols, which are at the same time absolutely real life, is a trait common to both writers. The vision of a lady who, before the eyes of her high-born family, suffers the sea-change into a dishonoured woman-in-child is by no means so far from that of the picture of a family son whose fate is a metamorphosis into a despised species of vermin—*The Metamorphosis*.

Ties with the experiences of boyhood, ties with the family, and a strict tradition that had unconscious after-effects—which in Kleist's case was Prussian, refreshed by Kant's system—in Kafka's case Jewish ethics of justice, brought to new life by later studies. On the question of the childlike air of Kleist's portrait I put forward for comparison what Kafka once said to me : " I shall never grow up to be a man, from being a child I shall immediately become a white-haired ancient." He often em-phasised, and noted in his diary, how young he was always taken to be. A certain temporary mistrust of his sexual capacity is part of the same story—Kleist reports the same of himself. Further, the overstrain of the demands they made on themselves, as though both of them were under an obligation to prove to their families that they were not good-for-nothings. Franz's dislike of any kind of tutelage which plagued him during the last year of his life in Berlin, because he had parcels of food sent him by his parents in Prague during the starvation winter of 1923. And Kafka's highest aim in life could not be better described than by Kleist's cry full of yearning : "To farm a field, to plant a tree, to father a child." For both of them, one must admit, life ran far from the farmer's life and the simple constructive outlook they desired. The analogy can be carried still further, and shown to go right into their way of writing, in doing which sight must naturally not be lost of the fact that Kafka consciously learnt from Kleist's style. But apart from that, the community of a special kind of fairy-story-like inventiveness and weaving of a story is certainly to be set down to their dependence on early days, in which the child casts a spell on and transforms into a dream-shape everything he plays with. Both of them really knew " the way back "—and passed along it often and with pleasure. The crystal-clear style and realism of detail of both thus turns out to be the counterbalance and defence of strong natures against this inclination to dreams and childhood. In the case of both writers what is fundamentally insoluble, most secret, most obscure, is related in the clearest, simplest, most clear-cut words possible.

II

THE UNIVERSITY

" TALK comes straight out of his mouth like a walking-stick "—that
is the first remark of Kafka's that I find noted down in my diary.
Kafka was describing with these words somebody or other—who it was
I have long ago forgotten—who could never be stopped talking.

In this little note of mine I can still feel to-day my admiring astonishment at Kafka's manner. For him nothing was ordinary, always and
everywhere he expressed himself with his own peculiar gift of pregnant
observation and simile. And this he did in a completely unforced manner
without preciosity, with the most charming naturalness.

Of any burden of strained, gloomy, boyhood impressions of the
decadence or snobbishness which might easily have offered themselves as
escapes from so much depression, of a troubled or a contrite soul, no one
who met Kafka could observe any trace. What Kafka set down in the
" Letter to my Father " didn't seem to exist on the surface—or rather
revealed itself only in hints, and then only in extremely confidential talks.
I only learnt of this great sorrow, and to understand it, by slow degrees.
At first sight Kafka was a healthy young man, admittedly remarkably
quiet, observant, reserved. His spiritual bent was not in the direction of
the morbidly interesting, the bizarre or the grotesque, but in that of the
greatness of nature, the curative health-giving, sound, firmly established,
simple things.

I have experienced over and over again that admirers of Kafka who
know him only from his books have a completely false picture of him.
They think he must have made a sad, even desperate impression in
company too. The opposite is the case. One felt well when one was
with him. The richness of his thoughts, which he generally uttered in a
cheerful tone, made him, to put it on the lowest level, one of the most
amusing of men I ever met, in spite of his shyness, in spite of his quietness.
He talked very little ; when there were a lot of people he often didn't
speak for hours on end. But when he did say something, everybody had
to listen immediately, because it was always something full of meat,
something that hit the nail on the head. And in an intimate conversation
his tongue sometimes ran away with itself in the most astounding manner.
He could be enthusiastic and carried away. There was no end to our
joking and laughing—he liked a good, hearty laugh, and knew how to
make his friends laugh too. More than that, if one were in a tight corner,

[34]

one could unhesitatingly rely on his knowledge of the world, his tact, his advice, which hardly ever failed to be right. He was a wonderfully helpful friend. It was only in his own case that he was perplexed, helpless —an impression that, owing to his self-controlled bearing, one did not get in personal contact with him except in rare, extreme cases, but one which is undoubtedly deepened, all the same, when one reads his diary. The fact that from his books, and above all from his diary, such a totally different, much more depressing, picture may be drawn than when it is corrected and supplemented by the impressions one can add from living with him day by day—that is one of the reasons that persuaded me to write these memoirs. The portrait-from-life of Kafka that remains in the memory of our circle stands alongside his writings, and demands to be taken into account in any final judgement of him.

I got to know Franz Kafka in my first year at the university, that is to say in 1902-3, I suppose as early as the winter term, 1902. Franz, who was a year older than I, was beginning his second year. After leaving school he first studied chemistry for a whole fortnight, then he took German for one term, then law—this last only as a makeshift, with no preference for it, as with most of us. A plan to continue his German studies in Munich with Paul Kisch was never carried out. Law he took up with a sigh because it was the school that involved the least fixed goal, or the largest choice of goals—the bar, the civil service—that is to say, the school that put off longest taking a decision and anyhow didn't demand any great preference. On the subject of Kafka's dislike of the study of law, which he never attempted to conceal, I find the following entry in his diary (1911): " Out of an old notebook : Now in the evening, after studying since six o'clock this morning, I noticed how my left hand clasped the fingers of my right hand for a few moments, in sympathy."

In the " Letter to My Father " he connects his choice of profession, too, with his feeling of being defeated by his father, with the " chief thing ". I consider this a later interpretation ; but the kernel, the haziness and aimlessness of our youth can be clearly glimpsed in Kafka's words, behind the scaffolding of interpretation. He writes : " There was no real freedom of choice of profession for me, I knew : compared with the main point everything will be as indifferent to me as the subjects I took in my secondary school, and so the only thing is to find a profession which will give the widest scope for this indifference, without hurting my vanity too much. So the law was the obvious thing. Feeble oppositional attempts of my vanity, of senseless optimism, like my fourteen days study of chemistry, my half-year of reading German, served only to strengthen my fundamental conviction. So I read law.

That meant that in the few months before the examinations, while wearing out my nerves at a great rate, intellectually I fed myself exclusively on sawdust—sawdust, too, which had already been chewed by thousands of jaws before me. But in one sense, this was just to my taste, as in one sense my schooling had been, and later my civil service, because it all fitted in exactly with my position. In any case, I showed remarkable foresight in this case ; when I was a mere child I already had sufficiently clear presentiments about my education and my profession. I didn't expect any deliverance in this direction, I had already abandoned all hope of any."

At bottom the state of affairs was this : both of us felt ourselves honestly drawn only to creative art, but that we did not yet admit ; furthermore, we had far too high a regard for art to care to connect it with all the sordidness that lay in the words and idea of " earning one's living "—besides we had no one to guide us, no one who could show us the way, if there was a way at all. We were so without guidance that to both of us the idea that there could be any other refuge than our hated studies never occurred seriously. Least of all to me. Kafka, it is true, had something more like a vague idea—which recurred in later periods of his life—that one " should get away from Prague and start on something altogether different ".

The place of our first meeting was the " Reading and Lecture Room for German Students "—the clubroom at that time was in Ferdinand Street, now Národní. Everyone who matriculated at a German secondary school in Prague—and in many places in the provinces— became a member of this big students-union as a matter of course unless he were an anti-semitic nationalist or a professed Jew. (I myself didn't take up Zionism till much later, some ten years after.) The " Hall " belonged to the German Freedom Party. We didn't wear any caps, it is true, but we did wear the black, red, and gold ribbon, with the date of the revolution, 1848. But how faded, how lukewarm was the memory of this revolution ; indeed it never rose above the horizon. The most important component of the " Hall " was the Hall Committee, between it and the members there existed a certain antagonism, in fact at times a kind of " battle ", which, however, invariably ended in the crushing and utter defeat of the members ; for at the general meeting there always turned up in a body the " Couleurs ", the corporations that wore colours, and which belonged to the " Hall " by a very loose tie, and who never otherwise bothered their heads about the life of the club. For the voting however they were there in full number and voted unanimously for the committee list—to our disgust, which we felt afresh each time, against this voting-machine which was run according to an exact, preconceived plan by the committee's great tactician, Bruno Kafka. They never took any part whatsoever in the debates, and complaints made by the despised "chaffinches"—that is to say, those who wore no colours—against the committee, however justified they might be, didn't interest them; they contented themselves with making their irrevocable wishes known through the mouths of their doughty whips. And the committee remained unshaken in their seats as always.

Franz took no interest in this childishly ambitious game, it was not until his later years that I first heard him mention even that he was related to Bruno Kafka—to the accompaniment of his admiration for the man's energy. And yet it was the conduct of this batrachomyomachia that brought us together for the first time. The centre of resistance to the committee was, in fact, the "Section for Literature and Art", which led an independent life in some respects, and was dependent on the vote of the committee only in matters of finance—which led to specially violent quarrels; I remember, for example, that the committee refused to approve the fee, or at any rate to approve a sufficiently high fee for Detlev von Liliencron, whom we had invited to lecture in Prague. As opposed to the committee with its ball-committees and its "Winers", we in our section, whether rightly or wrongly, considered ourselves the bearers of the spirit. The section held its regular debates and read papers regularly in its own circle. On one of these evenings I, straight from school, made my debut with a paper on "Schopenhauer and Nietzsche" which created some stir. As the bitter and fanatical adherent of Schopenhauer that I then was, and as such I considered the slightest contradiction of the tenets of the philosopher I worshipped as nothing less than lese-majesty, I spoke of Nietzsche quite simply and baldly as a "swindler". (I have, by the way, remained to this day true to my antipathy to Nietzsche, even if with reservations and in a different sense.)

After this paper Kafka, who was a year older, saw me home. He used to take part in every meeting of the "Section", but until then we had hardly taken any notice of each other. It would indeed have been difficult to notice him, because he so seldom opened his mouth, and because his outward appearance was above all deeply unobtrusive—even his elegant suits, which were mostly dark blue, were as unobtrusive and reserved as himself. But that evening something about me seems to have attracted him, he was more communicative than usual; anyhow the endless conversation that went on while seeing me home began with a strong protest against the extreme uncouthness of my way of putting things. From that we went on to talking about our favourite authors, and defended them against one another. I was enthusiastic about Meyrink. At school I modelled myself on the classics, and rejected everything "modern", but in one of the upper classes I swung round, and at this time in a proper "storm and stress" mood, I welcomed everything that was out-of-the-way, unbridled, shameless, cynical, extreme, over-caustic. Kafka opposed me with calm and wisdom. For Meyrink he had no time.[1] Well, I quoted him "purple passages" by heart. One from Meyrink's *Purple Death* compared butterflies to great opened-out books of magic. Kafka turned up his nose. That sort of thing he considered too far-fetched and much too importunate ; everything that suggested that it was planned for effect, intellectual, or artificially thought up, he rejected—although he himself never used labels of this kind. In him there was something of the "softly murmuring voice of Nature" of which Goethe spoke, and it was that he liked to hear in other writers. As a contrasting example—as what he himself liked—Kafka quoted a passage from Hoffmannsthal, "the smell of damp flags in a hall". And he kept silent for a long while, said no more, as if this hidden, improbable thing must speak for itself. This made so deep an impression on me that I remember to this day the street and the house in front of which this conversation took place. There may be a number of people who manage to find in Kafka's work an affinity with writers like Poe, Kubin, and Baudelaire, writers of the "night side of life", who will be astonished to hear that it was just to simplicity and naturalness of feeling that my friend guided me, and led me gradually out of my confused and corrupt state of mind, puffed up with childish pride and a completely false assumption of a blasé air. But that is how it was. Indisputable documentary evidence is the letter I quote below, I think the first Kafka ever wrote me. I can't give its exact date, because its envelope is missing, but it must be before 1906 (the year Kafka took his degree) because he mentions going to lectures still.[2]

It gives you some idea of Kafka's gracious character, ready to under-

[1] He had just as little for Wedekind and Oscar Wilde—but he loved Thomas Mann's *Tonio Kröger*, and reverently searched out every line of this author's in the *New Review* ; he read Hamsun, Hesse, Flaubert, and Kassner with enthusiasm. Among favourite authors of his later years I can name Emil Strauss, Wilhelm Schäfer, Carossa (in saying this I have no wish to express approval of their development after Kafka's death), also Hebel's *Little Treasury*, Fontane, Gogol, Stifter—and above all, constantly, Goethe and the Bible. Other authors of Kafka's preference are to be found in the appropriate passages in this biography.

[2] The handwriting, too, points to the letter being from the earliest period of our acquaintance, it is written in Gothic characters—later Kafka used Latin characters. His handwriting went through various stages of development in the course of years. The Gothic flourishes in the beginning accord with the rich, rounded off, decorated, occasionally precious, style of his prose. In accordance with this, the letters to Oskar Pollak, written in a still earlier period are written in a still more ornamental handwriting. The period of his spacious Latin handwriting is the period of comparatively peaceful maturity and mastery. MSS. from the last few years often reveal the use of a fine pen, tiny characters, speed, as though overwhelmed by the richness of his inspiration.

stand other people's views, tolerant, for all his severity about his own life, if you read how gently the letter puts me in my place, how he localises the attitude he reproves—one of cheap romanticism and gross seeking after effect—which he describes as a " Wolves' Glen "—not in myself but in the people who surrounded me at that time, and who recognised a ringleader in me.

" DEAR MAX—Particularly because I was not at lectures yesterday, I feel it is important to write to you to explain why I didn't come with you to the evening at the Redout, although I did perhaps promise to do so.

" Forgive me, I wanted to give myself the pleasure of bringing you and Pr. together for one evening, because I thought there would be bound to be some lovely combinations when you, carried away by the impulse of the moment, made hyper-sarcastic remarks—you do that when you are in company—and he on the other hand, with the sensible grasp he has of almost every point except art, would give you the right answer.

" But when I first thought of it, I forgot your crowd, the little crowd with whom you go around. To the first glance of a stranger it doesn't show you up to advantage. Because it is partly dependent on you, and partly independent. In so far as it is dependent, it stands around like a receptive mountain range with a ready echo. That puts the listener off. While his eyes would like to busy themselves peacefully with the object in front of him, he is attacked from the rear. In this case he cannot but lose his ability to enjoy either, especially if he doesn't happen to be more than usually agile.

" In so far as your companions are independent, they do you still more harm, because they caricature you. Through them you are not seen in your proper perspective ; as far as the listener is concerned, you are defeated through yourself, to which the wonderful moments when your friends are consistent contribute ; friendly crowds are only useful in a revolution when they all play their parts simultaneously and simply, but when there is a small uprising by a straggling light at a table, they ruin it. This is what happens when you want to show your conversation piece, ' Landscape at Dawn ', and put it up as the backcloth—but your friends think the ' Wolves' Glen ' would be more suitable, and they set your 'Wolves' Glen ' up in the wings. Of course you painted both pictures, and every onlooker can recognise that, but what disturbing shadows there are on the meadows of a ' Landscape at Dawn ', and foul birds fly over the field. That's what I think about it. It doesn't happen to you very often, but it does happen from time to time (and I still don't quite understand this) that you say, ' Look at Flaubert ! There you have nothing but discussions about facts, you see, there is no sentimental nonsense.' How odious I could make you appear if I used it in this way some time or other. You say, 'How beautiful *Werther* is !' I say, 'But if we are prepared to tell the truth, there is a lot of sentimental nonsense in it after all '. That is a ridiculous, unpleasant remark, but I am your friend when I say it, I don't wish to do you any harm, I only want to tell the listener your whole opinion on such matters. For it may often be a sign of friendship not to take a friend's pronouncements too seriously any more. But meanwhile the listener has become sad and tired.

" I have written this because it would be still sadder if you didn't forgive me for not having spent the evening with you than if you don't forgive me for his letter ; my love to you, Your FRANZ K.

" Don't put it away yet, I have read it through once more and see it is not clear. I wanted to write : What a wonderful stroke of luck for you that you can safely venture to grow careless when you are feeling tired, and yet be led to the point you are striving to reach without taking a step yourself, through the help of a friend who absolutely shares your thoughts ; that is just the thing, when it is made a display of—that was what I thought to myself at Pr.'s—that shows you as I don't want you to be. That's enough of that now."

Absolute truthfulness was one of the most important and distinctive features of his character. Another distinguishing feature was his un-imaginably precise conscientiousness. *Conscientia scrupulosa.* It revealed itself in all questions of a moral nature, where he could never overlook the slightest shadow of any injustice that occurred. From the very beginning one is reminded of debates in the Talmud ; this method of reasoning was foreshadowed there too ; at the same time, he didn't get to know the Talmud itself until much later on in life. Many of his works exhibit this trait, for example, " The Runners-by " (*Die Vorüber-laufenden*), in which the possibilities are discussed which could have led to one man's running behind another man in the night, but not running after him—or the great scene in *The Trial*, in which the motto, " Before the Law ", is discussed from various angles.

There were times when Franz himself could not get over tiny scruples, was afraid he had done this, that, or the other wrong, and admired, *e contrario*, every decision, particularly decisions concerning marriage, to an exaggerated degree. At the same time, as far as his own person was concerned, he was brave, a good horseman, swimmer, and oarsman. His conscientiousness therefore arose from no cowardice, but from an unusually developed sense of responsibility. I remember going out for the evening with him once immediately after the news that Italy had declared war on Turkey (Tripoli) had been published. We were in the theatre. Franz was unusually restless. During the interval he suddenly said, " Now the Italian battleships are taking up position before the undefended coasts ". And the sad smile with which he said it ! The condition of contemporary humanity seemed to him hopeless and desperate. And yet for all his deep pessimism one must not overlook his joy in everything that was healthy and growing, his interest in every kind of reform—e.g. in the methods of natural healing, in modern methods of education, such as the Montessori system. In the authors of the " night side ", of the decadence, he felt as we have already said, not the slightest interest. It was to the simple positive forms of life that he was powerfully attracted. Among his favourite books were Stifter's *Indian Summer* and Hebel's *Little Treasury*. In him there was a rare mixture of hopelessness and constructive urge which in his case did not cancel each other out but rose to endlessly complicated visions.

The artistic counterpart of the preciseness of his conscientiousness is the attention he gives to detail in his descriptions. You can see it in every one of his books. He loved detail. Under his influence I wrote a long descriptive novel which went into every detail, called *The Thousand Pleasures*—Franz and I sometimes called it also *The Happy Ones*. Franz used to be enormously pleased every time I read him a new chapter I had finished, and urged me to go on with it (1909). I finished the book, but I never published more than one chapter of it, in a magazine, " Under the Intoxication of Books," a description of the university library—because in the end, despite lively protests from Kafka, the whole thing seemed to me too monstrous. Kafka's preference for thoroughness, for descriptions that ranged far and wide, was characteristically displayed in his life too. He was often late for appointments ; not out of unpunctuality, but because he had felt the need to settle some other business absolutely exactly before leaving it. There was nothing that was unimportant, nothing that he would just " leave at that ". He could no more be unjust to a thing or an everyday piece of work than he could to a human being. That was why when one was with him one had the impression strongly that nothing vulgar or " common " existed at all. Saints and founders of religions are said to have affected people similarly—and going about with Kafka has convinced me that such reports are based on real experience. The category of holiness (and not really that of literature), is the only right category under which Kafka's life and work can be viewed. By this I do not wish to suggest that he was a perfect saint—that would be, even in his own sense, a thoroughly false, not to say iniquitous statement. But from the many indications, even taking all the proper caution that every step on this the last crest of human nature demands even from the observer himself, one may pose the thesis that Franz Kafka was on the road to becoming one. The explanation of his charming shyness and reserve, which seemed nothing less than supernatural—and yet so natural—and of his dismayingly severe self-criticism, lies in the fact that he measured himself by no ordinary standard, but simply measured himself up against the ultimate goal of human existence. Here, too, we can find one of the motives that held him back from publishing his works.

A characteristic that places him in the category of a saint was his absolute faith. He believed in a world of Rightness, he believed in " The Indestructible " of which so many of his aphorisms speak. We are too weak always to recognise this real world. But it is there. Truth is visible everywhere. It glints through the mesh of what we call " reality ". This explains Kafka's deep interest in every detail, every wrinkle of this reality. In the diary there are to be found pages and pages of notes on the appearance, features, etc., of indifferent people, people sitting opposite him in the train, for instance. Immediately bound up with this interest is a pervading irony. Even the most gruesome episodes in Kafka's writings (*In der Strafkolonie, Der Prügler* (Chap. V *The Trial*) stand in a curious twilight of humour, an investigator's interest and tender irony. This humour, which is an essential ingredient of Kafka's writing (and of his manner of living), points through the meshes of reality to the divine existence beyond. His faith in this existence, never expressed in formulae, and never in a clumsy appeal to emotion, expressed itself in all his actions, made him at heart inwardly certain of himself, although he was fond of presenting himself and others with a picture of the uttermost uncertainty, made him above all spread around him a sweet aura of certainty such as I have only very rarely felt elsewhere.

In everything he came into contact with Kafka looked for that which was important, that which came from this world of truth. That is why he was the best of listeners, the best of questioners, the best of readers and critics. How remote from his way of looking at things was all the talk about the " standards ", " literary hallmarks ", " distinction of rank ". In every case he hit upon the essential. He could be carried away by a turn of speech in a newspaper article ; with passionate enthusiasm he would dilate on the crowded life, the eye for drama, in some novel by some author or other who was generally sneered at as " cheap ". I remember how, that time we were staying together in Schelesen in the Stüdl boarding-house, he produced a novel by Ohnet from the boarding-house library and, with great enthusiasm, read me a passage—a conversation—which he praised for its unforced liveliness. Odd passages in a musical comedy or a conventional film that had somehow come off and taken on organic shape as if by a miracle (the Muse had thrust the wretched author's pen on one side, and written a few lines herself) could move him to tears. He was an entirely independent explorer, who had not the faintest idea of being tied down by the insensitive classifications of histories of literature.

He passed judgement on people and conditions in exactly the same way. He had neither a prejudice in favour of going with conventional opinion, nor a prejudice in favour of going against it on principle. The most refreshing thing about him was that he was completely unparadoxical—in fact antiparadoxical. His judgement had a certain elemental simplicity, naturalness, obviousness. It was easy and sure, although he delivered it with great care and was extremely, even passionately, ready to acknowledge a mistake.

In people, too, who were considered contemptible by the world in general, he saw admirable single qualities. He never lost patience, one might say, with any man. And in great men, whom he himself admired, he found ridiculous features. But when he emphasised comic details of this kind, there was never any suggestion of holding them up to derision in it, but rather a quiet tear and regret, or acknowledgment of something incomprehensible which passes our earthly understanding. The love he felt for Goethe and Flaubert never changed in all the two-and-twenty years I was a close friend of his. In the case of some writers, such as Hebbel and Grillparzer, Kafka liked their diaries better than their works— or so it seemed to me, at least. I have never heard him pass disrespectful remarks against the great, never heard him use the method of bluff which is so popular nowadays, and which consists in an impertinent and effectively delivered sneering reference to a writer's " youthful period " and his " puerilia ". In this respect one may well say that Kafka had a very clear idea of the difference in rank there is among people. Only he also knew how easily the divine—and also the devilish—sparks overleap these classifications according to rank. And since he was too conscientious ever to simplify the picture of the world for himself, he watched this " overleaping " with a zeal for knowledge which one can only describe as fanatical.

His preciseness did not come from any cowardice which had to hide behind ideas, and was also not pedantic like Zola's preciseness. It was a quite special preciseness of genius, the peculiarity of which at first dumbfounded one, striking as it did a road which had previously lain hidden and which one had least expected, and then following this road with astonishing consistency right to the end—but in such a manner that one admitted that it was not capriciousness, it *was* a road of natural importance. Every chapter in *The Trial*, in the other two novels *The Castle* and *America*, and in the unfinished short stories demonstrates this astounding peculiarity of Kafka's plastic gift.

He never pointed the way out to you by saying : " Look, that is the right road "—or even by saying as much as, " That is a road, too." He simply marched on with firm step, realistically, without using philosophical terms (for his thinking, as his wonderful diary shows, was generally done in the form of images), absorbed only in observing the detail which the everchanging vistas of the road crowded in on him.

The strangeness of Kafka's person and writing is only apparent. In fact, one should add, anyone who finds Kafka singular and attractive on account of his *bizarrerie* has not yet understood him, or perhaps may be in the first stages of understanding him. Kafka traced to their source the individual and the unobvious with such love and preciseness that things came to light which one had never before suspected, which seem strange indeed and yet are nothing but true. Such, too, was his way of looking at a moral duty, a fact of life, a journey, a work of art, a political movement—never bizarre, but only very exact, keen, right, and in consequence different from everyday talk, in consequence, perhaps, also quite often (though not perhaps always) unsuitable for what one calls " practical life."

There is no more pregnant contrast to Kafka than Balzac's sham preciseness, Balzac's superlatives and generalisations (something after this style : " She walked along with that light tread with which every Paris woman walks between ten and ten-fifteen in the morning ").

It is superfluous to point out (superfluous that is for anyone who has even half followed the above) that Kafka found much to admire in Balzac. For he never lost the grand line in the mass of details nor the sweep of a way of life. Kafka once said : " Balzac carried a stick with the motto, ' I break every obstacle '—my motto would rather be, ' every obstacle breaks me '."

This would be the right place to drag in a long list of remarks on Kafka's weaknesses which, however, on the whole, spring in the most tragic fashion from his good qualities. By discussing the one feature of his character " preciseness ", I have indicated only one side of his being. One could go on explaining and explaining (people will undoubtedly do so), but necessarily without coming to an end. It is like walking for ever along a wall without a door—one can never penetrate the inside of the building. But even this endless and vain explaining does give some kind of picture of Kafka's personality, gives a picture at the same time of its force, its weight, its inexhaustibility. This is the same method, by the way, in which Kafka portrays his characters, without ever explaining them to the end.

Of course I can now no longer sort out exactly how my opinion of Kafka developed and was perfected in the course of the years—what was there from the very beginning and how gradually it grew. I know only this ; in the beginning our relations developed very slowly, and it took some years before we became really intimate.

It began with a decision we made not to let the Greek we had picked up in our secondary schools get too rusty. Together we read Plato's *Protagoras* with the aid of translations and our school dictionary—often with a great deal of difficulty. At that time I never got as far as the real meaning which Plato was to have for me much later—long after Kafka's death ; what we enjoyed chiefly was undoubtedly nothing more than the vivid and scurrilous description of the life of the Sophists, and the Plato-Socratic irony. If the reading of Plato was due to my inspiration (for I have been drawn to this great star at various periods in my life), it was Kafka who, to my gratitude, brought Flaubert to my attention. This great love I inherited from him. We read *A Sentimental Education* and the *Temptation of St. Anthony* in the original. As we could find time for these studies only two or three times a week, we went on together with this work for years, and it provided us with continual fresh material for a long time. Our reading parties generally took place in Kafka's little room in his parents' house (in Zeltner Street) and sometimes at my place. Over Kafka's desk there hung a copy of the picture by Hans Thoma, " The Ploughmen ". On the wall at the side there was a yellowing plaster-cast of a little antique relief, a Maenad, brandishing a piece of meat—a leg of beef, to be precise. The graceful folds of her dress danced around the figure, which had no head. All that I still see before me just as my eyes swept over it countless times. I have described it in my novel *The Kingdom of Love*, in which Kafka appears as Richard Garta, together with the simple, almost miserly furnishings of the room which were of an almost provisory nature. " The whole not uninhabitable, but not perhaps comfortable for people who want the conventional ornaments and luxury." This modest furniture accompanied Franz to all his lodgings in Prague : a bed, a wardrobe, the little, old, dark-brown, almost black, desk, with a few books and a lot of unarranged note-books. His last room (in Niklas Street) had, at least, a second entrance, which Kafka generally used, through the kitchen and the bathroom. Otherwise he didn't live apart from the rest of the family, which was certainly not healthy for the conflicts that were ever inwardly consuming him. In later years he tried to get away from the spell of not being independent by taking a room of his own in a different district. (Proust lived in the room of his childhood until he died.)

The above-mentioned picture by Thoma, a " Kunstwart " print, bears witness to the great influence that a friend from his secondary schooldays, Oskar Pollak, had on Kafka at the time when I first got to know him.

Pollak had gone deeply into the theories of the " Kunstwart " series of handbooks, which were edited by Avenarius, and out of which later the Dürer League grew. At the university Pollak began by reading chemistry ; that Kafka, too, began with fourteen days of chemistry, happened most probably for the sake of Pollak, whose special gifts of leadership are hinted at also in Franz's letters to him. Pollak afterwards went to Vienna and Rome as a historian of art ; baroque and modern art, the architectural history of Prague and Rome were his chief fields of activity and he furthered them by important work of extraordinary scientific import, founded on meticulous studies of sources. The young professor fell on the Isonzo front as a volunteer in the Austrian army in 1915. Among the riches of his posthumous papers was found, ready for print, the manuscript of a two-volume work on " Art Activities under Pope Urban VII ", which has since been published, as well as drafts of MSS. on the papacies of Innocence II and Alexander VII, preliminary notes for a bibliography of the guide-books of Rome, and the beginnings of a collection of material for a monograph on Pietro da Cortona, and other fragments. One of the wild ironies of war—the scholar who had devoted most of his life to the love of Italian art, must needs end his life by Italian bullets ! In the *Neue Züricher Zeitung* of 27 August, 1915, J. A. F. Orbaan, of Geneva, paid honour to the man who died " crowned with the halo of science ". After praising several essays of his, e.g. the keenly critical tone of his " Architects' Fairy Stories ", he goes on : " It is no wonder that we so tensely awaited the publication of the *Sources of Baroque*, which he had planned in the grand manner, and the first volume of which, dealing with a section of the art life of Rome, he had reserved for himself, and which was to be followed in a reasonably short while by a critical edition of Baglione's *Careers of Artists*. We knew that our excellent colleague was, in the first place, on intimate terms with the actual works of art, through his many wanderings in Rome and about it, an advantage which not all art historians possess, because the libraries and the archives often claim all their strength. We knew it from our daily meetings with him when we saw his kindly, tanned face in the Vatican early in the morning, after he had the previous day collected together in out-of-the-way parts of Latium a rich booty of notes and negatives of the country seats and churches of the Barberini. With the same spirit of enterprise he would then sit down to a pile of books of the managing board of the Fabbrica di San Pietro, the Barberini library, the Papal Treasury, or of rare books of the Seicento, completely at home with the book-keeping of antiquity and able to decipher the cacography and technical language of master-builders and master-painters long since passed away. A learned conversation with the ever-interested Pollak on the remote theme of the palaeography of baroque was always worth while. He achieved astonishing results in the interpretation of entries written almost in shorthand, which you find here and there in some firm's books, where important information about Gian Lorenzo Bernini may be waiting round the corner at any moment. But with all this work, that demanded a severe daily dose of research into manuscript sources and other literature of the same kind, Pollak never had anything about him of the superfluous, and always awkward, self-importance of the savant. He was in deadly earnest, and he brought every ounce of effort and brain-power to bear on his work, but his studies did not make him any the less capable of enjoying the pleasures and excitement of the moment and these were offered him in plenty by his marriage with a witty and affectionate young wife, who showed a fine understanding for what he was striving to do, and by the time he spent in the company of a wide circle of friends and acquaintances including people of the country."

This, then, was the man who won a decisive influence over Kafka in his younger days. To complete the picture I shall quote from an obituary by Hugo Bergmann (*Bohemia*, 4 July, 1915). "The richness of his interests was inexhaustible ; but to whatever it might be that got hold of him and carried him away at one time or another, he devoted himself completely, forgot everything else for its sake, and in no time became a disciple and a gospeller. In this way he studied the Upanishad, the Bible, Luther, St. Francis of Assisi, the Italian short-story tellers of the Renaissance—with what purity he could read the *Decameron* to us—in this way he took up playing the guitar, and sport of various kinds." I hear he was one of the first to take up ski-ing in Bohemia.

I myself remember Oskar Pollak as a young man who passed severe judgements and knew his own mind. Despite his nineteen years he wore a full beard. This, I now discover after my researches, he later discarded together with a certain abruptness and stand-offishness of manner, which at that time made any approach to him no easy matter. Him, too, I met in the " Hall ". On that occasion he recommended to me the " Rembrandt-German ". The most serious Jewish intellectualism, unconscious of its origin, revealed facets, at that time, which had many analogies with, and tried to take lessons from, a Teutonism that was groping into the past for its pure wells of strength. So far as I know, Oskar Pollak never bothered himself with truly Jewish questions, and it was not until very much later that Kafka and I came to this our home-ground. The love of Teutonism led, in all honesty, and so to speak, innocence of heart, occasionally also to pure Teutomania. For example, in one of Kafka's letters to Oskar Pollak you may find the following passage, which sounds odd to the ear of a connoisseur of Kafka's later style :

"Just opposite the vineyard, on the road, deep in the valley, stands a tiny cottage, the first and the last in the village. There isn't much in it. Between you and me it's worth at the outside a miserable hundred shillings. And what is still worse even not Schultze-Naumburg could find a use for it, unless, at most, as a hideous warning. In all probability I and the owner are the only people who love it and weave our dreams about it. It is small and squat. It isn't even old. On the contrary, it's a modest five or ten years old at most. It has a tiled roof, a tiny door, through which one can obviously only crawl, and a window on either side. Everything is symmetrical, as though it had crept out of a school text-book. But—the door is of heavy wood, painted brown, the shutters are painted brown, and always shut, by sunshine or by rain. And yet the house is inhabited, too. And in front of the door is a broad, heavy, stone bench, which appears to be almost old. And when one day three apprentices come along with their sticks in their hands and their all-too-light knapsacks on their backs, and sit down on it to rest, and wipe the sweat from their brows, and then lean their heads together—I can see all this quite well from up above—then it is like a dear, old, peaceful German fairy story."

The influence of the works of art and art-values which "Kunstwart" propagated is here clearly revealed in every detail. When it concerns a writer who, like Kafka, so early developed his own quite personal attitude in which scarcely a trace of outside influence can any longer be felt, to know of this beginner's stage of dependence strikes one as nothing less than grotesque, and, at the same time, touching, it seems to me.

The letters to Oskar Pollak are from the years 1902 till 1904. In this case Kafka wooed the friendship ; in his friendship with me, which broke up this first strong spiritual tie, things were rather the other way round. At least, Kafka was the stronger partner in our friendship, if through nothing else than his calm and reserve, even though a foundation of equality of rights was cheerfully acknowledged on either side. It is with astonishment that I learn from Kafka's youthful letters to Pollak that he himself offered to send him his writings, or to read them to him. That never happened later—one had to plead hard with Kafka, and bring fervent pressure to bear on him before one could get him to show one anything in his MSS. This attitude was not, all the same, founded on pride, but on immoderate self-criticism. It began very early with him. Thus the fifth letter to Pollak is followed by an unpublished one, from which I quote with the additional inducement that they tell us something about these first works of Kafka's which have not survived : "Of the few thousand lines I am giving you there might be perhaps ten that I could listen to patiently, the flourish of trumpets in my previous letter was unnecessary, instead of a revelation is born childish scribbling. . . . The greatest part of it, I openly say, I find repulsive. ' Morning ', for example, and other bits, too—I find it impossible to read it all, and I am satisfied if you can stand odd samples. But you must remember I began at a time when one ' created work ', when one wrote high-flown stuff ; there is no worse time to begin. And I was so mad about grand phrases. Among my papers there is a sheet on which are written all the uncommon and particularly impressive names I could find in the calendar. You see I needed two names for a novel, and chose finally two, underlined, Johannes and Beate—Renate had already been snatched from under my nose [1]—because of the size of their halo. It is almost funny."

In this letter there are some mischievous remarks about another schoolfellow, who had an inexhaustible store of words—" they were bars of iron, and I was driven to despair when I saw how easily he threw them around. There was no hope of my approaching it, and I swear in all my life I have never again been so jealous as I was then." This is followed by even severer self-criticism. " There is one thing that is entirely missing in these copy-books, that is hard work, perseverance, and whatever all these strange things are called." In the next paragraph he writes again, " What I lack is discipline. That you half read the copy-books is the least I want from you to-day. You have a lovely room. The little lights from the shops below twinkle, tucked away, and busily. I want you to let me read to you there every Saturday, beginning from the very next Saturday as ever is, for half an hour. I am going to work hard for three months. Above all, I know this now : Art needs hard work more than hard work needs Art. Of course I don't believe that one can force oneself to give birth, but one can force oneself to look after the children."

I don't know how Oskar Pollak received the works of Kafka which were submitted to his severe judgement, whether he admired him as I did from the very start ; to be honest, as I felt I had to admire him. Oskar Pollak's interests certainly lay in rather a different direction from Kafka's fantastic microcosm, which, particularly at that period, had a specially whimsical air—it was just the extraordinariness, the unrepeatable newness of it that pleased me—the first friend of his youth, who left Prague very soon afterwards, was drawn to great things, to the laws of science. So Kafka's cry of longing fell at first on deaf ears—the cry that rings so movingly through the letters and thus early anticipates the later longing for community. " You will never do anything without other men " : " To become a hermit is abhorrent ", and the polemic, which affects one, one can only say like prophesy, against " the Mole ", which

---

[1] Allusion to an early work of Wassermann's.

became a symbol in Kafka's late period. " I know that, were a pair of stranger's eyes to look at it, they would make each thing warmer and more alive "—for me, that is the vital sentence of the young Kafka in this pursuit, in this friendship about which I first learned from a study of the letters, and to which, remarkably enough, Franz himself hardly ever made a definite allusion in my hearing. Perhaps it never got further than a trial friendship, and no real relationship ever came out of it ; Kafka's later silence—there is no mention of it in the diary—would seem to me to point to this. But that does not in the least affect the greatness of the moulding influence his first comrade had on him. He disappeared from our sight, first to take up a job as a tutor in the country, and then to his famous scientific work in Rome. From time to time we used to hear how he would show and explain the architectural monuments of Rome to friends, visitors to Rome, from our circle, in a particularly kindly way, with no trace of gruffness any longer, and of course extraordinarily knowledgably. Then the dreadful news of his death at far too early an age shocked us.

I went about with Kafka for several years without knowing that he wrote. I myself had already published several things in newspapers and magazines, and my first book appeared in 1906. Perhaps the first mention that my friend made to me of his literary activities was when he told me he had sent in a short story for a competition in the Vienna newspaper *Zeit*. He sent it in under the pseudonym " Heaven in Narrow Streets ". That may possibly have been the title of the story as well, I can't remember exactly any longer. The entry did not gain a mention in the competition, and has disappeared.

Then one day, in 1909, he read me the beginning of a novel which was called *Preparations for a Wedding in the Country*. Parts of the MS. survive in unpublished form. The hero's name was Raban. Here, too, is a reference to the " ego ", through the philological similarity of the two names Kafka and Raban,[1] like that which Franz himself analysed in the name of the hero of his short story " The Verdict ", which is Bendemann. Raban, as the first chapter tells us, leaves his workshop to go and see his fiancée who lives in the country. The first chapter describes, with great detail, in the twilight of humour, no more than the journey to the station, a rainy afternoon, and a few meetings with casual acquaintances. It is extraordinary. I was overpowered and delighted.[2]

---

[1] Kafka, remember, means Jackdaw, while Raban is similar to the German *Rabe* = raven
[2] The impression this made on me was increased, if that were possible, when he read me his short story, " Description of a Fight " (*Beschreibung eines Kampfes*). (The date of this in my diary is 14 March 1910.) The conception of this work, which Franz did not value very highly

I got the impression immediately that here was no ordinary talent speaking, but a genius. My efforts to bring Kafka's works before the public began from that moment—an endeavour that was stronger than myself, and which indeed I made no effort to fight against, because I considered it right and natural. Franz resisted sometimes with greater, sometimes with less violence, sometimes not at all : one cannot say that he always on principle adopted an attitude of disapproval (after all, apart from other things, his entering for the competition I mentioned above shows this). Naturally he, too, sometimes felt pleased over literary success. There was, I must admit, generally a deprecatory smile there at the same time ; but once I saw him very angry at an unfavourable un-understanding criticism in the Almanack of the Dürer League. In general his hopes and fears were directed towards quite other things than literary reputation, which was not exactly unpleasant to him, but un-important. The whole business of publicity didn't interest him very much, did not occupy his feelings very much—so that his shrinking from publication (apart from certain later periods in his life) was a matter of no great fuss, no passion.

I mentioned his works, which had not yet been published at all, in the Berlin weekly, *Die Gegenwart* (The Present), by adding his name to a list I gave of prominent authors (Blei, Mann, Wedekind, and Meyrink). This must have been the first public reference to Kafka's name (9 February 1907). Kafka wrote me a letter full of humour about this " carnival-like " first appearance before the public. I was certainly displaying a certain amount of high spirits in thus offering to the public the name of a writer a single line of whose had not been printed at the time, in the same breath with very big names, as though everyone should have heard of him. A little joke, of no importance. " Very well, so I have had one dance this winter after all ", Franz mocked.

It was not until 1909 that some of Kafka's prose works were printed for the first time, in Franz Blei's journal, *Hyperion*. (Blei had come out very warmly in favour of my first book, *Death to the Dead*, and afterwards often came to Prague, and I introduced him to Kafka.) The second published work was *The Aeroplanes at Brescia* (28 September 1909) which appeared in the Prague daily, *Bohemia*. The third was published in the Easter supplement to *Bohemia* on the 27 March 1910. In it, under the general title of *Betrachtungen*, will be found the following works : " *Am Fenster, In der Nacht, Kleider, Der Fahrgast, Zum Nachdenken für Herrenreiter.*

—in fact on 18 March 1910 he wrote to me, " Dear Max, the thing that pleases me most about the short story is that I have got rid of it "—and the MS. of which I took home with me, because he wanted to destroy it, dates back several years I am sure, and points distinctly to the period of family dances, to the time he was at the university. On studying my diary closer, I discover that this was not the first of his works that Kafka showed me.

Nobody took any notice of these writings which it cost me so much energy to get published. (In book form, *Betrachtung*, these pieces are called *Zerstreutes Hinausschauen* (Distracted Gazing), *Die Vorüberlaufenden* (The Runners-by), *Kleider* (Clothes), and then as above "The Passenger" and "Thoughts for Gentlemen Riders". Franz Blei had published two passages from the story *Beschreibung eines Kampfes* (Description of a Fight).)

In 1908 Max Bäuml, the friend of my childhood, died.

From then on my relations with Franz grew deeper. We met daily, sometimes even twice a day. The whole time Franz was in Prague (it was only later that his illness forced him to live in the country, in sanatoria), we kept up this custom. When we had both achieved the longed-for post "with a single shift" (i.e. with no afternoon duty), as chance would have it, we both went the same way home from our offices. So I used to wait for Franz every day at two o'clock in the afternoon by the Powder Tower—how well and thoroughly I studied the beautifully wrought, old double-headed imperial eagle on the gable of the provincial head office of the Inland Revenue, on the corner of Hyberner Lane, because Franz was always later than I—he had something extra to do in the office, or got lost in conversation with his colleagues—with my stomach rumbling, I used to stride up and down ; but my anger was quickly forgotten, when the slim, tall figure of my friend hove in sight, generally with an embarrassed smile that was intended rather to simulate than really to express utter fright, nay horror, at being so frightfully late. At the same time he would hold his hand clasped to his heart. This gesture meant, " I am innocent ". What is more, he came along at the run, so that one really couldn't say anything very furious to him. As we walked along together the same way from Zeltner Street to the Old Town Square, there was always no end of things we had to tell each other, and when we did reach Franz's house, it was still a long time before we could finish talking. And in the afternoon or evening we were together again.

In my novel *The Kingdom of Love*, in the figure of Richard Garta I have set down very much of what remains of Kafka in my heart and memory. Write an objective biography of Kafka !—that I felt I could not do at that time, four years after his death. It is only now, after nine more years have past, thirteen years, that is, after the catastrophe, that I can bring myself to do it. At that time, however, I *lived* still with my unforgettable friend, he was present with me in the truest sense of the word, always by my side, I knew exactly what he would have said in this or that situation, exactly how he would have thought about things that went on round about me. I asked him questions, and could answer myself in his name. That is how I came to feel the necessity of bringing my incomparable friend to life in the form of a living work of art, not in a historical study, collecting dates and carefully piecing facts together, but as an epic figure. Above all, I wanted to bring him to life for myself in this new way. So long as I lived in this book, in working at it, he was not dead, he still lived with me, and still exerted his influence on my life. (You will find that the whole treatment of the novel serves this purpose.) But this was misunderstood just as everything else is—people found it odd, or even incompatible with my reverence for Kafka. Nobody remembered that Plato in a similar, although of course much more comprehensive way defied Death and, all his life long, kept his friend and mentor Socrates alive and functioning still, as a companion who lived and thought together with him, by making him the protagonist of almost every dialogue he wrote after Socrates' death.

Here I shall take out of this novel (for otherwise I should have to repeat myself) the passage about the first books to which Kafka drew my attention. Apart from Flaubert, whom I have already mentioned, there were also Stefan George, two volumes of whose work Kafka gave me, one on each of two birthdays, the marvellous prose translation of Chinese lyrics by Heilmann, not to be mentioned in the same breath with later imitations in rhyme and watered-down versions by other authors, and further, Robert Walser. On the unobtrusive way Kafka had of making his friend (who is called Christof in the novel) fonder of his own favourite authors, on the whole spirit of the first years of our friendship, and on the way it was intensified after Max Bäuml's death, I could not find anything more apt to say than what I wrote in *The Kingdom of Love* :

" Garta does not persuade one, that is not his way, and he does not evolve a system—systems are not much in his line. What he does is read to you over and over again this or that passage from his favourite authors in his rapid, unemotional voice that, at the same time, creates a sense of rhythm and climax, with a throbbing chant in the background, with his eyes flashing, surrendering himself utterly to joy in human greatness ; except that now and then he quietly curls his lip, not at all mischievously, but rather in gleeful scepticism—well, well !—when some bit seemed to him not quite to have come off, or to be painfully exaggerated. Anything forced, in any artistic expression, he always thrusts as far away from him as possible, unless it be that as an effort it is at least genuine, and the writer cannot avoid it, in which case it admittedly betrays his occasional weaknesses and demands only sympathy with what his other deeds show him capable of. In short, he does not canvass for his chosen ones, he always sees clearly, there is clarity even in his most unbounded enthusiasm, he never attempts to rush Christof off his feet ;

on the contrary it often comes to Christof, being the one who is all aflame for the works that Garta revealed to him, and who even feels he must rush to the defence on behalf of some parts of them, against Garta. All this is done with the pleasantest earnestness, it is a gracious mutual education on the part of each ; there is no breath of vanity or pretence ; both have the feeling that at this very moment the whole world differentiates itself into purest truth and worthlessness. Not only that, but this feeling does not make them proud, or excessively worried, or crushed under responsibility. It is quite a simple feeling—the Good is there, and it lies in our power either to follow after it, or, which would be senseless folly, to reject it. But who, who would do that ! So they enter joyfully into the land of " The Spirit " which is otherwise hidden from the poor children of men by millions of reservations, chances, sorrows, passions, considerations ; but in this case it has revealed itself for once quite simply in all the bright, health-giving light of its eternal splendour, it lies there—invitingly great.

Then comes the decisive turn of events—Christof's first friend, who passed through all the eight classes of his secondary school with him, dies. A few days after the funeral Christof, sad unto death, goes for a walk with Richard Garta in the evening. It is the " Kleinseite ", dark castle stairways rise above them. " Will you . . . fill his place for me ? " he asks, stammering, knowing in the deep distress of his heart that he is asking an impossible question—and yet feeling that there was something justifiable, courageous, and good about the question, and that this was fully recognised by Garta. Only there is no other way in which it can be recognised than by a long, deep silence. Then they walk through many a narrow, winding street, side by side, still in silence, and Christof thinks he can feel the presence of his good, loving friend who is dead, and with whom really his whole boyhood died—the memory of countless things they went through together at school, of first perceptions and sorrows, narrow but deep scars in the heart. When one is at school, friendship comes of itself, but afterwards it must be won, fought for indeed, and finally even this becomes impossible. That is the law of the world of men. . . . The question, and the answer that was never given, were never mentioned again. But from this night on the parting handshake of the two friends is heartier and longer."

Reading together and exchanging our favourite authors may have been the first thing that brought us clearly together, but alongside this great and noble circumstance there was from the beginning an immense number of little circumstances, almost unnoticeable, in which we formed the complement to one another. If I don't wish to pretend false modesty, I must at this point confess that Kafka felt he benefited just as much from me as I did from him. My initiative and energy were the characteristics that especially appealed to him in me. Looking at things objectively, I was not at all so unreflectively bold and unconcerned as he perhaps saw me. If I were writing my own biography now, I should know how to explain and illustrate that in great detail. As it is, it is enough to state that, in comparison with Kafka, it was I who was the adventurer and that I really was. What fascinated me about Kafka I am at liberty to explain in greater detail. He had an unusual aura of power about him, such as I have never met anywhere else, even when I met very important, famous men. I have often tried to analyse this peculiarity, after Kafka's death that is, because while he was alive it made itself felt in a way so naturally and so completely taken for granted, that the idea of thinking about it never struck one. Perhaps the best way to express this remarkable, extremely personal characteristic is this ; the unintermittent compactness of his ideas could not endure a gap, he never spoke a meaningless word. Everything that came from him, came in a way that became less and less forced as the years went on, a precious expression of his quite special way of looking at things—patient, life-loving, ironically considerate towards the follies of the world, and therefore full of sad humour, but never forgetful of the real kernel, " The Indestructible ", and so always far from being blasé or cynical. Yes, that was it—in his presence the everyday world underwent a transformation, everything was new, new in a way that was often very sad, not to say shattering, but which never precluded the possibility of final consolation because it was never dull, and never flat. In a thousand easy ways, so it seemed, his powers of observation caught connections, of which one had never dreamt, but which had nothing arbitrary, nothing " surrealistic ",[1] or wayward about them, but were true connections, minute but faithful perceptions, from which one felt a strong urge to build up a completely new system of knowledge— without failing to realise that the attempt to know the world and the souls of men in such meticulous detail is of course justified and even very essential and yet may easily have to be reckoned among those things which, like Kafka's *Building of the Chinese Wall*, or *The Trial* can never, by their very nature, come to an end.

In addition, it was not only on me, but on many others that Kafka had the effect I have described. Among the friends and in the hospitable house of Mrs. Bertha Franta, where precise philosophy was discussed, with the lady of the house taking a zealous part in the discussions, Kafka had a very high reputation—simply by virtue of his personality, his occasional remarks, and his conversation—because no one at that time beyond

[1] The word did not exist at that time. The surrealists of to-day claim Kafka as one of themselves without foundation.

myself knew his literary work. There was no need of his works, the man produced his own effect himself, and despite all the shyness of his behaviour, he was always quickly recognised by men of worth as someone out of the ordinary. At all periods of his life women felt themselves drawn to Franz—he himself doubted he had this effect, but the fact cannot be disputed.

How markedly a special spell pervaded every living utterance of Kafka's, how you can except from this not a word, not a line that he wrote—be it on a casual picture postcard, or just wishing someone many happy returns, or dedicating a book—appears from the following express messages and short notes which he wrote to me. Generally they contain only cancellations of a rendezvous, or apologies—as we saw each other every day there was no other reason for writing to each other, except when one of us occasionally failed to turn up. Even for these everyday bits of information, Franz never had a conventional, ready formula. And that is why just these writings hastily tossed off (they deal with the period of our studies, the law examinations and then first work in the office) appear to me to be especially characteristic documents of a boundlessly rich spirit which never succumbed to routine or convention. Here are some specimens :

I

" I am now half delighted that I am actually studying at last, and for that reason will not come to our café this week. I would very much like to be there, because I never study after 7 o'clock ; but if I do take a little change of this kind, it disturbs my studies all day the next day. And I daren't waste any time. So it's better for me to read my *Kügelgen* [1] in the evening, a splendid occupation for a little mind and for sleep when it comes. Love to you.—FRANZ."

2

" DEAR MAX,—Now I was nearly forgetting it after all. To write and tell you, I can't go to the Exhibition to-morrow, I can't go at all any more. You see I've let myself be led astray, and elected to sit for my finals at a stupidly early date, while my knowledge is not even infinitesimal. Now that would be irresponsible, and for that reason very nice, if I didn't keep on thinking of the doctor's certificate that I shall soon have made out for me, to enable me to withdraw. How are things with the *Amethyst* ? [*Note.*—A periodical published by Franz Blei that we subscribed to between us.] I've got my money prepared already.

[1] A famous book of memoirs by Wilhelm von Kügelgen.

—So take a look round at the Exhibition, and see if there isn't anything attractive that you can buy for a small sum. Perhaps it might do for a wedding present.—Yours FRANZ."

3

" Now, my dear, I shan't be able to go out anywhere for a bit. The Dean has been so irresponsible as to fix my finals a little earlier and as I was ashamed to be more cautious than he, I've made no protest. All my love.—FRANZ."

4

" DEAR MAX,—Forgive me for yesterday evening, please ! I shall come to your place at five o'clock. My excuse will be a little comic, so you are quite sure to believe it.—Your FRANZ."

5

" MY DEAR MAX,—I am a completely useless person, really, but nothing can be done about it. Yesterday afternoon I sent you a letter by special messenger : ' Here in the tobacconist's in the Graben I beg you to forgive me for not being able to come to-night. I have a headache, my teeth are falling out, my razor is blunt, I am an unpleasant object to look at.—Your F.'

" And now in the evening I go and lie down on my sofa and reflect that I have made my excuses anyhow, and that there is again a little order in the world, but as I am thinking it over, I suddenly remember that I wrote Wladislaw Street [Note.—Oskar Pollak's address. I was living in Schalen Street at that time], instead of Schalen Street.

" Now, please, I beg of you, be annoyed about it, and don't speak to me any more because of it. I am utterly on the downward path, and—I can see far enough for that—I can't help going to the dogs. Also I should love to cut myself, but as that is impossible, there is only one thing I can rejoice about, and that is that I have no pity on myself, and so I have at last become egoistic to that extent. We should celebrate achieving this height—you and I, I mean ; just as a future enemy, you should celebrate it.

" It is late. I should like you to know that I wished you a very good night to-night.—Your FRANZ."

6

" By speedy work in the office, we have earned our lunch. Forgive me if I don't come to-day, I should have done something on Sunday, and neglected to do it, because Sunday is short. In the morning one sleeps, in the afternoon one washes one's hair, and in the evening one goes for a stroll as though one were a lounge lizard. I always use Sunday as a spring-board for pleasure, which is rather ridiculous. Write and tell me when you are free except for Thursday and Friday. All the best.—Your FRANZ."

7

" MY DEAR MAX,—We are beginning a race for unreliability and unpunctuality. Of course I don't hope to be first in this race, because I am only simply unpunctual through Italian industry,[1] but you through your lust for pleasure. But since you are trying to make it up by being ready to come and see me (Wednesday, I believe ?) that is all right with me again. But perhaps you are only doing it because it is easier to put off a visit than a visitor.—Your FRANZ."

8

" MY MAX,—I am in such a bad way that I think I can only get over it by not speaking to anyone for a week, or as long as may be necessary. From the fact that you won't try to answer this postcard in any way, I shall see that you are fond of me.—Your FRANZ."

9

" MY DEAREST MAX,—I am kissing you here on a picture postcard which is dirty, but my most beautiful one, and that in front of the whole populace. As I believe you much more than I do myself, I thought yesterday it was really my fault, only I considered it didn't make so much difference, because we still have a long time to live. But if things are as you write, and I am already again convinced that they are, then it is all the better, and you will soon be coming up in the lift after all. Besides, I am in such a good mood to-day, as though I were beginning to live, and your card fits in so nicely too, for what a nice friendship it must be if it begins in such a way. You don't frighten me at all with the date, because after all you will get your job before then, and if not, ' The Maid '[2] is coming out—it is coming out in any case, apart from every-thing else, so what more do you want, I ask you ? In the night one can wish for still more : but in the morning ? "

10

" MY DEAR MAX,—It looks as if I shall not be able to come. This morning, just as I was looking forward to the afternoon and evening, I

---

[1] He was taking Italian lessons before going on his journey to Riva.
[2] A short novel by me, *A Czech Maidservant*.

was told I must go to the office in the afternoon ; lunch-time, as I was looking forward to the evening only, I was told I must be in the shop in the afternoon and the evening. There is a lot to do, one of the assistants is ill, and father is not too well. There would be murder if I didn't stay in the shop till eight, and probably there would be if I went away at night.

" So forgive me nicely, please ! "

11

" MY DEAREST MAX,—Look, if I go on like this, all the people I like will be angry with me except the one, and she doesn't love me anyhow. The story of my life yesterday is simple. I was there until 10 o'clock, and in the bar until 1 o'clock. At half-past seven, when your music had already begun, I suppose, I got a few more blows. My mother and my father are not feeling well, my grandfather is ill, they are distempering the dining-room, and the whole family is living in my room as though it were a gipsy caravan. This afternoon I must go to the shop. I haven't the courage to make my excuses to Baum. Don't desert me.—Your FRANZ."

12

" But your memory, dear Max ! I remember so exactly. In front of your house on Sunday night, I shook myself and said, ' Tuesday, I am going to such-and-such a place'. You said, ' Come on Wednesday'. I, ' I shall be tired, and I want to go and see Pr. . . .' ' Come on Thursday then.' ' All right.' So Thursday I did come to see you. In any case I am in such a state that even justifiable reproaches would be too much for me."

13

" MY DEAR MAX,—You are lucky you are not at home ; you are getting out of several little kindnesses you might have liked to have done for me. I am lucky, because I can all the more easily and firmly beg you to forgive me, and to make my excuses to the world if I can't manage to get to Baum's before nine o'clock. We have some relations staying with us. What is more, on Monday at five o'clock I am coming to see you for a moment. If I am disturbing you in any work, please refuse to see me.—Your FRANZ."

14

" DEAR MAX,—You know I have a job, so a New Year has begun, and my worries, granted that up till now they went on foot, now follow suit and go on their hands. I should very much like to see you at 2.30

near the statue of the Madonna in the Square, punctually. Please, make it possible !—Your FRANZ K."

15

" DEAR MAX,—Written in the street, as we shall always write to each other from now on, because the shoves you get from people passing by gives life to the writing.

" I am in front of a photograph of Paula K. Yesterday I saw her in the flesh several times. She stood for a while, and for a while she walked all white along Hyberner Street with a young man who was wearing trousers with a crease. Just to get hold of something solid : her teeth are all over the place in her mouth, on the right cheek only she has a dimple, her complexion is fairly mouldy, covered with ashes, not with powder at all ; obviously her complexion takes a rest by day. I am coming on Thursday. Do me a favour and work hard.—FRANZ."

If one tried to quote verbal utterances of Kafka's, to complete these occasional written utterances in which it is just the fact that they are occasional that lights up and makes clear the genius that is in them, one could go on for ever. But let me quote a few examples. He was coming to see me one afternoon—I was still living with my parents then—and his coming in woke up my father. Instead of apologising, he said, in an indescribably gentle way, raising a hand as if to calm him and walking softly on tiptoe through the room, " Please look on me as a dream ". Once he went to the Berlin Aquarium with a lady, who told me the story later with emotion. Suddenly he began to speak to the fish in their illuminated tanks, " Now at last I can look at you in peace, I don't eat you any more ". It was the time that he turned strict vegetarian. If you have never heard Kafka saying things of this sort with his own lips, it is difficult to imagine how simply and easily, without any affectation, without the least sentimentality—which was something almost completely foreign to him—he brought them out. Among my notes I find something else that Kafka said about vegetarianism. He compared vegetarians with the early Christians, persecuted everywhere, everywhere laughed at, and frequenting dirty haunts. " What is meant by its nature for the highest and the best, spreads among the lower-classes." In the same notes, which I made while Kafka was still alive, I find : " Theosophy is nothing but a surrogate for literature " (literature in our use of the word at that time, was used in Flaubert's sense of the word—meant real literature). " Insurance [1] is like the religions of primitive peoples who believe they can ward off evil by all kinds of manipulations." " Karl

---

[1] The reference is to Kafka's daily work.

Kraus confines the Jewish writers up in his own hell, guards them well, and keeps them under stern discipline. The only thing he forgets is that his proper place is in the same hell with them." He told me that his " loveliest dream " was that he " was sitting in a boat, and flying along an empty river-bed ". Talking about his headaches, a frightful tension in the temples, he said, " It's the sort of feeling a pane of glass must have in the spot where it cracks." Talking about a fir tree lightly covered with snow, when he was taking a walk with me, in Schelesen in the winter, he said, " They haven't yet had a headache so long as I have " ; at the time his deep black hair had gone grey at the temples. Talking about a play he had written—probably *Der Gruftwächter*—when we very much wanted to hear it, he said, " The only thing about the play that is not dilettantish, is that I shall *not* read it to you ". (From Oskar Baum's " Memories of Franz Kafka ", in *Witiko*, 1929, Part 3.) At the beginning of 1911, I made this note : On Sundays Kafka goes for walks by himself, without any objective, without thinking. He says, " Every day I wish myself off the earth ". " There is nothing wrong with me except myself." He has done no work. In the afternoons he sleeps or looks at the papers in the Arts and Crafts Museum. In company, he is cheerful, full of humour, as a critic, unsurpassable for his witty observa-tions ; with his conversation it is the same ; it could and should all be written down. When asked what after all was responsible for his sad condition, and why he couldn't write, he said, " I have hundreds of wrong feelings—dreadful ones—the right ones won't come out—or if they do, only in rags ; absolutely weak ". I protest (in reply) that when one is writing one sometimes has to work one's way through one's first worthless ideas in order to come to the nobler thoughts that lie beneath them. He answers, " That's all right for you, but not for me—that would mean giving these wrong feelings the upper hand ". Here is another conversation I noted down that I had with him on 28 February 1920. He : " We are nihilistic thoughts that came into God's head ". I quoted in support the doctrine of the Gnostics concerning the Demiurge, the evil creator of the world, the doctrine of the world as a sin of God's. " No," said Kafka, " I believe we are not such a radical relapse of God's, only one of his bad moods. He had a bad day." " So there would be hope outside our world ? " He smiled, " Plenty of hope—for God—no end of hope—only not for us ".

But it was not only when it was a question of themes of such greatness that Kafka revealed his powerful intuitive command of imagery, but at all times—that was just the remarkable thing about him. What seems peculiar to us in his remarks was, for him, the natural and absolutely unavoidable shape of life and thought. He couldn't speak or write in any other way than this. It *was* natural, it can be found again partly even now in the way in which his sisters express themselves. Quite peculiar to him were his dream-poetical and his paradox-humoristic turns of expression. Talking of a man who worked in the same office, he said, half in recognition, half in mockery, " He doesn't mind how long his office hours are "—and then went on reflectively, " But one might perhaps persuade him to." As we were coming home once after one of our nights on the tiles, in the early hours of the morning, and the first awakening sounds of town life were making themselves heard— milkcarts, etc.—he stopped and listened and said, " The crickets of the metropolis ". Once when he was taking up some of my time, and asking me to do something for him, he said, " You forgive me for this, for I can't forgive myself for it ". One of his very last words has this same tinge of paradox. When Dr. Klopstock, who was treating him, refused to give him any morphia, he said to him, " Kill me, otherwise you are a murderer." When he had his first attack of blood-spitting, which heralded his tuberculosis, he exclaimed—and he used these words to describe his disease as a way out, which was even not unwelcome, from the difficulties he was then faced with on the question of the marriage he had been planning—" My head has made an appointment with my lungs behind my back."

However revealing the citation of details may be, it cannot give the sum total of the effect that Kafka's personality produced. It was not the wit he displayed but the deep sureness on which it was based, and the peacefulness there was in his physical movements, that was the real thing that made itself felt in his vicinity. I shall once again call my " Garta " to the rescue and quote : " In his presence one felt directly that what is great must prove to be as great, even when every appearance speaks against it—that the noble kernel of the world remains untouched by all the abuses and perversions that exist. He didn't say this, it is only very rarely that he speaks about things like that, and when he does it is only hesitatingly, in fleeting images that often sound almost like jokes. But his whole behaviour, down to the smallest detail, even if you only watch the way he brushes his hair, is based on the belief that there is, as a premise taken for granted without discussion, a mode of life which is right, thorough, clean, and unshakeably natural. It is there. But to find it, to arrive at it—that is the difficulty. Deny this enormous difficulty— that he is far from doing. On the contrary : he sees all the confusion and all that is in a nasty way comic in the world more intensively than any other man. He knows one can't take a step without getting into complications, without stumbling. And yet there is this deep confidence that the inner excellence will mature."

III

To Earn One's Living or Live One's Life?

ON 18 July 1906, Kafka obtained his Doctorate in Jurisprudence at the Imperial and Royal Karl-Ferdinand German University of Prague.

He did the usual so-called year in the courts, i.e. the unpaid practice in the law-courts which those lawyers who intend to take up the Bar have to go through. Kafka never had any intention of being called to the Bar—he used this year only as a breathing space after the strain of the examinations, and also as a breathing space in which to look round for a properly paid job. For it was taken as settled that he wouldn't be a burden on his parents' pockets a day longer than was necessary. That his father would never have understood anyhow, and would have regarded it as the worst of impositions. As I have said, the question whether this exceptionally gifted son (but did his parents have any clear idea of his gift, had it manifested itself at all?) should not be granted some exceptional liberty, such as a few years' study in foreign countries, for example, was not raised. The financial prospects of the family were favourable enough at that time. But Franz would have needed push to have won such a favour for himself. And what was there that Franz lacked more than push? His energy was directed inwards only and, anyhow, manifested itself as stubbornness, a passive tenacity. Herein perhaps lay the fatal weakness of his life. He suffered and kept silent. At the same time one must also not forget that the special nature of his gift, in fact, and not only in the minds of his parents, precluded its being turned to any practical value. Furthermore, to turn it to any such practical value was utterly and completely incompatible with the purity of Franz's idea of Art. " Writing is a form of prayer," the diary affirms. Indeed, when it came to the point of choosing a profession, Franz postulated his job should have nothing to do with literature. That he would have regarded as a debasing of literary creation. Breadwinning and the art of writing must be kept absolutely apart, a " mixture " of the two, such as journalism, for example, represents, Kafka rejected— although at the same time he never laid down dogmas, but merely withdrew, as it were, with a smile on the explanation that " I just can't do it ". He influenced me and my choice of a profession for years with these views of his and, like himself, out of respect for Art, I went through agonies, in the most hideous, prosaic, dry, profession of the law and didn't find the road to theatrical and musical criticism until years later.

To-day I regard Kafka's severity on this point as a noble error, and regret the hundreds of joyless hours I let slip by in a mood almost of despair, wasting God's high creation, time, in offices just like those in which Kafka now set out on his martyr's way.

What we both strove after with burning ardour was a post with a "single shift"—that is, office from early morning till two or three in the afternoon—now I can write this "or" so easily as though to us at the time it didn't seem as if the whole health of our souls depended on this *one* hour—and none in the afternoon. Jobs with commercial firms, which meant being in the office mornings and afternoons, didn't leave any continuous stretch of the day over for literary work, walks, reading, the theatre, and so on. And even when one came home after three, by the time one had eaten, recovered a little from the soul-destroying work, and was ready to switch over into the state of freedom one had been looking forward to—there was already very little of the day left. The desired office hours till two o'clock only were offered by extremely few offices, however, being almost exclusively in Government offices which even then, under the old Austrian Empire, were open to Jews only if they had influence in very high quarters. I don't want here to go into the story of all our disappointed hopes of suitable jobs which haunted our conversation at that time. It will suffice to say that Kafka, after a short prelude in the most strenuous of commercial offices (the Assicurazioni Generali), finally achieved the longed-for job in July 1908, in a semi-Government office, the "Workers Accident Insurance Institute for the Kingdom of Bohemia, in Prague".

In both posts Franz had men over him who were well disposed towards him. Nevertheless it soon became evident that he couldn't get on with it, in spite of all his experiments in dividing up his time in such a way as to allow him to indulge unrestrictedly in his passion—writing. For that he needed a succession of many hours, to permit the great impetus which his creative power gave him to soar to its proper climax and then die down again. But this was impossible for Kafka in one short afternoon with the prospect of the next barren day in the Insurance Institute always in front of him—for me, who had to go through the analogous experience shortly afterwards, it was only half possible by the application of extreme energy and concentration. So hard times began for both of us. Significant of what we suffered is the poem I wrote during one of the holiday tours we made together, and which I dedicated to my friend. Kafka tried sleeping in the afternoon and writing at night. That always went all right for a certain length of time, but he was not getting his proper sleep—Franz suffered from poor sleep, and an unusual sensitivity to noise anyhow—conditions of exhaustion set in, and so he had to call upon his last reserves of strength to get through his work in the office. A lot was expected of him there, among other things jobs that he described—and this is the strongest word of disapproval I have ever heard from him—as " disgusting ", as for example a kind of press campaign against not unjustified attacks to which social insurance was then exposed. This explains an entry in the diary, " A sophistical article written for and against the Institute ". (What irony that he didn't after all completely escape journalism !) Here is the poem I mentioned above :

LAKE LUGANO

To Franz Kafka

With their delicate wings outspread,
Dragonflies glittered above our legs
Dangling in the water as we sat on the sunbaked wall,
To them we might seem like rocks.

High above us wound the road
Bright with lime-dust scorched clean and white.
And from the vineyard rich grapes did greet us
And coolth descended caressing like a gentle woman.

Our bodies bore the warm tan of the generous sun.
But our souls, dear Friend, knew no peace or richness
And shook with thoughts and words, dark distant but searing,
Despite the beauty that cradled us
We knew that near days would bend us and bleach us
With the same relentless burden.

The years that I spent as an official in the Post Office, and during which I wrote, among other things, in the afternoons and evening, my *Tycho Brahe*, remain so dimly in my memory that I can hardly see a single detail any more. It has all been forcibly crammed into the maw of the subconscious. Perhaps it may yet emerge once again. What remains is a direct sympathy for the almost unrealisable suffering that weighs on the working-classes—that weighs on all who have to do work that does not interest them. Suffering that has been raised to a degree that one can only describe as fantastic by the Taylor System and the " continuous band ". How can such suffering be borne at all ? Perhaps we are all only dreaming that it is borne—this almost unimaginable suffering—because in reality it surpasses the limits of human powers of resistance, and of what is unfortunately the same thing in this case, of the possibilities of human degradation. The attitude towards social problems which wants to see a fair distribution of the burden of labour

E

meets with my full approval—but my own experience points to a quite different problem that lies much deeper, to the question of the happiness of labour, joy in one's work, in one's own handicraft. Perhaps I shall have more to say on that point later.

A few days ago, after an interval of many years, I was once again on the premises of the Workers' Accident Insurance in Poříč Street, at the scene of Franz Kafka's daily work. How often I had been to see him there, walked up and down with him in one of the bleak, echoing corridors. This time I spoke to one of the head officials who once worked with Kafka. Franz Kafka, so the gentleman told me, was popular with everyone ; he hadn't a single enemy. His devotion to duty was exemplary ; his work was very highly thought of. The gentleman emphasised that Franz Kafka attacked every question from the opposite end to that from which every one else generally did. (A very apposite remark on the part of the gentleman, who, be it noted, did not know that Kafka had since become world-famous.) Another thing he emphasised was a certain naïveté in Kafka's make-up. He was " our office baby ". He told me a story that is very characteristic of Kafka. " One day he came into my office just as I was eating a slice of bread and butter. ' How *can* you swallow that fat ? ' he said, ' A lemon is the best food '."

His department in the Workers' Accident Insurance Institution was the studying of the prevention of accidents and the appeals in respect of the classification of trades under the various degrees of risk.

He himself never considered his professional work was first-class. His superiors, however, thought very highly of it. He used to talk of the specialised knowledge, and the " cleverness " of his boss—Marschner —with an admiration that bordered on enthusiasm.

His social conscience was greatly stirred when he saw workers crippled through neglect of safety precautions. " How modest these men are ", he once said to me, opening his eyes wide. " They come to us and beg. Instead of storming the Institute and smashing it to little pieces, they come and beg."

The annual report of the Accident Institute for the year 1909 contains an article which I am giving below which Kafka wrote as a clerk of the office. Naturally, Kafka is not mentioned by name in the report itself. But I remember exactly Kafka bringing me the annual report that year, and telling me this article was his work. His boss had corrected his draft, but Kafka's style can be seen unmistakably in passages here and there even in this technical work. The high official who was kind enough to see me also pointed out the passage, as well as another one in the annual report for 1910, and told me they were Franz Kafka's work.

Here is an extract from this document which is interesting in more respects than one :

"Our illustrations show the difference between square spindles and cylindrical spindles as it affects the technique for the prevention of accidents. The cutters of the square spindle are connected by means of screws direct to the spindle and rotate with exposed cutting edges at speeds of 380 to 400 revolutions per minute. The dangers to the operator, presented by the large space between the cutter spindle and the surface of the table, are obvious. Such spindles were used either because the danger was not recognised, which may incidentally have increased the danger, or with the knowledge of the presence of a permanent danger which could not be avoided. Although an extremely cautious operator could take care not to allow any joint of his fingers to project from the timber when guiding it over the cutter head, the main danger defied all caution. The hand of even the most cautious operator was bound to be drawn into the cutter space if it slipped, particularly when, as often happened, the timber was hurled back (by the cutter block) while the operator was pressing the article to be planed against the table with one hand and feeding it to the cutter spindle with the other. This lifting and recoiling of the timber could not be anticipated nor prevented as it may have been due to gnarls or knots in the timber, to an insufficiently high cutting-speed, to warped cutters, or to uneven pressure of the operator's hands on the article. In such accidents usually several joints, and even whole fingers, were severed. Not only every precaution but also all protecting devices seemed to fail in the face of this danger, as they either proved to be totally inadequate or, whereas they reduced the danger on the one hand (automatic covering of the cutter slot by a protecting slide, or by reducing the width of the cutter space), they increased it on the other by not allowing the chippings sufficient space to leave the machine, which resulted in choked cutter spaces and in injured fingers when the operator attempted to clear the slot of chippings.

"By turning back the spindle according to Schrader's patent and flattening it in a gentle slope right up to the cutters [i.e. by making it eccentric—TRANSLATOR], clogging up of the cutter block will be avoided, whereby easy feeding of the timber to the cutter spindle and sufficient space for the chippings to leave the machine will also be effected.

"The most important point in this connection, however, from the point of view of the prevention of accidents is that only the cutting edges of the cutters should be permitted to project, and that these cutters, forming as it were an integral part of the spindle, can be very thin without danger of fracture."

It is clear that Kafka derived a great amount of his knowledge of the world and of life, as well as his sceptical pessimism, from his experiences in the office, from coming into contact with workmen suffering under injustice, and from having to deal with the long-drawn-out process of official work, and from the stagnating life of files. Whole chapters of the novels *The Trial* and *The Castle* derive their outer covers, their realistic wrappers, from the atmosphere Kafka breathed in the Workmen's Accident Institution. Compare too the sketch " New Lamps ", and an entry in the diary dated 2 July 1913 : " Wept over the account of the trial of twenty-three-year-old Marie Abraham, who, through want and hunger, strangled her almost nine-months' old child with a tie which she was using as a garter and which she unwound for the purpose. A thoroughly typical story." Compare also the following scheme for reform, which is almost unique in Kafka's work, drawn up towards the end of his life, the plan of a workers' collective, voluntary of course, almost monastic.

" GUILD OF WORKMEN WITHOUT POSSESSIONS

" *Duties.*—(1) To own or accept no money, no valuables. The following the only possessions allowed : the simplest clothing (details to be settled), materials necessary for work, books, food enough for one's own needs. Everything else belongs to the poor. (2) To earn one's keep only by work. To shrink from no work for which one has the strength without damage to one's health. Either to choose one's work oneself, or if that is not possible, to submit to the orders of the work committee, which is under the orders of the Government. (3) To work for no other reward than one's keep (to be settled according to the district, for two days). (4) The most temperate life. To eat only what is absolutely necessary, for example, as minimum recompense, which is in a certain sense also maximum recompense ; bread, water, dates. The food of the poorest, the lodgings of the poorest. (5) To treat the relationship with one's employer as one of trust, never to demand the intervention of a law-court. Any work taken on to be finished under all circumstances, except when serious considerations of health prevent it.

" *Rights.*—(1) Maximum period of work, six hours ; for manual labour, four to five. (2) In the case of illness, and when a man is too old to work, acceptance in a State Home for Old People, Hospitals.

" The working life to be a matter of conscience and faith in one's fellow-man.

" Property a man brings with him to be given to the State for building hospitals and homes.

" For the present at least, exclusion of married men and women.

" Advice—heavy responsibility—to be given by the Government.

" Where a man can help, in forsaken districts, workhouses, as teachers. . . .[1]

" Limit, 500 men.

" One year's novitiate."

Not that Kafka ever took any active part in political movements. But his reflective interest was claimed by any efforts that aimed at improving the lot of man. That is why he zealously attended Czech mass meetings and debates. I have often heard him describe the characteristics of great popular speakers like Soukup, Klofáč, Kramář in detail, and generally very critically. It wasn't until after his death that I found out by accident, while I was collecting the material about the Czech anarchic-revolutionary movement of before the war (1914) for my novel *Stefan Rott*, that Kafka was personally known to one of the survivors of this movement, old Kacha. On the basis of his authentic reports, confirmed also by other sources, I was able to write these lines in my novel : " With another group of Czechs seated at the table in this big inn-room sat another German guest, who looked very thin, and very young, although he was apparently over thirty. He didn't utter a word the whole evening, only looked on attentively with his great grey gleaming eyes, which stood out in strange contrast to his brown face under his thick coal-black hair." It was Franz Kafka the writer. He often came and attended this gathering quite peacefully. Kacha liked him, and called him a " klidas ", that is, a " shut-mouth ", if one may be allowed an attempt at creating something like Prague-Czech slang. The gathering in question was the famous " Klub Mladých ", the " Young People's Club ", to which the Czech writers Gelner, Toman, Šrámek, Stanislav Neumann, Mareš, and Hašek also belonged.

Naturally Kafka's office life was not always overshadowed entirely by completely dark overtones. He had the ability to make firm friends with his colleagues and subordinates, even with some of them who were very simple or very confused. For example, I find among my papers an extraordinary memorandum written by one of these men that he brought to me. It begins with the words " *Nos exules filii Evae* ", and at the end it has a note on it in Franz's handwriting, " From an experience of the fifty-year-old author, which he hints at in the beginning, grew this further programme, ecstatically conceived, according to which a uniting of Polish Jews (Dalila—the present Jewish mother) with the Slavs (Ursus—the present Slav-man) shall effect the salvation of both, and the creation of Samson, who will create a new religion ". Franz brought

---

[1] At the beginning of the third sentence from the end there is a line in which I cannot make out the shorthand signs.

the author of this curious memorandum along and introduced him to me, and then we went all three of us to one of the performances given by the Polish Jewish Theatre company, about which I shall write more later.

In one of his letters, putting me off, his office work is described in the following humorous fashion which anticipates a Charlie Chaplin film. " If you only knew how much I have to do ! In my four district headquarters—apart from all my other work—people fall, as if they were drunk, off scaffolds and into machines, all the planks tip up, there are landslides everywhere, all the ladders slip, everything one puts up falls down and what one puts down one falls over oneself. All these young girls in china factories who incessantly hurl themselves downstairs with mountains of crockery give one a headache. By Monday I hope to be over the worst. . . ."

In his diary he wrote down in detail the experiences of a young book-keeper. But he found the dignity of those who sit on high hard to bear. One day he came to me in the greatest excitement. He told me he had just done the silliest thing—which might cost him the wonderful job he had managed to ferret out with so much trouble— and which he valued for his parents' sake. What had happened was he had been appointed drafting-clerk. A high personage on the Board of the Institution had summoned the new drafting-clerks to his presence and given them a talk which was so solemn, and so full of fatherly sanctimoniousness, that he (Franz) had suddenly burst out laughing, and couldn't stop. I helped the inconsolable Franz to write a letter of apology to the high official, who luckily turned out to be a considerate person, not without a sense of humour. It is altogether remarkable how Franz, as if in compensation for his inner repressions, hit upon people who were well disposed towards him, who helped him on, or at least did not knowingly get too much in his way—whereas other people, who have achieved their own inner balance in life, have to scuffle almost the whole time with obstructionists. Thus everything is reduced to some kind of order—that is, it is all arranged for nobody to have an easy time of it.

The happy and encouraging episodes in his profession must, however, be considered as rare exceptions in the course of a burden that daily grew heavier because it was daily felt to be less and less bearable. The diary says such shattering things on the subject of office work preventing him from writing, that there is nothing more one can say on the subject. But there is one utterance of his which must be underlined, coming as it does from one who was otherwise so modest, that he had to force a piece of writing for his office out of himself, as if he were tearing a piece of flesh out of his own body, and who then in " great fear " sets forth

" that everything in me is ready for creative work, and such work would
be a solution of my problems and a real coming-to-life, while here in the
office for the sake of such a miserable bit of an official document I must
rob a body which is capable of such happiness of a piece of its flesh ".
There are, of course, in the still unpublished parts of the diary other
passages in the same vein. And they rise to a really mighty climax when
the time comes for him to take up formally a share in a factory in the
interests of his family, and later to be constrained to show, if only
occasionally, a practical interest in this undertaking. That he finds
unbearable. He knows, in fact, what tremendous creative powers there
are in him, which are clamouring to be unleashed and which are pent
up by responsibilities of this kind. His complaint sounds very similar to
that letter from Paris in which Mozart wrote the following refusal to his
father who was urging him to start taking on pupils. "You must not
think it is laziness—no !—but because it is utterly against my genius,
against my way of life. . . . You know that I am, as one might say, stuck
fast in music—that I am busied with it all day long—that I love to
speculate—to study—to think things over. But now here I am prevented from doing so by this way of living (i.e. the lessons). I shall, it is
true, have a few hours free, only—these few hours I shall need to rest in,
rather than to work in." Unfortunately there will always be Philistines
who are of the opinion that it is enough if genius has " a few hours free "
—they don't understand that all the available hours barely suffice to
guarantee an even tolerably uninterrupted ebb and flow of inspiration
and repose the right and proper far-flung arc of oscillation.

To those who are of the opinion that Kafka in all seriousness considered his literary work bad or indifferent, and that this was the reason
for his refusing to publish anything, it will come as rather a surprise to
find him making the following entries in his diary concerning his
" capacities ", and "How they are irritated by the pernicious daily
drudgery ", with exactly the same confidence with which Mozart speaks
of *his* " genius " in the above letter. It is truly ridiculous also to suppose
that genius—clear-sighted, form-bestowing genius—should be in doubt
about the powers which are most peculiarly its own. To the outer
world Kafka did, it is true, display a certain amount of self-depreciation—
in comparison with that which he strove after, with religious enlighten-
ment, which was what finally concerned him most, he felt himself petty—
but that did not in the least prevent his estimating at his true worth the
divine grace that had been conferred upon him and how perverse it was
that it should meet with temporal obstructionism. He writes :

" 15/11/1911. Last night it was already with a certain presentiment
that I took the spread off my bed, lay down, and again became conscious

of all my capacities, just as if I were holding them in my hand ; they tightened my chest ; they set my head on fire ; for a while, to comfort myself for not getting up and working, I said over and over to myself, ' It can't be good for you ; it can't be good for you ', and tried, with an almost visible effort to pull sleep over my head. I kept on thinking of a cap with a brim which I was pulling hard down over my forehead, to protect myself. How much I lost yesterday ; how my blood pulsed through my tight-packed head, capable of anything, and only held back by forces which are indispensable for just keeping alive, and are being thrown away here !

"Certain it is that everything that I have conceived beforehand, although with a clear apprehension of every word, or even only approximately but in definite words, when I sit at my desk, when I try to set it on paper, seems dry, perverse, stiff, embarrassing to the whole neighbourhood, timid, but above all full of gaps, although I have forgotten no jot of my original conception. The explanation lies, of course, largely in the fact that I conceive good things only when I am not tied to paper, at the time of inspiration, which I dread rather than long for, and that then the richness is so great that I must renounce it, and so just follow blindly my luck, and take things out of the flood, in handfuls, so that what I have acquired, when I come to write it down in reflexion, is nothing to compare with the richness in which it lived, is incapable of summoning this richness up and is therefore bad and disturbing because it only entices one in vain."

" 28/12/1911. What agony the factory costs me ! Why did I not protest when they made me promise to work there in the afternoons ! Of course no one makes me do it by force, but my father does by reproaches and K. by silence and my guilty conscience. I know nothing about the factory, and this morning when I was being shown over the factory I stood around helpless and like a whipped schoolboy. I swear I shall never be able to get to the bottom of all the details of the workings of the factory. And if, after asking endless questions and being a nuisance to all concerned, I were to do so, what would the result be ? I should not know any practical use to put this knowledge to; I am built only for cooking up something that looks all right, to which the sound common sense of my boss [1] adds salt and makes it look like a really good piece of work. But through this useless expenditure of energy on the factory, on the other hand, I would rob myself of the possibility of using the few hours of the afternoon for myself, which could only lead to the complete destruction of my existence, which is getting more and more circumscribed as it is."

[1] i.e. in the Workers' Accident Insurance.

" 21/6/1912. The tremendous world I have in my head ! But how can I release it and release myself without tearing myself apart ? And it is a thousand times better to tear myself apart than to keep it in check or buried in me. That is what I am here for, of that I am quite clear."

" The tremendous world I have in my head ! " The diary is alive with plans, sketches, and beginnings—only the very smallest part of them carried out. Mozart resisted, and stood up to his father. Kafka kept silence. But I have a letter of his in which he makes the evil of his being caught up in his daily work completely apprehensible. It is here, and not in his relations with his father, that, in my opinion, lie the roots of his later absorption into the world of sorrows that finally led to his illness and death. And only in so far as his exaggerated feeling of his tie with his father held him firm in the bonds of his profession did it contribute to the disaster—but the disaster was essentially caused by the fact that a man so tremendously richly gifted, with such a rich creative urge, was forced just at the time when his youthful strength was unfolding itself, to work day in day out to the point of exhaustion, doing things which inwardly didn't interest him in the least. This is what he says in his letter to me :

" After some good writing in the night from Sunday to Monday—I could have gone on writing all through the night, and all day, and all night and all day, and finally flown away—and to-day I am sure I could have written well, too—one page, really only the last dying breath of yesterday's ten, is even finished. I must stop for the following reason : Mr. X, the factory owner, early this morning went away on business, which I, in my fond absent-mindedness, hardly noticed, and will be off for ten or fourteen days. While he is away the factory is really left in control of the works manager alone, and no employer, least of all one so anxious as my father, will doubt that the most utter fraud is now being perpetrated in the factory. I myself in fact believe it too, although not so much for the sake of the money, but because of my ignorance and pangs of conscience. But after all, even an impartial person, so far as I can imagine such a person, couldn't have very much doubt that my father's fears are justified, even though I must not forget that I myself, at bottom, cannot comprehend why a German works manager from Germany, even during the absence of Mr. X, whose superior he is by far in every technical and organising question, should not be able to keep everything running in the same good order as usual ; for after all, we are men, not thieves. . . .

" When I was trying to tell you some time ago that nothing from outside can disturb me when I am writing (which was said, of course, not as a boast, but to comfort myself), I was only just thinking how my

mother whimpers to me almost every evening, that I should after al
take a look at the factory now and again just to keep father's mind easy,
and how father has said the same thing, on his side, in a far nastier way
with looks and in other indirect ways. All this whimpering at me and
reproaching me wouldn't, for the most part, amount to stupidity were
it not that—and that, one can't deny it for all the world, is where the
stupidity of all this talk lies—I can't bear such a control even in my
brightest moments.

" But it's not a question of that for the next fortnight, when all
that is necessary is that any pair of eyes, even mine, should wander about
over the factory. I can't make the slightest objection to this demand
being made of me, of all people, because everybody thinks that I am
chiefly responsible for founding the factory—though I must have taken
this responsibility on in a dream, it seems to me at least—and moreover,
there is no one here besides me who can go to the factory, because my
father and mother, of whose going one couldn't dream, anyhow, are
now in the middle of their busiest season (business seems to be going
better in the new shop, too) and to-day, for example, mother didn't
even come home for lunch.

" So when Mother once more began the same old story this evening,
and, apart from the reference to making my father unhappy and ill by
my behaviour, produced the further reason of Mr. X's business journey
and the complete desertion of the factory, a wave of bitterness—I don't
know if it was only gall—passed through my whole body, I saw perfectly
that I had only the alternatives of either waiting until everyone had gone
to bed and then jumping out of the window, or of going every day to
the factory and sitting in X's office every day for the next fourteen days.
The former would have given me the opportunity of rejecting all
responsibility both for interrupting my writing and for deserting the
factory, the latter would have interrupted my writing without any
doubt—I can't just rub fourteen nights' sleep out of my eyes—and would
leave me, if I had enough strength of will and hope, the prospect of
perhaps being able to begin again where I stopped to-day, fourteen
days later.

" So I didn't jump out through the window, and also the temptation
to make this letter a letter of farewell (my motives for writing it lie in
quite a different direction) is not very strong. I stood at the window a
long time, and pressed my face against the glass, and I more than once
felt like frightening the toll-collector on the bridge by my fall. But I
felt too firm a hold on myself the whole time for the decision to dash
myself to pieces on the pavement to be able to depress me to the necessary
level. It also seemed to me that by staying alive I should interrupt my

writing less—even if one does nothing, nothing, but talk of interruptions —than by dying, and that between the beginning of my novel and its continuation after a fortnight, I might somehow in the factory, in full view of my satisfied parents, move and have my being in the heart of my novel.

" My dearest Max, I am putting the whole case before you, not because I want you to judge it, for you are not in a position to have any judgement on it, but since I had firmly decided to jump from my window without writing a letter of farewell—after all one has the right to be tired just before the end—now that I am going to walk back into my room again as its occupant, I wanted to celebrate it by writing you a long letter of meeting again, and here it is.

" And now a last kiss and good-night, so that to-morrow I can do what they want of me, and be the boss of the factory."

When I read the letter, I was gripped by cold horror. I wrote freely and openly to Franz's mother, and pointed out to her the danger of suicide in which her son stood. Of course, I asked her not to mention my intervention to Franz. The answer which I received on 7 October 1912, is full of touching mother-love. She begins, " I have just received your letter, and you can see from the way my writing shakes how much it has upset me. I, who would give my heart's blood for any of my children, to make them all happy, am helpless in this case. But nevertheless I shall do everything in my power to see my son happy." The mother then outlines a scheme for a white lie. She wanted to pretend to the father, who had to be kept from any shock because of his illness, that Franz was going to the factory every day, and in the meantime look around for another partner. " I shall speak to Franz this very day, without mentioning your letter, and tell him he needn't go to the factory to-morrow any more. I hope he will listen to me and calm himself. I beg you, too, dear doctor, to calm him and thank you ever so much for the way you love Franz."

One's verdict on the affair depends upon what relation it bore to Franz's writing, and the importance one gives to that.

" Writing is a form of prayer " is, as I have said, the most revealing entry in the diary. From the account that Franz has left, unfortunately only in a fragmentary form, of his interview with the anthropologist Dr. Rudolf Steiner, it is clear that while he was working Franz experienced conditions that " very clearly resemble the conditions of second sight " which Dr. Steiner has described. He compares his creative work with a "new occult doctrine, a kind of Kabbala ". Literary work was his " sole desire ", his " sole profession ", he says in the draft of a letter to his presumptive father-in-law, which is not only remarkable in itself but also significant in more directions than one. And on 6 August 1914, he writes in his diary : " My preoccupation with portraying my dream-like inner life has relegated everything else to a secondary position and it is all embittered in the most dreadful fashion, and never stops embittering me. Nothing else can ever make me happy. But it is impossible to calculate how much strength I have for this portrayal. It may already have vanished for ever ; it may come back to me once again, but the circumstances under which I live are not favourable to it. So I vacillate, fly incessantly to the peak of the mountain, but cannot rest on the height for a moment." " I have a mandate ", he explained in another passage, and at first it would appear that it was a question of a purely literary mandate, were it not that fundamentally one feels right from the star t that it is a religious question that lies at the back of the literary one—a religious question after the peculiar quality of Kafka's religion, which was a religion of the life fulfilled, of work, good work, that fulfils life significantly, of co-ordination in the right and proper life of national and human community.

" To be alone brings nothing but punishment "—this sentence from the diary is a *leitmotiv* that occurs again and again with Kafka, and finds its strongest positive expression just in the last piece he wrote, in the story called " Josephine the Songstress—or The Mice-Nation ". On 6 January 1914, after reading Dilthey's *Das Erlebnis und die Dichtung* he wrote down, " Loving one's fellow-man, having the highest respect for everything in its perfected forms, standing back calmly on the most suitable observation platform ". The letters to Oskar Pollak (" It's better to bite Life than to bite one's tongue ") repeatedly bring out the motive of active participation.

And at the end of 1913 we find the following formulation : " The uniformity of mankind, which every man, even the best of mixers and the most adaptable of men at one time or another begins to doubt, even if only sentimentally, on the other hand reveals itself, too, to every man, or at least appears to reveal itself in the complete community of the development of mankind as a whole, and as individuals, which we come across again and again. And this even in the most isolationist feelings of individuals." Is this written by the same man in whose work descriptions of the most utter human distances and loneliness occur o ver and over again, such as in all the animal stories (the soul of the anima' cannot be got at by a human being), such as the ideology of the mole in " The Molehill ", or the still unpublished fragment from August 1914 which begins with the sentence, " At one time in my life I had a job on a side-line in the heart of Russia ", and which then goes on, " The wider the loneliness that surrounded me, the better pleased I was " ? Two opposite tendencies fought for supremacy in Kafka : the longing for loneliness, and the will to be sociable. But you don't understand Kafka properly until you realise that the tendency to loneliness (which undeniably existed in him) he disapproved of, and it was life in the social community and significant work that meant the highest goal and ideal for him—the life into which K., the hero of the *Castle* novel, tries in vain to thrust himself.

So, too, all the many pictures of a bachelor's life which play so great a part in his work are absolutely to be apprehended as the image in reverse of what is right and what is to be striven for. It is true that Kafka needed loneliness for his literary work, he needed a high degree of self-absorption, such as could sometimes be disturbed by a conversation—as his diary tells us—such as even communicating it to a friend could endanger. But he examined himself minutely. In 1911 he makes this discovery about himself : " In periods of transition such as I have undergone the last few weeks, and of which the present moment is yet even more marked, I am often seized with a sad but calm astonishment at my lack of feeling. I am separated from everything by a space to whose limits I can't even force my way out." And in March 1912, " who will confirm for me the truth or probability of the fact that solely as a result of my literary bent I am without interest in anything else, and heartless ".

Oh all too conscientious friend ! Your literary work itself was after all for you only the symbol of a life well lived, but it was at the same time something much more too ; it was the thing itself, it was your life, it was the right and proper use of the powers you were born with. It was that which you demanded of yourself and of all mankind : not to misuse the good powers one has been given, not to let them decay, but to make every use of them to fulfil the " Mandate ", and in this way to enter into the " Law ", thrusting aside the wicked man at the gate who tries to keep one from entering in. It is difficult, all the same. The temptations are many. " Once you have followed the false notes of the bell in the night—you can never put it right again." " Nobody, nobody can point you the way to India. Even then (in the time of Alexander) the gates of India were inaccessible, but the King's sword pointed the way. To-day the gates have been conveyed elsewhere, to a more distant, a higher place ; nobody points the way ; many carry swords ; but only to flourish them, and the gaze that would follow them is dazzled." (From the collection *Der Landartz*, *The Country Doctor*.) And yet the " incorruptible ", " indestructible " in us remained. We look for it " Far from the battle of Alexander ", we read and turn over the " pages of our old books ", wait for the arrival of the " Imperial Emissary ". It is just as the

Rabbi Tarfon in his *Sayings of the Fathers* taught us with exactly the same elastic tension between pessimism and optimism, " It is not granted you to complete the task—and yet you may not give it up ".

His literary work was not the be-all and end-all for Kafka, however much many passages in his diary, if taken literally, might seem to say so. His business was a little different from that of Flaubert, for whom art really meant the essence and the proper meaning of existence, which was almost always (almost, please !) looked on sceptically and with hostility by Flaubert. But look at Kafka in contrast : " Our art consists of being dazzled by the Truth. The light which rests on the distorted mask as it shrinks from it is true, nothing else is." Art is a reflexion of religious experience. But with Kafka art is a way to God, not only in this sense— he who shrinks back also sees the way, indeed it is the way from which he shrinks back—but also in the positive sense explained above—as a midwife for a man's powers, as a governess teaching the fulfilment of life according to one's natural abilities. Thus Kafka affirmed on 15 August 1914 : " I have been writing for a few days, may it continue ! So completely protected and wrapped up in my work as I was two years ago,[1] I am not now, but all the same I have got the feeling that my regular, empty, mad, bachelor life has some justification. I can once more hold a conversation with myself, and am not gazing into such a complete blankness. This is the only way in which I can ever get better."

Thus art serves the religious principle of giving a meaning to life. As work, as an unfolding of good creative abilities given by God, it has the same rights as other work which men do, which is significant and constructive and leads the writer out of the desert of idleness back into the circle of the active communal existence. All the same, writing, of however high a standard, was not enough according to Kafka's lights. Other things were needed to become a fully qualified citizen of this earth, e.g. founding a family. I shall never forget the deep emotion with which Kafka read to me the last paragraph of *Souvenirs intimes* by Flaubert's niece, Caroline Commanville. The passage describes how Flaubert sacrificed to his idol " La Littérature ", everything—love, tenderness—everything, and the author asks if he never towards the end of his life, regretted this departure from the " route commune ". She is inclined to believe he did. A few excited words that Flaubert once said to her on one of their last walks together led her to think so. They had been to see a woman friend of theirs, and found her in the middle of her charming children. As they were walking back home along the Seine, Flaubert said, " Ils sont dans le vrai " . . . en faisant allusion à cet intérieur de famille honnête et bon. " Oui ", se répétait-il à lui-même

[1] In 1912 Kafka wrote *The Verdict*, " The Stoker " (*Der Heizer*), and *The Metamorphosis*.

gravement, " ils sont dans le vrai " . . . Kafka often quoted this sentence. Art alone then had not been enough for him on which to build a proper life. But it was an indispensable part of the foundation of it, it was at the same time the beginning, the innermost circle, upon the health of which other circles depended. One can understand from this the deep tragedy that lay in the fact that circumstances prevented him from taking this first step towards a fulfilled, which is to say in his sense a good, religious life, from properly saying the prayer which he felt he was capable of saying. Had he been allowed to let his artistic capabilities have their full run, undoubtedly many other things would have gone better for him later on. As it didn't happen, the harmful effect, of having a profession in which he found no pleasure forced upon him, gradually worked down into the metaphysical depths.

That is obviously not to say that, had one first step succeeded, Kafka would have solved all the other problems of his life smoothly. But without the first step, failure was certain. Only that can be recognised, and no more. It seems indeed that many of Kafka's problems bordered at least very closely on the absolutely insoluble. Nevertheless—given a maximum of physical and spiritual inviolacy (a maximum which was precluded in advance by the slavery of his profession) we should—of that I am convinced—have experienced in Kafka's later development things which go far beyond our present stock of ideas.

UP TO THE PUBLICATION OF *BETRACHTUNG*

THE brief summer holidays which freed us from the thrall of our office work for two or three weeks, gained a double significance for us through this association. To be free for a few whole days, to be able to meet the world and fresh people without bothering and with open minds—we enjoyed this happiness with the unbroken strength of youth. We went on our holidays together, and looked forward to them for months beforehand, made our preparations for them with a care that we ourselves laughed at more than anyone, but which lit up the grey work-day like a ray of sunshine. The day we could leave came at last ! Never in my life have I been so equably cheerful as during weeks of holiday spent with Kafka. We turned into happy children, we hit upon the queerest, loveliest jokes—it was a great happiness to live in Kafka's neighbourhood and to enjoy at first hand his lively thoughts as they bubbled forth—even his hypochondria was still entertaining and full of ideas.

Moreover, it was not only the long summer holidays that we spent together, but all the year round there were lots of excursions in Prague's immediate and farther neighbourhood. Many a summer we did long walking-tours every Sunday. At Easter and Whitsun we stayed away two or three days, and at other times, too, we often left the town as early as Saturday afternoon. Felix Weltsch was generally a third in the party. We marched (so I find out from my diary, alongside the adjective " indescribably beautiful ") seven or eight hours a day ; it was our sport. Bathing in brooks and rivers was part of it. We used to swim, we used to sun ourselves, we got hardened. One day the young Franz Werfel, still a schoolboy then, was taken along with us to Senohrab, and introduced to our uninhibited Nature-life. He got horribly sunburnt in doing so. The poems of his which he read aloud to us on the reedy banks of the Sazawa moved us to enthusiasm. I shall quote here one of the many original letters I have in which Kafka used to propose excursions like this. " MY DEAR MAX,—Don't rush into a great outlay of cash on an express letter to say you can't be at the Franz Joseph Station at 6.05, because you must be, since the train we are going to take to Wran leaves at 6.05. At 7.45 we shall walk the first step towards Davle, where we shall eat a gulash at Lederer's. At 12 o'clock we shall lunch at Stěchowitz, from two till a quarter to four we shall walk through the woods to the rapids on which we shall row about a bit. At 7 we shall take a steamer back to Prague. Don't think any more about it, but be at the station at a quarter to six. Apart from that, you may after all write an express letter to say you would like to go to Dobřichowitz or somewhere else." We spent countless happy hours on the boards of the bathing establishments of Prague, in rowing-boats on the Vltava, in doing climbing stunts on the mill weirs, many an echo of which you can find in my novel *Stefan Rott*. I admired Franz's swimming and rowing. He was particularly clever at handling a so-called "man-drowner". He was always less clumsy, bolder than myself, and had a special trick of leaving one to one's fate in neck-breaking situations with an almost cruel smile which seemed to say something like "Help yourself". How I adored that smile, in which, after all, there lay also so much confidence and encouragement. Franz was inexhaustible in finding out new lines of sport, or so it seemed to me. In this too his personality expressed itself, this too he did, as he did everything, with complete abandon.

Our first summer holiday together began 4 September 1909, and took us to Riva. Kafka, my brother Otto, and I spent many hours of contemplation in the little bathing-place under the Ponale Road, at the "Bagni della Madonnina". When I came back to Riva after the war, I no longer found the lovely sunny grey boards, and no longer saw the gleaming lizards gliding over the garden paths that had led the way down from the dusty road full of cars to the cool place of the spa. Unforgettable, modest little establishment, under the towering walls of cliffs, I have dedicated an obituary to you and the happiness we found in your bay—here we ourselves were guests of peace, of the classic simplicity of the South. Never since has the South revealed herself to us so kindly and so exalted at the same time. Kafka, too, in later years was drawn once more to visit Riva ; but he lived there alone, in 1913, after his first great unhappy love affair, in the Hartungen Sanatorium on the other side of the lake.

In 1909 we were all still doing very well. And even the discussions we had with Dallago, the poet and apostle of Nature, who came to visit the same bathing-resort as ourselves, failed to disturb our comfort. The travelling experiences of my brother, who was much more useful in practical things than I, and whom Kafka very much admired, helped us out of many a difficulty. My brother had, so to speak, "discovered" Riva for us, had been there already the year before, and now took us the easiest way to everything that was beautiful and of interest. One photograph is of Franz under the colonnades of Castell Toblino, another shows him with my brother sitting on his haunches on a slab of marble in the green wilderness on the shore of the lake.

F   [81]

Into the idyll of the Madonnina Spa burst the newspaper story—of course we were reading nothing at the time except the Italian local papers from Riva—that the first flying meeting was to take place at Brescia. We had never yet seen a flying machine, so we decided with great enthusiasm, although funds were low, to go to Brescia. Kafka was keener than anybody on making the trip—and this is I think a good place once again emphatically to point out how false the view is that considers Kafka was at home in an ivory tower, a world of phantasies, far removed from life, and imagines him as an ascetic consumed by nothing other than religious speculations. He was entirely different : he was interested in everything new, topical, technical, as for example, in the beginnings of the film ; he never proudly withdrew himself, even in the case of abuses and excrescences of modern development, he went down to their roots with patience and inexhaustible curiosity, preserved his hopes in man's common sense, never, in proud " distinction ", never, in the attitude of Stefan Georg, rejected contact with the inferior, organised world around him. Only what was dirty, immoral, seemed to have no attraction for him. He had the wonderful gift of finding it just boring. Thus, for example, I could never persuade him to read more than a line or two of Casanova—whom I then rated more highly than his deserts perhaps, but whom I still find significant and worth reading.

Brescia was crowded out. As we had to be very careful of our money, we finally spent the night in a room which we thought must be a den of robbers, and in the middle of the floor of which—even to-day I ask myself if it can't be a trick of my memory perhaps—was a large circular hole, through which one could look down into the taproom which lay underneath. We thought Sparafucile was bound to join us at any moment. But the next day, in the sunlight on the aerodrome, we laughed the unpleasant hours of the night to smithereens. On our way back, when we spent a night at Desenzano, I must admit we were driven into the streets by the bugs that lurked behind hundreds of pictures of saints, and we sat shivering on the benches on the quay by the lake side waiting for the morning. Yes, that is how we travelled in those days ; we knew nothing of first-class hotels, and yet were uneffortlessly jolly. It was, one must admit, a time which had its great advantages. Riva was Austrian, Brescia Italian. There was occasionally some talk of tension ; there were rumours about the underground fortresses of Monte Brione near Riva, but fundamentally nobody took it seriously ; war was an unreal idea, something like the philosopher's stone and, when we crossed the frontier on our walks, we didn't even notice it.

The first flights we saw made a great impression on us. I told Franz he must immediately take notes of everything he observed, and gather them together into an article. By the idea of making it a sporting competition between him and me, I made the idea attractive to him. I was going to write an article, too, and we should decide who had succeeded in making the best remarks. Playful, not to say childish aims of this nature seldom failed in their effect on Kafka. For example, it gave him tremendous pleasure when we made this excursion and took great pains to hide our first reactions from each other, and to betray nothing of what we felt about the things we saw. Only at the end one might see who had hit the mark.

But behind all this solicitation I had a secret plan. At the time Kafka's literary work was lying fallow ; for months he had not produced anything, and he often complained to me that his talent was obviously seeping away, that it had completely and utterly gone from him. Indeed he sometimes lived for months in a kind of lethargy, in utter despair ; in my diary I find note after note on his sadness. *Le cœur triste, l'esprit gai* —this description fits him excellently and explains how it was that, even when he himself was in the most depressed state, he never, except perhaps in the hour of extreme intimacy, had a depressing, but rather a stimulating effect on those with whom he went about. But how deeply he suffered, I knew even then from many a confession, and so I wanted to give him a concrete example of how one must pull oneself together, wanted to prove to him that his fears of literary barrenness were without foundation, that it only needed a certain amount of will, a certain amount of concentration, to bring his gift into working order again.

My plan succeeded. The article " The Aeroplanes at Brescia " Franz wrote with joy, finished it, and then had it published, very much cut, at the end of September 1909, in *Bohemia*. I had handed it to Paul Wiegler, at that time editor of *Bohemia*—and later succeeded in persuading Franz to let me publish it without cuts next to my own essay on the same theme in my book *On the Beauty of Ugly Pictures*. In this book I introduced Franz's essay with the following remarks :

" It is really an extremely far-fetched, and at the same time also banal idea that only *one* author should get a hearing in *one* book. And if we two friends, inseparable in our thoughts on this journey and in other things, have always stood so near to each other in a foreign land, shall we not dare do so in this book in our own home ? And what if these two variations on the same theme would not have come into being the one without the other, although the two authors kept their ideas secret from one another with comic and purposely exaggerated fear, or even, in the heat of rivalry, attacked the third fellow-traveller, my brother Otto, for advice ? What if these variations, then, belong to one another, complete one another, make one another clearer, beautify one another ?

And what if we wish it ? And what if nothing can be done about it anyway ? " I have the galley proofs of the two essays in front of me. I was proud to have effected the first publication of Kafka in book form in this way. But, alas, it never got further than goodwill. In the end the book turned out to be far too long, and at the wish of the publisher, along with several other essays, these two had also to be cut out of the final set-up of the book. Kafka's essay is now published as an appendix to this book.

The article as such was not, of course, the end I had in view, it was to serve only as an incitement to bring Franz's pleasure in creation into flow again. This success I achieved. Albeit always against the strong resistance the stubborn author put up against me. At times I stood over him like a rod, drove him and forced him, not directly naturally, but again and again by new means and new tricks ; at any rate I didn't let his gift break down again. There were times when he thanked me for doing so. But often I was a burden to him with my prodding and he wished it to the devil, as his diary informs one. I felt that, too, but it didn't matter to me. What mattered to me was the thing itself, the helping of a friend even against the wish of the friend.

I claim that it is thanks to me that this diary ever came into being ; even Franz's quartos grew directly out of our little notes on our journeyings, were in fact in a certain sense sequels to them. A conscious and already cultivated tendency of Kafka's to render such an account of his experiences found fresh nourishment in the reportage of the journeys we did together, and was now systematically developed. That is exactly what I had wished for. The diaries have a significance for Kafka which is not only autobiographical and an aid to the mastery of his soul ; in between remarks of a personal content stand the pieces which he then later took for his first book, *Betrachtung*. In fact many of these pieces published by himself are, in their substance, indistinguishable from the entries in the diary ; we don't know why the author considered one worth publishing and kept back the other.

In the context of the diary [1] there are also many fragments of short

---

[1] Here are some beautiful passages from entries in the diary : " One advantage of keeping a diary is that one becomes conscious, with comforting clarity, of the changes one is constantly undergoing, which one also, in general, believes, guesses at and admits, but which one unconsciously denies, when it comes to extracting hope or peace out of any such admission. In a diary one finds the proofs that one has oneself lived, looked around, written down observations, under circumstances which to-day appear unbearable ; that, in fact, this right hand went through the same movements as it does to-day, when we are of course wiser about the conditions at that time, since we have the possibility of having a bird's-eye view of them, but are therefore all the more obliged to recognise the fearlessness of our strivings at that time, which persisted despite all our lack of knowledge." Another extract reads :

stories which have got thus or thus far ; they pile up, until suddenly out of the throng the first finished story of considerable length, *The Verdict*, shoots out like a jet of flame. With it, during the night 22 to 23 September 1912, the writer succeeded in breaking through to the form that suits him, and a powerful genius of the art of storytelling, unique in his genre, finally found his freedom.

Next year, October 1910, we went to Paris for our holidays. There were Kafka, Felix Weltsch, my brother, and I. Our circle of friends had grown, a development which had already begun some years previously. I brought Kafka along to Felix Weltsch and Oskar Baum. The clear-sighted philosopher (*Favour and Freedom*, and *The Risks of the Via Media*, are his most important books, and there is also the—philosophical—treatise, *Perception and Concept*, which was written in collaboration with me)—as well as the writer—who in addition to the list of works quoted elsewhere has just written the impressive historical novel, *The People Who Slept Hard*—felt drawn towards Kafka. Our foursome was also unique in that between each pair of friends there existed an intimate friendship, in whose harmony no jarring note was ever felt. The four of us came together regularly, and this for many years gave our lives a firm rhythm.

Oskar Baum, the writer, describes how he first met Kafka in the following words : " Our first meeting still remains quite clear in my memory. It was Max Brod who brought it about. He brought Franz Kafka along to my place and read to us, that autumn afternoon in 1904, his short story, " Excursions into the Dark Red " which he had just finished. We were little more than twenty at the time. I can still remember many of the things we said during the enthusiastic exchange of opinions in which the problems of the story involved us, and which was carried on with the extremely controlled economy of words which was then the fashion with us. Kafka, for instance, among other things, said, ' When there is no necessity to digress from the action through tricks of style, the temptation to do so is strongest '.

" Kafka's first gesture as he came into my memory left a deep impression on me. He knew he was in the presence of a blind man. And yet, as Brod was introducing him, he bowed silently to me. It was, you might think, a senseless formality in my case, since I couldn't see it. His hair, which was smoothed down, touched my forehead for a moment as he bowed, probably because the bow that I made at the same time

" On the way back home after saying good-bye, regret for my falseness, and pain at its inevitability. Intention : to begin a note-book of my own on my relations with Max. What one doesn't write down flickers before one's eyes, and optical accidents determine the result."

was a little too violent. I was moved in a way that for the moment I could see no clear reason for. Here was one of the first people in the world who had made it clear that my deficiency was something that concerned nobody but myself—not by making allowances or being considerate, not by the faintest change in his bearing. That was what he was like. He stood so far from the accepted utility formulae, that he affected one in this way. His severe, cool reserve was so superior in depth of humanity to the ordinary run of kindness—which I otherwise recognise when I am first introduced to people in a pointless increase in warmth of words, or tone of voice, or shake of the hand.

"This co-ordination of every involuntary movement, of each every-day word with his whole personal outlook on life made his behaviour, his outward appearance, unusually full of life, despite the abstract battles that continuously dominated his mind. When he read aloud—and that was his particular passion—the emphasis on each separate word was completely subordinated, although every syllable was perfectly distinct—with his tongue sometimes working at a speed which almost made one giddy—to a musical breadth of phrasing, with enormously long breaths, and mightily swelling crescendi of the dynamic levels—just as you find them in his prose, where you occasionally find that a complete separate piece like the "Equestrienne" (*Auf der Galerie*) has arisen in the form of one marvellously constructed sentence."

I don't wish, however, to create the impression that Kafka was to be met only in the innermost circle of the "Prague Four". On the contrary, it was much more in accordance with his nature to try and meet everyone who seemed to share his feelings, or at any rate, at least as long as his health lasted, not to refuse to. Among the men who consorted with Kafka are Martin Buber, Franz Werfel, Otto Pick, Ernst Weiss, Willy Haas, Rudolf Fuchs, in later years the elocutionist Ludwig Hardt, Wolfenstein, and many others. Perhaps a few of them will still take up the tale, and complete the picture of the life of Kafka (cf. Supplements II and IV).

Our holiday in Paris was a failure owing to a small carbuncle that Franz developed, and a few terrifying experiences at the hands of French doctors. After a few days he went back home to Prague. Kafka was always very sensitive on the question of any risk to his health. Every imperfection of the body tormented him, even, for example, scurf or constipation, or a toe that was not quite properly formed. He distrusted drugs and doctors. He demanded that Nature herself should restore the balance, and despised all "unnatural" medicines.

This tendency was strengthened in 1911, when, on a journey—probably on behalf of the office—to Warnsdorf, he met the industrialist

Schnitzer, who preached the "Nature Cure". I find the following entries on the subject in my notes dated May 1911. "Kafka came back to Prague on Friday, but didn't come to see me or Baum. Finally, the following Thursday, I rang him up in a temper." He was, "So weak, felt so rotten ; his stomach was out of order ; he wasn't going out at all, he was so miserable ". On Friday afternoon he came to see me and told me a lot of wonderful things about the Garden City of Warnsdorf, about a "Magician ", a believer in Natural Healing, a rich industrialist, who had examined him, had looked only at his throat in profile, from the front, and had then talked to him about poisons in his spinal marrow and almost up to his brain already, which had developed through living on the wrong lines. To cure them he recommended sleeping with the windows open, sunbathing, working in the garden, joining in the activities of a club for Natural Healing and subscribing to a magazine published either by the club or by the industrialist himself. He speaks against doctors, medicines, and injections. He explains the Bible from a vegetarian standpoint : Moses led the Jews through the desert so that they might become vegetarians in these forty years. Manna as a meatless diet. The dead quails. The longing for the "Fleshpots of Egypt ". Even more clearly, in the New Testament Jesus addressed bread with the words, "This is My body ". Franz's attitude to the "Natural Health Methods " and reform movements of a similar nature was one of very intense interest, nicely tempered by making good-natured fun of the follies and fads which go along with these movements. Fundamentally he saw in the efforts to create a new healthy man, and to use the mysterious and freely proferred healing powers of Nature something extremely positive which agreed with many of his own instincts and convictions, and which he widely put into practice too. He slept with the window open all the year round. When you went to his place to see him, the cool fresh air there was a thing that struck you. He always wore light clothing, even in winter, went for long periods without eating meat and drank no alcohol. When he became ill he infinitely preferred being looked after in a private house (in Zürau), in a primitive country district, to any sanatorium, and only went to sanatoria when he was finally forced to do so.

In 1910 there was another important meeting. For 1 May of this year I find this entry in my diary : "Café Savoy. Theatrical company from Lemberg. Very important for J. F. "—the novel I was planning at the time. For 4 May : "Went with Kafka to the Savoy this evening. Marvellous ! " Franz's notes about this Polish Jewish troupe of actors who acted folk-drama in Yiddish, and sang in Yiddish, don't begin until the following year, but from then on they fill many pages of the copy-books, and the greatest actors have seldom been written about with such love and such penetrating understanding, not only with regard to their art, but also to their private lives, as Kafka devoted to describing Mr. and Mrs. Klug, Mr. and Mrs. Tschissik, Mr. Pipes, and above all, the young Isak Löwy.

I was the prime mover in this case. That was just the beautiful thing about our friendship, that I learned from Kafka in many points, as I have already explained, but in other questions Kafka followed my lead. Generally, I must admit, in these cases, he guided the first impulse which he received from me into a depth and a breadth I had never before suspected. I, for example, was a frequent member of the audience at the performances in the Café Savoy, and learnt a lot there towards appreciating Jewish folk-lore. But Franz, after the first time I took him there, entered into the atmosphere completely. It was the same intense and creatively fruitful dogged determination with which he himself did everything. A curious kind of shy love and veneration bound him to one of the actresses, who is hardly likely to have noticed anything of it,[1] and he treated the actor Löwy as a friend, often took him back home with him—to the intense annoyance of his father, who never could get on with any of Franz's friends—made this passionate person tell him all about his life, his surroundings and his development, and gained deep insight into the customs and spiritual crises of the Polish-Russian Jews. His diary makes it clear what he got from Löwy ; in this way, too, Kafka was brought to the study of Jewish history (Graetz) and the study of the history of Yiddish literature—in the French edition of Pines' book.[2] Long portions of the quarto copy-books contain extracts from the latter book, followed by discussions, rich in ideas, on the structure and peculiarity of the literatures of small nations. In this way many a sidelight is thrown on the way in which Kafka followed up the development of Czech literature in every detail. The many-sidedness of Kafka's interests is shown by the fact that the extracts from Pines are followed by extracts just as full from Biedermann's *Conversations with Goethe*. (It should be mentioned here that in later volumes of the diary Kafka's entries include excerpts from *The Memoirs of Countess Thürheim*, " which have been my joy for the last few days ", from *Memoirs of General Marcellin de Marbot*, and from Paul Holzhausen's *The Germans in Russia in 1812*. Kafka preferred reading biographies and autobiographies to

[1] In his literary plans he writes in his diary, " Love of an Actress ", and several dreams about the theatre.

[2] *Histoire de la Litterature Judeo-Allemande*, Paris 1911, which was later published in German too. In his diary Kafka writes he is reading this history of literature " with such a thoroughness, speed, and pleasure as I have never done other books of this kind ".

anything else. The diaries of Grillparzer and Hebbel, the letters of Fontane, were among his favourite books, and he knew them much better than he knew these writers' fiction.)

Perhaps the following postcard may give some idea of the enthusiasm and joy with which Kafka threw himself into this world of the Polish-Jewish folk-energy which was so new to us : " DEAR MAX,—We are in luck ! They are doing *Sulamith* by Goldfaden. With pleasure I am wasting a card to write you what you have read already. I only hope you have written it to me too." Franz began to write a kind of auto-biography of Isak Löwy, using the material the latter gave him, and giving a survey of the Yiddish theatre. The beginning of the book has survived. Short as it is, it gives a good picture of the kind of conversa-tions the two used to hold, and in which I often took part, and of the circle of interests which was busying Kafka at the time, and which was able to show us the question of Jewry from a more living and colourful side than the abstract theories of Zionism could. It was the time when I first came into contact with Zionists and the Zionist outlook, and I passed their influence on to my friend, influences which came from the Prague club Bar-Kochba, and particularly from the wonderful Hugo Bergmann. At first Kafka's attitude was one of rejection. I too, was not at first in agreement with everything that was preached to me on this side—often in a form all too fine and polished—and in the beginning used to go to the tiny, not very inviting Café Savoy on Ziegen Square, where they gave the generally despised melodrama as a direct protest against Zionistic academics. I zealously championed the thesis that however near to unconscious humour and trash they might come, from the performances of these actors more could be learned about the essence of Judaism than from the philosophic deductions of Jews of the West who were, it is true, striving to get to the people, but who were at heart already estranged from them.

It was not until much later by the laborious accumulation of know-ledge that I learned how interdependent East and West, Zion and Diaspora [1] are. Kafka held out against these views much longer than I did, in fact. Later when I had become a convinced Zionist and was vainly trying to convert Kafka to recognising the necessity of the Zionist policy—while we were rowing on the Moldava—we often came to an argument and once to the only quarrel we ever had, a short and passing one. In my diary for 18 January 1913, for example, I find entered in my diary the record of a conversation with Buber, Werfel, Kafka, Pick, Baum, and myself, which was obviously on this theme, and on 23 August 1913, there is this entry : " Afternoon with Kafka. Bathing,

[1] i.e. " The Dispersion " (of the Jews).

rowing. Conversation about feelings of community. Kafka says he has none, because his strength just about suffices for himself alone. Argument in the boat. My change of heart on this point. He shows me Kierkegaard, and Beethoven's letters." In December there is the little note that we had quarrelled. But on the 24 December it was all right again : " Kafka talked about social questions. In the Town Park."

From then on Kafka gradually came distinctly nearer my Zionist standpoint, and in the eventful days in 1918, 1919—the founding of the Jewish National Committee, and of the Jewish School, he stood by me with advice, interest, encouragement, and loving agreement, his recognition of my work was my greatest support—finally, by studying Hebrew deeply, he left me far behind in this field too.

But I am anticipating. Let us go back again for a moment to the poor Yiddish troupe from which we both of us received the impulse which set us on to reach later stages of development which seem so far removed from it. Kafka was unwearying in the service of these artists who were always in need. According to his diary, he drew up a circular to all the Zionist Clubs in Bohemia to make a tour possible for this company ; he had it duplicated himself, too. In this affair he revealed how much energy and activity slept pent up in him, before earning-his-living and marriage plans, etc. had quite crippled him. On 18 February 1912 he organised an evening of recitations for Löwy in the banquet hall of the Jewish Council Chamber, and the whole burden of getting everything ready and the technical arrangements rested on him. He bore it with a groan, and yet with grace, not without pride. The speech with which Kafka opened the evening has been preserved in my wife's notes : it begins :

" Before the Polish Jews begin their lines, I want to tell you, ladies and gentlemen, how very much more Yiddish you understand than you think you do. I am not really afraid of the effect that is waiting for each one of you this evening, but I do want it to be given free play as soon as it has deserved it. But this can't happen if some of you . . ."

That the Russian friend in *The Verdict* bears traces of the actor Löwy is clear. And how deeply the heart is moved by this beautiful sentence in the diary : " The pity we feel for these actors who are so good, and earn nothing, and apart from that receive nothing like enough gratitude and praise, is really nothing but pity for the sad fate of so many noble efforts, and above all of our own ". From Prague, after breaking with his company, Löwy turned to Budapest. Among the papers Kafka left behind I find Löwy's letter from Vienna dated 28/10/13. It runs, with its characteristic original spelling and grammar : " Think you, how deep am I sunk that even with you I have lost touch. . . . And how I miss your letters ? I have now been torne [*sic*] away from everything for a long time, no friends any more, no parents, no family . . . and the dearest of all, Dr. Kafka, also lost. . . . Of this loss I never dreamt. . . . You were after all the only one what was so good to me . . . the only one what spoke to my soul, the only one what half understood me. And you I must also lose, I'm sorry. . . . You mustn't write to me, I'm sorry. You mustn't be good to me. Please don't think I'm ' mad ', I am normal, cold as death." . . . Further on in the letter is the sad sentence : " What have I to wait for ? Another shot of morphia." Franz's draft of an answer either to this or some other letters lies next to it.

" DEAR LÖWY,—I was very pleased you remembered me, as one might guess from the fact that I have taken so long in answering. I am in great confusion, and work, without myself or anyone else getting much out of it.

" Anyhow, here is some good news for you. I've got engaged, and think I've done something good and necessary in doing so, even if the world is, of course, so full of doubts that nothing is safe from them.

" That you are still in trouble, and can't find a way out is very sad. That you are staying so long in Hungary is strange, but probably has its bad reasons. I imagine we were both much more hopeful when we walked about in Prague in the evenings. Then I thought you must make good somehow, and at one stroke too. Anyhow, I am not giving up hope for you at all, let me tell you. You despair easily, but are easily happy, too ; remember *that* in your despair. Only look after your health in preparation for better days. What you have gone through seems bad enough, don't make it worse by damaging your health.

" I'd like to hear more about you and your friends. Aren't you going to Karlsbad this time ? All my best wishes.—FRANZ K."

I don't know whether this letter reached Löwy and what has happened to him. I wonder if he is still alive.

1911. End of August. Rejoicings, holidays ! The journey to Zürich. Then Flüelen, then Lugano. Everywhere the thing that we are keenest on is bathing in the lake. They were days of sunshine and every glorious thing in the world. Our friendship was growing more and more intimate at this time ; the working year that had just ended had brought us again many a dizzy height, including moments of sympathetic solicitude. Thus I find in my notes on 13 March : " Kafka rang up, because the light in his room was going on and off ". I showed my love for my friend, too, by setting to music his poem, " Little soul— thou leaping dancest ", to a simple melody accompanied by variations on the piano. Here let me remark that Kafka, as if to compensate for the remarkable gift he had of musical speech, had no talent for pure music. I have frequently noticed that many an author whose verse or prose bears all the characteristics of good music in its rhythm and dynamic, at the same time expends all his musical energy on speech, so that no specific capacity is left for the world of musical sounds. Kafka played no instrument. He once told me he couldn't tell the difference between *The Merry Widow* and *Tristan and Isolde*. There is this amount of truth in these words, that he never took much trouble to get to know the higher music. And yet he was not without a natural feeling for rhythm and tune. I often heard him sing Löwe's ballad, " Count Eberstein " to himself—it was his favourite piece.

I often used to drag him along to concerts until I gave it up, when I found his reactions to them were of a purely visual character. " Listening to music, by its nature, sets a wall around me ", he writes in his diary after a Brahms concert, " and the only lasting musical effect is that, shut in in this way, I am anything but free." There follow descriptions of the singers, the public, some clergymen in a box ; not a word about the music. All the more receptive was Franz to plays and recitations. How many evenings we spent together in theatres, cabarets—and also in wine bars with pretty girls ! For the idea that Kafka was a kind of stylite or anchorite is completely wrong. He asked not too little from life, but rather too much, perfection in fact, or nothing—and the result of that, of course, was that in later years he steered clear of dalliance, looked at the erotic side of life only from the most serious angle, and never told a dirty story or even stood for one being told in his presence. That is to say, he never protested against one ; it simply would not have occurred to anyone to tell one in his presence. But in those young days this strict way of thinking had not yet developed so markedly. I remember his passion for a barmaid called Hansi, of whom he once said that whole cavalry regiments had ridden on her body. Franz was very unhappy while this affair lasted. You can see that, too, in a photograph taken of him together with Hansi, but in which he looks as if he would like to run away the next moment. An entry in my diary runs : " Trocadero wine bar. There he [Franz] is in love with a Germania from the German postage stamps, Chambre Séparée. But he is so extraordinarily shy. When he says, ' I'll pay your rent for you ', he laughs as if he meant it ironically." Many of his letters refer to this and similar contacts. These ambiguous and one may say, even in his opinion, in fact most of all in his opinion, unclean affairs with women have left many traces in his three great novels and in other parts of his writings. I shall quote here another postcard, from Spitzberg in the Bohemian Forest, and three letters, which bear witness to his craving and unsatisfied feelings as far as the world of women is concerned. (The book Franz mentions is my novel, *Nornepygge Castle*, 1908.)

Postcard :

" MY DEAR MAX,—I am sitting under the roof of the verandah. In front of me it is about to begin to rain. I'm protecting my feet by lifting them up from the cold brick floor and putting them on a rung of the table, and I am exposing only my hands as long as I am writing. And I am writing to tell you I am very happy, and that I should be glad if you were here, because there are things in the woods that one could lie in the moss for years and think about. Adieu, I shall be back soon.— Your FRANZ."

(Notepaper headed " Assicurazioni Generali ".)

9/6/1908.

" DEAR MAX,—Thank you. I am sure you forgive unhappy me for not having thanked you before, when you hear that Sunday morning and early afternoon I was trying for a job in vain, dreadfully in vain, of course, solely on account of my physical appearance, and the rest of the afternoon I was sitting with my grandfather, although from time to time affected by the idle hours ; and then in the evening let me admit I was on the sofa near the bed of my dear H., while she twisted and turned her boy's body under her red blanket. In the evening with the rest of them at the exhibition, in the night in a wine bar, home at half past five. That was where I first looked at your book, for which I thank you again. I have read only a little, the parts I knew already. What an uproar, a kind of controlled uproar !—Your FRANZ."

" MY DEAR MAX,—It's half past twelve in the night, that is to say, an unusual time for writing letters, even on a night as hot as this. The moths won't even come to the light. After my light happy days in the Bohemian Forest—the butterflies there fly as high as the swallows do at home—I have now been in Prague four days, and so helpless. Nobody can stand me, and I can stand nobody, but the second is only a result of the first ; only your book, which I am now reading straight through, does me good. It is a long time since I was so deep in misery without any explanation for it. As long as I go on reading it I hold tight on to it, even if it is in no wise intended to bring help to the unhappy ; but if I don't do this, I must go and look for someone who will only just give me a friendly pat so urgently that yesterday I went to a hotel with a whore. She is too old to feel melancholy any more ; but she is sad, even though she doesn't wonder at it, that one is not so loving with a whore as one is with a mistress. I didn't bring her any comfort, because she didn't bring me any."

" DEAREST MAX,—Not because it is in itself anything that must be said without delay, but because it is after all an answer to your question, for which our way yesterday (not really ' yesterday ' because it's quarter past two in the morning) was not long enough any more for me to find the right answer. You said she loves me; Why did you say that ? Was it a joke, or the seriousness of over-sleepiness ! She loves me, and it doesn't even occur to her to ask me who I was with in Stechowitz, what I am doing these days, why I can't go for a picnic on a week-day, and so on. Perhaps in the bar there wasn't time enough, but when we went on the excursion there was time and everything else you want, and yet any answer was good enough for her. But one can plausibly refute anything; yet in the following case one can't even attempt a refutation. In D. I was terribly afraid of running into W., and told her so, and then she immediately got afraid on my behalf of meeting W. That gives us a simple geometrical figure. Her attitude to me is the greatest friendliness, as incapable of developing as anything you can think of, and as far from the highest, as from the lowest love, because it's something quite different. Myself I naturally don't need to obtrude into the figure at all, if it is to remain clear. Now I have really earned my sleep.—Your FRANZ."

It is obvious that we often had a lot of other things, too, to tell each other about our first experiences with women, and on a few of these occasions Franz would sometimes remember something he had with a French governess, which happened a long way back. He used to talk, too, about a woman he once met in Zuckmantel. And I found a puzzling postcard from Zuckmantel in my possession, from very early days : my address is written on it by Franz. The writing under the view of a walk through the forest is that of an entirely unknown woman. " This *is* a forest, in this forest one can be happy. So come along here, then ! " The signature is in shorthand, absolutely indecipherable. It is to this episode and another later one in Riva, in 1913—about the latter Franz preserved an inviolable silence, he had vowed to the girl he would do so—that this entry in the diary of the year 1916 refers : " I had never yet been intimate with a woman apart from the time in Zuckmantel. And then again with the Swiss girl in Riva. The first was a woman, and I was inexperienced ; the second was a child, and I was completely and utterly bewildered."

In Lugano we lived happily in the open air. Franz was a master of that joy in Nature that bestows life and as in a dream marries Earth to

Heaven. (Read again the lines he wrote me when he came back from the Bohemian Forest. " The butterflies there fly as high as the swallows do at home ".) At the Hotel Belvedere au Lac (Lugano) and the bathing-place near by, as well as on our long walks, we enjoyed our good idle days, in the evening on the terrace of the hotel. We kept our diaries fervently ; but this time not keeping it secret from each other, but in communion. Out of this came the plan for a novel in collaboration, *Richard and Samuel*, in which we had a little good-natured laugh at each other. With Kafka, when he was happy, nothing was carried out without a touch of mischief, which was always, however, combined with a great amount of affection. At that time we worked out, besides from our habit of keeping diaries, a whole theory of how to enjoy life, or at least travel. I remember going on a steamer on the Lake of Lucerne and pitying those tourists who took " only " cameras with them, and obviously had no idea of the higher art of recalling one's travels through the medium of diaries.

And there was yet another plan which came out of that short but so endlessly significant journey—which took us to Milan, too, and from there, diverted through a cholera scare, to Stresa and Paris—a plan that bordered on lunacy but which was worked out by the two of us with determination and continual new jests. We hit upon the idea of creating a new type of guide-book. The series was to be called " On the Cheap ". There were to be titles like " On the Cheap through Switzerland ", " On the Cheap in Paris ", etc. Franz was untiring and took a childish pleasure in compiling, down to the finest details, the principles of this type that was to make millionaires of us and above all take us out of the hideous routine of office work. I then wrote in all seriousness and put our plans for " The Reform of Guide-books " up to publishers. Negotiations always broke down on the point that we refused to deliver up our precious secret without an enormous advance.

Franz took special delight and displayed a high degree of virtuosity in balancing in this way on the line between seriousness and the comic. It was often impossible to tell whether he meant what he said seriously or as a joke : he himself didn't always know, I am sure, but simply surrendered himself to the creative imagination of a great teller of fairy stories. Just so, with me too, he played this game of our new Baedeker —our " On the Cheap ", which we could see already posted up on the walls of the Paris Metro alongside Byrrh and the other most widely advertised apéritifs. Well, " On the Cheap " was above all to save tourists from having to choose, so that it needed imperative routes, only *one* hotel in each town, only *one* means of travel, the one that gave the best value for money. There was to be an organisation to check our information frequently. " Exact amount of tips ", Kafka writes in the memorandum we wrote together. And a note saying " Neither tourists that want to go too fast or too slow, but a certain in-between class. Departures from plan are easier to arrange because they can be linked on to something precise." " On the Cheap " was also to devote a separate chapter to each of the following questions : " What to do on a rainy day " ; " Travel souvenirs " ; " What to wear " ; " Free concerts " ; " Where and how does one get free tickets for the theatre, like a native of the place ? " ; " In picture galleries see only a few important pictures, but study these thoroughly." We got particular fun out of a guide to conversation, " On the Cheap ", which worked out on this principle : " It is impossible to learn a foreign language properly. We therefore prefer to teach it you badly straight away. This gives you less trouble, and is quite enough for making yourself understood. It is a kind of Esperanto, bad French or bad English, invented by us. In addition, we give dialects and the language of signs in current use locally." All the plans we developed with so much fun and friendship, and at which we laughed ourselves sick, contained, of course, an undercurrent of irony, which was directed against our own shortcomings—we neither of us had any talent for languages—and against the economies we were unfortunately compelled by circumstances to make.

To cast a faint shadow on those days, which perhaps shine all too brightly in my memory, I shall be conscientious and quote another passage from my diary : " What a thought, that Plato several times tried to put his teachings into practice (Sicily). What on earth can have been going on in him and round about him ? The very sound of reasonableness which one associates with the name of Plato doesn't fit in with this undoubtedly lunatic reality. And must not his contemporaries lawfully have looked upon such a man, who after all was wrong on so many points, as a fool and a nuisance. Posterity suffers less, or not at all, from his extremes, and so the ' Ideal ' in him shines clearly forth—but we forget that these extremes and this ideal are part and parcel of one another. If I may be absolutely honest, didn't I find Kafka a nuisance now and then ? For instance, in Lugano, when he refused to take any laxative, faithful to his Nature principles, but ruined the days for me with his moanings ? At the same time Kafka was an exception among geniuses, he was so indescribably gentle and considerate. He went to personal trouble to damp down until they were completely unfelt the dissonances which had their root in the principle of genius. They were also really hardly noticeable, nothing but rudiments of them, e.g. unpunctuality."

For the journey to Weimar in the following year, 1912, we were

CHILDHOOD

WITH OTTO BROD (*Centre*), 1909

ABOUT 1918

IN LATER LIFE

especially well prepared by our love of Goethe, and the study we had been making of Goethe's works for years. To hear Kafka talk about Goethe with awe was something quite out of the ordinary, it was like hearing a little child talk about an ancestor who lived in happier, purer days and in direct contact with the Divine. And now again let me sound the little note of mischief at once : Kafka sometimes emphasised that he was amazed that some authors are so incautious as to quote Goethe—a sentence from Goethe, after all, cannot fail to stand out all too dazzlingly from the rest of the prose of any author. To the unusual reverence Kafka felt for Goethe the following passage from his diary bears witness. (I am putting alongside it another passage on one of Lessing's characters which will at least suggest the outline of the whole complexity of Kafka's position with regard to the German classics) : " Goethe by the power of his writings probably retards the development of the German language. Even if prose has often travelled away from him in the intervening period, yet it has always, as it is doing just at this moment, finally returned to him with increased longing, and has even taken to itself archaic turns of speech which are to be found in Goethe, but otherwise have nothing to do with him, in order to enjoy the completest picture of their unbounded dependence on him." On Tellheim in *Minna of Barnhelm*, he quotes Dilthey : " He has that free movement of the life of the soul which, as the circumstances of life change, takes us by surprise again and again by showing us quite new aspects that only the creations of true poets possess."

In this mood of reverential gratitude we paid our first and last visit to Weimar. Kafka's diary covering this most important journey I have now published. To complete the picture I shall here repeat the appropriate passages from my *Kingdom of Love*, making only one correction. That is, that we two poor lower-grade civil servants had not one whole month, but only a little over one week to spare for Weimar.

" They go for their summer holidays together. Only to Weimar, just one month in Weimar ; from the very first they had been one in their reverence for the primaeval force of Goethe, and both of them were quite uninfluenced by the fashionable pooh-poohing of his greatness. In this case there was no need for any mutual influence, the only result was perhaps a strengthening of their feelings. Moreover, they have no wish to do any such thing as study Weimar, but they live there just as in any summer resort, bathe every day in the town swimming-pool, in the evening eat dishful after dishful of good strawberries in a restaurant in the Town Square ; above all, they intend to have a good rest. But as with everything that touches Garta, this stay in Weimar also takes on a special shape—at the same time without Garta's wishing it, only from the fundamental characteristics of his nature, a special honesty and accuracy (not of the head but of the heart). You see, a tiny, ever so tender relationship springs up between him and the lovely daughter of the caretaker at Goethe's house in the Frauenplan. To call it a love affair would be saying too much ; it is nothing but a shy, teasing, perhaps also gently painful, pleasure in seeing each other on the part of the two young people. The result of it is that Garta, and Christof with him, are asked in to the caretaker's flat, that they then go in and out of Goethe's flat as though they were at home ; that they have the entry into the garden, which is otherwise out of bounds, and can wander about in Goethe's rooms out of the visiting hours, that is to say, undisturbed by the trampling of tourists. They feel as if they belonged even, in the most distant, Ancient Roman sense, to Goethe's ' family '. Like a ghost, something of Goethe's music echoes through their merry meetings with the caretaker's daughter, on these summer evenings crowned with green and ringed with roses in his garden with its ancient ivy-covered walls. He is there, the kingly old man ; he is invisibly there ! Of all the sights of Weimar, even of those which have to do with Goethe, they see very little else. Garta's experiences are always full of gaps ; it is only single things he grasps always, but these with loving penetration to their very depth, but there is never any question of completeness. This also could easily be turned into stereotyped praise : the intensive life that does not wish to record impressions. But Garta does not consider it an advantage, but only as a personal weakness, as a defect, that his capacities are insufficient for a complete comprehension, and when he finds a man who has this complete grasp of experience, or thinks he can presuppose in him a forceful striving to achieve it, he admires him beyond measure. From many things he said one can see that he took Christof for a first-class man of this kind—perhaps not altogether correctly. Anyway, they supplement one another in the most salutary fashion. It hurts them a little when they have to part after the days they spent together in Weimar— Christof to go home, Richard to go back again to a home for Nature treatment in the Harz Mountains. They go together by train a little way. At the junction where their lines part, Christof in a sudden wave of affection embraces his friend and kisses him—just this once—lightly on the cheek. When they both get home, not a day passes without their speaking at least for a fleeting moment. Many weeks they spend, afternoon after afternoon, at the good old Prague ' Zivil ' swimming-baths, lying on the burning boards under the autumn chestnut trees, or in the Vltava which has already grown cooler. Worries about work, families, first meetings with girls—everything they confide in one another."

The journey to Weimar was also important for the reason that it took us through Leipzig, where I brought Franz together with Ernst Rowholt and Kurt Wolff, who were then running the publishing house of Rowholt. For I had long cherished the burning desire to see a book of my friend's in print.

Franz's attitude towards this wish of mine was very divided. He wanted to—and again he didn't want to. At times his disinclination won the day, particularly at the time when, having returned to Prague, he had to set to work and choose those short pieces of prose, which he considered were ready to be printed, out of the wealth of his MSS., that is to say, the diaries, and give them the final polishing up—which took place not without a lot of hesitation, looking-up of dictionaries, and despair at his uncertainty of the rules of spelling and punctuation. The publishers had already expressed their readiness—these were happy days !—after seeing the specimens I had taken with me to Leipzig. It was only up to Franz to submit a definite MS. And that was just the point at which he began to kick good and proper, and discovered that everything he had written was bad, and that piecing together these " worthless " old fragments prevented him from getting on and producing better work. But I wouldn't let up any more. Kafka's diary is a witness to the resistance he put up against me, but it didn't help him in the least. The book had to be finished, and finished it was. When the amount of material chosen by Franz as worthy of publication turned out to be incredibly small, the publishers decided to have the *Betrachtung*—that was the title of the book —set in unusually large type. The first edition, now very rare, consisted of eight hundred numbered copies, and the ninety-nine pages with their gigantic lettering resemble ancient votive tablets. And thereby, by one of those rare accidents which according to Schopenhauer have nothing accidental left in them, the innermost character of this great prose was after all unsurpassably brought out.

Thus Franz's resistance was overcome, and turned to a healthy purpose by good forces which in those legendary days at least maintained an equilibrium with the bad forces of the world. Here I must insert the remark that Kafka had led me a similar dance the year before. I insisted on carrying out the plan we had made in Lugano to write *Richard and Samuel*. We began ; the work soon came to a standstill. I wouldn't give in, however, until at least a respectable slice of the book had been written. A part of it then appeared in the *Herderblättern* (Herder Papers) published by Willy Haas. The continuation was to show that the course of friendship was exposed to the same ups and downs and complications as that of true love. The two friends were to get really angry with one another on the journey, their incompatibilities were to come into the open, and only the danger of cholera they shared in sultry, torrid Milan —where I moved Franz almost to tears by begging him not to let me be buried without putting a bullet into me, should I die there away from home—was to fan the ashes of their old feeling for each other to its highest glory. " The journey ends in the two friends putting their forces together to produce a new work of art with a character of its own ", says the preface to the published chapter. The two friends were not, of course, drawn true to Nature, above all not Samuel, who was intended to be practical, rich, and independent—yet we got a great deal of fun out of using for Richard preferably Kafka's characteristics and notes on the journey, and mine for Samuel—although we sometimes followed the opposite procedure. But Franz struggled against this work, too, and yet it is a good thing that I held his nose to the grindstone for a while at least. He got used to regular work, overcame internal inhibitions, forcibly tore himself away from a period of sterility—it is just in the period in which we were writing *Richard and Samuel* that his own diary begins to flow more richly—he even occasionally, as an exception, found some pleasure in the work on *Richard and Samuel*, and the discipline he subjected himself to opened up to him the idea that " the transformation of emotion into character " which Schiller postulated was beginning to take place in himself. Thus the quantity and quality of his production grew until the final break-through was achieved in the night of the 22 to 23 September 1912, when he wrote down the whole of " The Verdict " at one sitting. In moving words Kafka describes this night in his diary—I believe that this self-revelation will for ever remain an important document for the understanding of what a true artist is. " This is the only way to write, only in a coherence like this, with such a complete flinging open of body and soul." By saying this Franz at the same time, without complaining, utters the severest criticism of the pestilential necessity he found himself under of earning his daily bread.

The redeeming moment that brought about this sudden break-through, was a visit paid to us by a girl from Berlin, Miss F. B.—his relations with her were the guiding principle in Franz's life for five years. With the words, " When I went to see Brod on 13 August, she was sitting at the table "; the diary begins the story of this fateful meeting, and then follows the sentence, " As I was taking my seat, I took a good look at her for the first time, and by the time I had sat down, I had already formed an unshakeable opinion ". This meeting is also noted down in my diary for 13 August, and in connection with the note on the meeting in my parents' house there follows : " Café City. Kafka brings the finished book and it pleases me immensely. Miss B. Then I read *Betrachtung* once again. Divine. Wednesday 14 August, sent *Betrachtung* to Rowholt."

The year 1912 is a decisive one in Kafka's life. And two important events took place on this same one day, 13 August. I have preserved a little note that Franz sent me by messenger the following morning. It shows, among other things, that it would be wrong to picture me only in the role of the one urging publication, and Kafka only in that of the one striving against it. The letter runs, " Good morning, dear Max. While I was arranging the pieces yesterday, I was completely under the influence of the girl, as a result it is quite possible that some stupidity has crept in, some sequence that may strike one as comic only in secret. Please see if this is so, and let me add my thanks for that, to all the great thanks I owe you." There follow two small directions for changes to be made.

When I came back on 29 September from Portorose where I had been working with my friend Felix Weltsch on the book, *Perception and Concept,* Franz came to the station to meet us, and began at once telling us about the short story " The Verdict " which he had just finished, and which he willingly gave me for my annual *Arcadia.* In this it duly appeared—in the only year in which the publication itself appeared, 1913 —with a dedication to his fiancée.

Immediately after " The Verdict ", Franz set to work on the first chapter of his novel, which he had most probably begun before, but which was only now getting into its stride. It was *The Man Who Disappeared,* or *America.* I shall quote my diary notes from this period : 29 September : " Kafka is in ecstasy, writes whole nights through. A novel, set in America ". 1 October : " Kafka in unbelievable ecstasy ". 2 October : " Kafka is still greatly inspired. One chapter finished. I am happy about it." 3 October : " Kafka is doing well ". On the 6 October he read me " The Verdict " and " The Stoker ", the first chapter of his novel *America.* Immediately after that on 8 October took place the correspondence between his mother and myself (concerning his contemplated suicide). On 14 October the great Vienna novelist, Otto Stoessl, for whom Kafka and I had special admiration, was staying with me, and we went for walks together, all three, in the streets of the Mala Strana of Prague. But on 28 October there is already the foreboding entry that Franz has written a twenty-two page letter to Miss F., and is troubled by worries about the future. That was the beginning of the tragedy of their relations. (Franz's own diary reveals a gap from October 1912 till Feb. 1913, which is why I am quoting my own diary just for this period.) On 3 November I find : " Went to Baum's where Kafka read us the second chapter of his novel. He is completely in love with

F., and happy. This novel of his—an enchantment." And as early as 24 November of this unusually rich end-of-year, Kafka read to us at Baum's, " His glorious short story about a noxious insect "—i.e. *The Metamorphosis*. Thus between the end of September and the end of November 1912, that is to say, within two months, three of Kafka's chief works came into being, or at least, as far as the novel is concerned, had reached the decisive stage.

On " The Verdict ", this stormy tale of how the good and dutiful son is, in spite of all that, found refractory and diabolical by his father, and condemned to " death by drowning ", whereupon he throws himself into the river with the cry " Dear parents, after all I have always loved you "—on this story which at first sight seems quite clear from the psycho-analytical point of view, but which, when you take a second and third look at it becomes more and more veiled in its meaning, Franz himself has left three commentaries. One was in a conversation with me. He told me, in fact, and to the best of my recollection, more or less in so many words, " Do you know what the last sentence means ? When I wrote it, I had in mind a violent ejaculation." [*Note*.—It followed the description of the suicide, and ran, " At this moment passed over the bridge a truly unending stream of traffic ".] The other two explanatory hints are to be found in the diary, and were written while the story was being printed :

" 11/2/1913. I am taking advantage of the proof-reading of ' The Verdict ' to jot down, as far as I can remember them now, all the relationships that became clear to me during the course of the story. This is necessary, because the story came out of me like a real human birth, covered with dirt and slime, and I am the only person that has the hand that can reach the body itself, and that cares to do so. The friend is the link between father and son, he is the greatest thing they have in common. Sitting alone at his window, Franz takes a sensual pleasure in rooting about in this common possession, believes he has his father in himself and, but for a fleeting, sad hesitation, considers that everything is peaceful. The development of the story now shows how out of this common thing, the friend, the father comes to the foreground, and sets himself up as Georg's opposite, strengthened by other lesser common possessions, such as by the mother's love and devotion, by the loyal memory of her, and by the customers whom, it is true, the father originally cultivated for the sake of his business. Georg has nothing, the fiancée who lives in the story only through her relations with the friend, i.e. with the common possession, and who just because there has not yet been even a marriage, cannot enter into the blood-bond that is drawn round the father and the son, is easily driven away by the father. The whole of what they have n common is built up on the father, Georg finds nothing in it but what is foreign, what has come to be taken for granted, something he has never sufficiently looked after, something exposed to Russian revolutions, and it is merely because he himself has nothing else left save the sight of his father, that the verdict that shuts his father off from him completely has such a powerful effect on him.

"Georg has the same number of letters as Franz. In Bendemann, the ' man ' is there only to strengthen the syllable ' Bende ' (bonds) in case of any unforeseen possibilities in the story. But Bende has the same number of letters as Kafka, and the vowel ' e ' is repeated in the same positions as the vowel ' a ' in Kafka.

"Frieda has exactly the same number of letters as F, and begins with the same letter ; Brandenfeldt begins with the same letter as B. and has a certain connexion of meaning too. Possibly, too, the idea of Berlin was not without influence, and the Brandenburg province may have had something to do with it.

" 12 February : While writing my description of the friend abroad, I thought of St. a great deal. When I ran into him by accident three months after this story, he told me he had got engaged about three months before.

"After I had read my story out to them at Weltsch's yesterday, the old man Weltsch went out of the room, and when he came back after a little while praised particularly the descriptive passages in the story. Pointing with his hand, he said, ' I see this father in front of me ' ; and as he said so, he was looking exclusively at the empty chair in which he had been sitting while I was reading it.

" The sister said, ' It's our house '. I was astonished at their getting the setting of the story so wrong, and said ' Well, then the father must have lived in the lavatory '."

In January 1913 *Betrachtung* appeared. The book is dedicated " To M. B. " and in the copy that Franz gave me these lines have been written in under the inscription : " Just as it now stands here in print, for my dearest Max—Franz K ". One year later I was able to return thanks by dedicating my novel *Tycho Brahe's Road to God* to him.

I wrote about his only book and about his literary work in general in the first long essay that appeared during Franz's lifetime, in the *Neue Rundschau*, November 1921, and among other things said, " Where shall I begin ?—It doesn't matter where. For among the peculiarities of this phenomenon is that one can approach it from any angle and reach the same conclusion.

" This already shows how true, how unshakeably genuine, how pure it is. For a lie offers a different aspect from every angle, and what is impure is irridescent. But there, in the case of Franz Kafka, and let it be said in his case alone in the whole literary circle of the " moderns ", is no irridescence, no changes of view, no scene-shifting. Here is truth, and nothing but the truth.

"Take his language, for example. The cheap means, coining new words, compounds, playing chess with the clauses, he despised. "Despised" is perhaps not the right word. They are inaccessible to him, just as the impure is inaccessible to the pure, is forbidden to it. His language is clear as crystal, and on the surface one can, as it were, detect no other aim than that of properly and clearly suiting the subject. And yet underlying the serene mirror of this well of pure language are dreams and visions of unfathomable depth. One peers into it and is enchanted by its beauty and individuality. But one cannot say, least of all at the first glance can one say, wherein lies the peculiar quality of this simple sentence construction which is after all nothing except right, healthy, and simple. Read a few sentences of Kafka aloud, and your tongue and your breath will feel a sweetness never experienced before. The cadences, the breaks, seem to follow mysterious laws ; the little pauses between phrases have an architecture of their own, a melody is heard that has its roots in other material than that of this earth. It is perfection, simply perfection, that perfection of pure form that brought Flaubert to tears in front of the ruins of the walls of the Acropolis. But it is perfection on the move, on the march, at the double, even. I am thinking of things like " Children on a Country Road " which was the introductory story in his first book, *Betrachtung*, this classically beautiful prose that nevertheless derives so completely from the cottage. There you have fire, the completely restless fire and blood of a tense childhood, full of forebodings ; but the walls of fire obey the baton of an invisible conductor ; they are not ragged sheets of flame but a palace, whose every stone is a roaring blaze. Perfection—and just for that reason not *outré* and not extravagant. One turns somersaults only so long as one has not reached the utmost limit, the line that embraces the universe. The all-embracing does not need to turn somersaults. But don't things get dull at this level ? This is the heart of Kafka's importance as an artist. I said before, he is perfection on the move, on the road. Hence the all-embracing consorts without effort with the minutest, yes, the most scurrilous detail. Oceanus with the comic tricks of the trade of office life, the sweetness of redemption with a new lawyer, who is, however, really the war-horse Bucephalus, or with a worried country doctor, or a little commercial traveller, or with the pink tinsel of a little equestrienne. Hence these great sentences full of artistry, and this simplicity of style, which is yet shot through with ideas in every phrase, in every word.

Hence the inconspicuousness of the metaphors which nevertheless—it is only some time after one notices it with surprise—say something new. Hence calm, perspective, freedom, as if above the clouds—and yet good natural tears and the compassionate heart. If the angels made jokes in heaven it would have to be in Franz Kafka's language. This language is fire, but it leaves no soot behind. It has the sublimity of endless space, and at the same time it palpitates with every palpitation of things created.

" That the pure dare not touch the impure is its strength, but also, at the same time, its weakness. Its strength, because it means the perception, the full perception of the distance between it itself and the absolute. But this distance is something negative, is weakness. And so the strength of the pure can only express itself by insisting that it will not try to lie away its distance from the absolute, but rather exaggerate it directly, as though through a spy-glass that magnifies a thousandfold. But that just to do this is strength, it may and dare not admit, if it wishes to maintain its position. Thus there results a double foundation and, as there always is where there is a double foundation, humour. Yes, even in the midst of the terror of such self-will, such persistence in the most dangerous of all attitudes—for it is a question of life and death in this case—there plays a loving smile. It is a new kind of smile that distinguishes Kafka's work, a smile close to the ultimate things—a metaphysical smile so to speak— indeed sometimes when he used to read out one of his tales for us friends of his, it rose above a smile and we laughed aloud. But we were soon quiet again. It is no laughter befitting human beings. Only angels may laugh in this way—angels that we certainly cannot picture in the likeness of Raphael's cherubs—no, angels, seraphim with three great pairs of wings, daemonic beings between man and God.

" In a quite special way, then, strength and weakness, rise and fall, interpenetrate in Kafka's writings. At first sight it is weakness that meets the eye—something that on the surface puts one in mind of decadence, and satanism, of the love of decay, death and horror that breaks out in Poe, in Villiers de l'Isle Adam, and other later writers. But this first sight is entirely misleading. A short story like Kafka's *In the Penal Colony* has nothing whatever in common with Poe, although scenes of horror occur in it along the same thematic line. A comparison of the style, if nothing else, should teach one that, or at least give one to think. What has the brightly coloured narrative of Kafka, with its sure line, like a drawing by Ingres, in common with the vibrating prose, sometimes indeed violently set in vibration, of these specialists in making one's flesh creep. They are specialists in the deep-sea exploration of hells, having a more or less scientific interest in their explorations ; a little religious end-resolution, a kind of ' moral of the tale ', is stuck on more or less out of embarrassment. Writers, certainly great writers even, and honestly confounded—but don't you hear throughout a note of being ' proud of confusion ' ? But in Kafka's case after all it is the deep earnestness of a religious man that fills the scene. He shows no curiosity about the abysses. It is *against his will* that he sees them. He does not lust after decay. He falls into decay, although he follows the narrow path, sees and loves determination and coherence, and there is nothing he loves so much as the blue unclouded heaven above him. But this heaven begins to pucker like the forehead of a scowling father. And as much more terrible and more shudderingly gruesome the fear for keeping heaven unclouded is than making a study of a tolerable couple of hell's abnormities and turning them into capital, so much more powerful is the shattering effect of Kafka's polished work of art than the sensations to be got from those sketch-books of ' interesting ' pathology of the ' uncanny ' type.

" That is exactly why his books—' The Metamorphosis ' or ' The Verdict ', etc.—give the reader such a shudder. Because all around them, and really in the midst of them, too, the whole of the free world is revealed. But they are not ' on principle meant to horrify '—but rather on a principle that is the opposite of ' horror-making '—on a principle that is perhaps idyllic or heroic, in any case honest, healthy, positive, inclined to everything that desires to live, everything gentle and good, the blooming girlish body that shines over the corpse of the hero at the end of ' The Metamorphosis ', farm labour, everything natural, simple and fresh with a child's freshness, full of striving after joy, happiness, decency, physical and spiritual strength, on the principle then on which a well-meaning God worked when He created the world—but ' not for us '. Against the background of a good Divine Will this ' only not for us ' has a doubly terrifying effect, as a confession of sin of the utmost possible force. It is not life that Kafka rejects. He does not strive with God, only with himself. Hence the dreadful severity with which he goes to law. All through his writings there are judge's chairs, sentences are executed. The ' Metamorphosis '—the man who is not perfect, Kafka degrades to an animal, to an insect. Or, what is still more horrible (' A Report for an Academy '), he lets the animal be raised to the level of a human being, but to what a level of humanity, to a masquerade at which mankind is unmasked. But even that is not enough ! Mankind must sink deeper still—it is a question only of ' all or nothing '—and if a man cannot raise himself to God's level, if the Father has found him guilty, if entire union with the fundamental morality, entry into the ' Law ', is forbidden him by a hefty doorkeeper, or rather when the man has not the courage to thrust this doorkeeper on one side, when the ' Imperial messenger ' of the dying sun-prince never comes to you—very well, then change yourself into some useless object that is neither animate nor inanimate, into a reel of cotton, which as ' something in the care of the heavenly householder ' wanders upstairs and downstairs without stopping. ' What's your name, then ? '—' Odradek '—and a whole range of Slav words is set ringing, which all mean renegade, renegade from one's race, ' rod ', renegade from the council, ' rada ', the divine decision of the creation, ' rat '. ' And your address ? ' ' No fixed abode.' From this you can understand that Kafka writes, alongside the general tragedy of mankind ,in particular the sufferings of his own unhappy people, homeless, haunted Jewry, the mass without form, without body, as no one else has ever done. He writes it, without the word ' Jew ' appearing in any one of his books."

In May 1913 appeared "The Stoker" (*Der Heizer*), the first chapter of the novel *America*, not published until after his death. This time Franz put the whole thing through without any assistance or urging on my part. I shall quote a letter of a later date, which shows the unusual relations that existed between Franz Kafka and his publisher Kurt Wolff, and which do the author and the publisher equal personal honour. It may also lay claim to be praised for having, in itself, the charm of rarity. Kurt Wolff writes, 3 November 1921 :

" DEAR AND HONOURED MR. KAFKA,—Fourteen days ago I happened to meet by accident, in Leipzig, Ludwig Hardt, who came from Prague, and travelled in his company from Leipzig to Berlin. On this journey we made together, Ludwig Hardt told me about the lectures he had given in Prague, and about the special pleasure it had given him to be in your company.

" Talking to Ludwig Hardt gives me an opportunity of giving you another proof that I am still alive. Our correspondence is rare and frugal. None of the authors with whom we are connected comes to us with wishes or questions so seldom as you do, and with none of them do we have the feeling that the outward fate of their published books is a matter of such indifference as it is with you. In this case it would seem to be the right thing for the publisher to write and tell the author from time to time that this lack of interest on the author's part in the fate of his books, does not lead the publisher astray, and make him lose his faith and trust in the special quality of what he has published. From the bottom of my heart comes the assurance from me that I personally have so passionately strong a feeling as I have for you and your work, in the case of perhaps two or at most three of the writers

[107]

whom we represent, and whom we are permitted to bring before the public.

" You must not take the outward results achieved with your books as a standard to assess the work we put into selling them. You and we know that it is generally just the best and most valuable things that do not find their echo immediately, but only much later, and we still have faith in German reading circles that they will one day have the receptive capacity that these books deserve.

" It would be an especially great pleasure for me if you would care to make it practically possible for us to demonstrate tangibly the unshaken confidence that unites us with you and your work, by entrusting us with further MSS. for publication. Every MS. that you can bring yourself to send us will be welcome, and will be published in book form with love and care. If, in the course of time you could once send us, together with collections of short prose pieces, a long connected story or novel—I know, after all, from yourself and from Max Brod how many MSS. of this kind are nearly finished, or perhaps quite finished—we should welcome it with special gratitude. It must also be taken into consideration that the public for a connected, comprehensive prose work is naturally much greater than that for a collection of short prose pieces. That is a banal and senseless attitude on the part of the reader, but there it is. The stir which a longer prose work would make would at least enable us to achieve incomparably greater sales than we have so far done, and the success of a book of this kind would also make possible a livelier trade in those already published.

" Please, dear Mr. Kafka, do us the pleasure and let me know if and what we may hope for in the near future.

" I hope your health is again passable, and greet you with unchanged feelings, as your honestly and heartily devoted KURT WOLFF."

Despite encouragement of this kind Franz could not bring himself to finish even one of his three long novels. Of the way he planned to finish the novel *America*—which I am dealing with here, because the first two chapters of it were written still in the period which falls before the publication of *Betrachtung*—I remember that it was to be the sole work of Kafka's that was to end on an optimistic note, with wide-ranging prospects of life. On the other hand Franz seems at other times to have pictured a different, tragic end for his hero, Karl Rossman. This we see from a note in his diary, dated 29 September 1915, in which he compares his two novels *The Man Who Disappeared* and *The Trial*, of which the hero is called K. " Rossman and K., the guilty and the innocent, finally without distinction destroyed by legal sentence, the innocent man with a lighter hand, more pushed on one side than hurled to the ground."

The novel *America* is kept with a lighter hand, in brighter colours, and with more joy in hopes than the two later long books. On this book, too, there is to be found a short commentary, a self-portrayal in the diary. I quote the following lines also because in them is clearly revealed the great discretion with which Kafka combines admiration for Dickens with keen criticism of him. Just through a direct insight of this kind one gets perhaps an inkling of the wealth and the surety of judgement one met with in the company of a man who, with all his devotion to the unfathomable, remained sober and aloof from excursions into the temptations of cheap mysticism, who never allowed himself to be so blinded by the good qualities of a man or a writer as to fail to see the bad side, and for whom, on the other hand, openly displayed vices and failings in any phenomenon never distracted his attention from a just appreciation of the virtues it possessed at the same time. As clearly, truly, and complicatedly as he here values Dickens, Kafka looked at the whole world.

The page in the diary runs : " Dickens's *Copperfield*. ' The Stoker ' a sheer imitation of Dickens, the novel I have planned even more so. The story of the trunk, the happiness-spreading and charming hero, the menial tasks, the loved one on the country estate, the dirty houses, and so on. Above all, the method. It was my intention, I now see, to write a Dickens novel, only enriched by the sharper lights I have taken from my period, and the duller ones which I dug out of myself. Dickens's wealth and carelessly powerful sweep, but in consequence passages of horrible powerlessness, in which the only thing he does is to muddle up together what he has already achieved. Barbaric is the effect of the senseless whole, a barbarism which I have at least avoided through my weaknesses, and profiting from the lessons of my being of a later generation. There is heartlessness behind this manner, overflowing with rough characterisations which are artificially injected into every person, and without which Dickens would be unable to scramble up his stories even for a fleeting moment."

FRANZ KAFKA had the highest conception of marriage. In the "Letter to My Father", he writes about it in these terms : " To get married, to found a family, to accept all the children that arrive, to maintain them in this uncertain world, and even to lead them a little on their way, is, in my opinion, the utmost that a man can ever succeed in doing. That so many people succeed with apparent ease in doing it is no proof to the contrary, because, in the first place, not many really succeed ; and secondly, these ' not many ' don't generally ' do ' it, but it just ' happens ' to them. This is not that utmost that I mean, it is true, but it is nevertheless a very good thing and worthy of all respect— particularly as ' doing ' and ' happening ' cannot be separated absolutely one from the other. And finally there is no question at all of this utmost, but only of some kind of distant, but respectable approach to it ; after all, it is not necessary to fly right into the middle of the sun, but just to crawl to some clean spot on the earth on which the sun sometimes shines and where one can warm oneself a little."

Similarly in a story like " The Eleven Sons " this high esteem for the family, one may even say for the patriarchal way of life, such as Franz so admired as the natural attitude of his father, stands out clearly. The enormous joy of a father, who told everybody in the house that a grandson had been born to him, is once described in the diary with that mixture of astonishment, deep approval, and light, critical mockery which characterises the relations between son and father in " The Verdict." The prose piece " Eleven Sons ", which has already challenged several powerful explanations of its meaning is, in my opinion, to be understood as a wishful picture of fatherhood, of founding a family, which can be held up against the father's example as something of equal value, that is to say, something just as magnificent and patriarchal, something bordering on the mystic in all the simplicity of its life. This explanation is not contradicted by the fact that Franz once said to me, " The eleven sons are quite simply eleven stories I am working on this very moment ". After all, stories were his children. In his writing he was accomplishing, on a remote territory, but independently, something which was analogous to his father's creative power. I am following Franz's conception of this point, not my own—and which could be set alongside it. The ideal that hovered before his eyes once when he was reading " with suppressed sobs " a book on the war of 1870–1871 was " to be a father, and talk quietly with one's son. But then one may not have a little toy hammer in place of a heart."

After all that one may well understand how the meeting with the girl who for the first time awakened in him the desire to get married stirred him to the very depths of his being. He got to know F. in August 1912. As early as 9 November 1912, we find in the papers he left behind him the draft of a letter ; I do not know whether the letter corresponding to it was ever posted, but it at least reflects sharply enough his first mood of fear and retreat. " DEAREST YOUNG LADY,—You mustn't write to me any more, and I, too, shall not write to you any more. I could not help but make you unhappy by my writing, and I myself am past all help. To admit that to myself, I didn't really need to count the chimes each hour all last night, I was fully aware of it in fact before my first letter, and if in spite of that I tried to cling to you, I should deserve to be cursed for it anyway, if I were not cursed for it already. If you want your letters back I shall of course send you them, much as I should like to keep them. But if you do really want them after all, write me a postcard with nothing on it as a sign that you do. Quickly forget the ghost that is me and live in happiness and peace as you did before."

Despite this letter, or draft of a letter, the correspondence between Prague and Berlin went back and forth with great liveliness. Things hung in the balance for a long time. The girl began to have doubts, Franz seemed to her—and one cannot hold it against her—uncanny and impossible to fit into the ordinary course of affairs. She wanted to break it off. That made him redouble his efforts to keep her. When no news came he was miserable. When news came he tormented himself with doubts. How was he going to manage to live in a menage of two ? At the same time he experienced then an epoch of the highest literary productivity. Immediately after " The Verdict ", in addition to the works which were published later, he began a story, the chief character of which was called Gustav Bleukelt, the tale of " a simple man of regular habits ", who dies at the age of thirty-five. " Kept myself from writing by force ", he writes twice following in his diary. And, " the rush of blood to the head and this useless drifting past ! What harmful things." At Baum's he read to us " The Verdict " and had tears in his eyes. " The indubitability of the story is confirmed." Those are strong words of self-conviction, rare enough in the case of Franz. In May 1913 he attempted to counterbalance his mounting worries by garden work. On 1 July he was seized by " the wish for solitude undisturbed by thought. To have only myself to face. Perhaps I shall find it in Riva." But on 3 July again we find, " the extension and heightening of existence

[111]

through marriage. Text for a sermon. But I can guess it almost." On 21 July he draws up for himself a list of all the points "for and against my marriage". The deeply affecting document closes with the appeal in large letters : " Miserable me ! " and " What Misery ". It lists the following points :

" 1. Inability to bear living alone, not any inability to live, quite the contrary ; it is even unlikely that I understand how to live together with someone ; but to bear the onslaught of my own life, the onset of time and old age, the vague pressure of the itch to write, my sleeplessness, the near approach of madness—to bear all this alone I am unable. Perhaps I should fit in naturally. My connection with F. will lend my existence greater powers of resistance.

" 2. Everything immediately gives me to think. Every joke in the comic papers ; every memory of Flaubert and Grillparzer ; the sight of the nightshirts laid out on my parents' twin beds made for the night ; Max's marriage. Yesterday N. N. said, ' All the married men (among our friends) are happy, I don't understand it '—when he said this, it also gave me to think, and I became frightened again.

" 3. I must be alone a great deal. All that I have accomplished is the result of being alone.

" 4. Everything that is not connected with literature I hate ; it bores me to carry on conversations (even when they are concerned with literature) ; it bores me to pay calls, the joys and sorrows of my relatives bore me to the very soul. Conversation takes the importance, the seriousness, and the truth out of everything, I think.

" 5. Fear of being tied to anyone, of overflowing into another personality. Then I shall never be alone any more.

" 6. In front of my sisters, this was especially so in my earlier days, I was often a quite different person than with other people. I laid myself open, was fearless, strong, unexpected, carried away, as I otherwise am only when I am writing. If I could only be these things before all the world through the intermediation of my wife ! But wouldn't it in that case be at the expense of my writing ? Only not that ! Not that !

" 7. Single, I might perhaps one day really give up my job. Married, it would never be possible."

On 13 August he made the note, " Perhaps it is now all over, and my letter of yesterday (i.e. to F.) may be the last. That would undoubtedly be the right thing. What I am suffering, what she will suffer—it's nothing to compare with the mutual suffering that would result. I shall slowly pull myself together ; she will get married, it is the only way out for mortals. We two cannot blast a road through the rocks for our two selves, it is enough that we have wept and tormented our-

selves for a whole year trying to do so. She will see that from my last
letter. If she doesn't, then I shall certainly have to marry her because I
am too weak to stand up against what she thinks about our mutual
happiness, and quite unable not to put into practice, as far as in me lies,
what she considers possible."

But the affair developed along different lines. On 14 August : " The
opposite has happened. Three letters came. The last I couldn't resist.
I love her, as far as I am capable of that, but my love is buried almost to
suffocation under fear and self-reproaches." On 18 August, during a long
walk, he told me he had proposed to F. I had gone and fetched him at the
nursery garden in Troja, and then he had given me some very worldly
wise, positive advice to help me to get rid of the worries which were
piling up on me at that time. Finally, with less assuredness this time, he
began to talk about his own affairs. I made this entry about our conversation in my diary : " Franz on the subject of his marriage. He has
proposed. His unhappiness. Everything or nothing. His justification,
pure emotion, without analysis, without the possibility or need for
analysis. A complicated situation, which engages my deepest attention.
He talks of Radeschowitz [1] where the married women are bursting with
sexuality, with children, the unborn too, who rule everything. He
counsels complete retirement from the world." The same mood of
despair expresses itself in entries in his own diary. For example, on
15 August : " Tormented in bed towards the morning. The only
solution I can see is to jump through the window. Mother came to my
bed and asked if I had sent the letter [2] off, and if I had stuck to the same
wording. I said the wording was the same, only still sharper. I said she
didn't understand me in any case, and not only in this affair. Later she
asked me if I was going to write to Uncle Alfred—he deserved to be
written to. I asked her how he deserved it. He has wired, he has
written, he means so well by you. ' Those are only outward things,'
I said, ' he is a complete stranger to me, he misunderstands me utterly,
and has no idea of what I want and need, I have nothing to do with
him.' ' Well then, nobody understands you ', said Mother. ' I suppose
I am also a stranger to you, and so is your father. We all wish nothing
but your harm.' ' Certainly, you are all strangers to me, it's only blood
that connects us, but that doesn't express itself. You don't wish me any
harm, of course.'

" From this and a few other observations of myself, I am led to the
conclusion that in my ever-increasing inward determination and confidence there lie possibilities that I could after all stand the test of marriage,
and even guide it towards a development favourable to my vocation. It

[1] A summer-house near Prague.   [2] To F's parents.

is however a belief I have clutched at, in a certain sense, standing on the window-ledge."

" I shall shut myself up away from everything until I have lost all recollection. I shall set myself at enmity with everybody, speak to nobody."

He was reading a Kierkegaard anthology, *The Book of the Judge.* The similarity between Kierkegaard's fate and his own becomes clear to him.

In September 1913 he took refuge in Riva, at the Hartungen Nursing Home. " The very idea of a honeymoon fills me with horror ", he writes to me. He experiences the curious episode with the Swiss girl. It remains obscure. " Everything struggles against its being set on paper. Were I sure that her command not to say anything about it had any influence on this—I have obeyed her command strictly, almost without effort—I should be satisfied." Then later the words, " Too late ! The sweetness of mourning and of love. To be smiled at by her in a boat. That was the most beautiful thing of all. Always the longing to die and yet keeping oneself alive, that alone is love."

In November " an ambassador from F. " appeared in Prague, a girl friend who later played a role in this relationship which is not quite transparent. In the most tactless way I was plaguing him just at this time with my *Education for a Community* for Zionism. It is the only small cloud on our friendship, which I have already mentioned. " The day before yesterday in the evening with Max. He becomes more and more of a stranger ; he was often that to me, now I am becoming it to him too." And a little later comes the outcry—later recanted by word and deed—" What have I to do with Jews ? I have almost nothing to do with myself, and should hide myself quietly in a corner satisfied with the fact that I can breathe." His diary swarms with dreams, beginnings of short stories, sketches. Everything seems to be caught up in a tremendous fermentation. And among them we find this important note, which makes clear one root of his spiritual housekeeping and economy, directing him away from the over-indulgence in self-analysis, which was also sapping his marriage plans, towards the realm of story-telling and of fiction : " Hatred of active self-observation, explanations of one's state of mind, such as : Yesterday I was so, and the reason was such ; to-day I am so, and the reason is such. It is not true, the reason was not such, and the reason is not such, and therefore also not so, and so. Conduct yourself with calm, without being hasty, and live as you must, and do not chase round after your own tail like a dog."

In the following year, 1914, a crisis broke out in his relations with F. She wanted to have nothing to do with him. On the 5 April he entered in his diary, " If it were only possible to go to Berlin, to become independent, to live from day to day, even to go hungry, but to let one's whole strength gush forth, instead of conserving it here, or rather turning oneself away towards nothingness ! If only F. wanted it, if she would stand by me ! " He wanted to live in Berlin as a journalist, as a free-lance. At the end of May or the beginning of June—I can't make our dates agree—the official engagement took place in Berlin. A flat was taken in Prague. The engagement, which took place under the most unfavourable auspices (" I was bound like a criminal ", etc.) was followed at the end of July, by the break, which also took place in Berlin. " The court of law in a hotel ", he writes about it. It was, so he told me, the hotel " Askanischen Hof " near the Anhalter Station. Present at the decisive talk were not only F. but also her girl-friend. Then the scene with his parents. " Solitary tears on my mother's part. I told the whole story. Father understood it rightly from every side. Came in fact from Malmö for my sake. Travelled overnight. Sat in his shirt-sleeves. They admit I am in the right, there is nothing, or at least not much that can be said against me. Devilish in all innocence."

I believe I am not going wrong when I look in those terrible upheavals, during which Kafka was always troubling his own conscience with questions (" To have to bear and to be the cause of such suffering ", he laments in his diary), for the origin of two new long works which were written after the breaking-off of the engagement. In September he read aloud to me the first chapter of the novel *The Trial*, and in November, *In the Penal Colony*. They are documents of literary self-punishment, imaginative treatment of sins. What K., the hero of *The Trial*, had done is never said. By ordinary bourgeois standards he is undoubtedly innocent. There is " nothing, or at least not much that can be said against him ". And yet he is " devilish in all his innocence ". Somehow or other he has not lived up to the laws of the good life. He is called to account by a mysterious court, and finally the sentence on him is carried out. " On the eve of his thirty-first birthday ", says the last chapter. As a matter of fact Kafka, when he began his novel, was thirty-one. There is a girl who appears in the book several times, Miss Bürstner—in his MS. Kafka generally writes this character's name abbreviated to Fr. B., or F. B., and then the connection is surely quite clear. At the end, K. is still trying to keep the bailiffs off. " Then in front of them, from a little alley that lay deep in the shadows, up a short flight of steps, Fräulein Bürstner came out into the square. It was not quite certain that it was she, the resemblance was certainly great. Whether it was really Fräulein Bürstner or not, however, did not matter to K. ; the important thing was that he suddenly realised the futility of resistance." It is really of no importance whether the apparition is Fräulein Bürstner or is only like her. The whole failure of his attempt to get married, indeed, was important for the life of Kafka, as will soon become clear, as a pattern, and not individually—independent of the person of his fiancée—or rather as a pattern that, as the last year of his life shows, could be broken through by the personality of a woman of unusual character.

About a journey he made to the Danish seaside place on the Baltic, Marienlyst, in the company of a writer whom he esteemed very highly, Ernst Weiss (who seems to have played a certain part, by his advice, in the happenings in Berlin), he drafted a revealing letter to his parents, revealing also because it shows that there were periods when Kafka had counted on the possibility of earning a living by his literary work. In this letter, among other things, he writes, "I have not finished with Berlin, however, in so far as I believe that the whole business, for your good and for mine (for they are certainly one and the same thing) prevents me from going on living as I have done. Look, really serious pain I have probably never caused you till now, unless it were that this breaking-off of my engagement is one, at this distance I can't judge it as such. But really lasting pleasure I have given you still less, and that, believe me, solely for the reason that I couldn't give myself this pleasure continuously. Why that is so, just you, Father, although you cannot recognise the real thing I want, will understand the easiest! You sometimes relate how badly things went with you when you were making your first beginnings. Don't you think it is a good training for self-respect and satisfaction? Don't you think—anyway you have already told me so in so many words—that I have had things too easy? So far I have grown up in complete dependence and outward well-being. Don't you think that that was not at all a good thing for a nature like mine, kind and loving as it was on the part of all who saw to it that it was so? Of course there are men who know how to ensure their independence anywhere, but I am not one of them. You must admit that there are also people who never lose their dependence, but to put it to the test as to whether I don't perhaps belong to that class, seems to me an attempt which can do no harm. Even the objection that I am too old for such an attempt doesn't hold water. I am younger than would appear. The only good result of dependence is that it keeps one young. That of course only in the case that it comes to an end.

"In the office I shall never be able to achieve this improvement. Not anywhere at all in Prague. Here everything is arranged to keep me, a man that fundamentally asks for dependence, in that state. Everything is so nicely laid to my hand. The office I find very burdensome and often unbearable, but at bottom, all the same, easy. In this easy way I earn more than I need. What for? Whom for? I shall go up in the scale of salaries. To what purpose ? If this work doesn't suit me and doesn't even bring me independence as a reward, why should I not throw it up ? I have nothing to risk, and everything to gain if I hand in my resignation and go away from Prague. I risk nothing, because my life in Prague leads to nothing good. Sometimes you say for fun I am like Uncle R. But my way of life will not lead me so far apart from his if I stay in Prague. I shall presumably have more money, more interests, and less faith than he has ; I shall be correspondingly more dissatisfied, because other differences there will hardly be. Away from Prague I can gain everything, that is to say, become an independent man at peace with himself, who is employing all his faculties, and as a reward for good and genuine work gets the feeling of really being alive, and of lasting contentment. A man like this—this will not be the smallest gain—will also behave better towards you. You will have a son whose every single action you will not perhaps approve of, but in whom, as a whole, you will be well pleased, because you will be obliged to say, ' He does his best '. This feeling you have not now, and rightly.

" The way to carry out my plan I imagine is this : I have 5,000 crowns. That enables me to live somewhere in Germany, in Berlin or in Munich, for two years, if needs must, without earning anything. These two years will enable me to go on with my literary work, and to produce from out of myself that which I cannot produce in the same clarity, wealth and coherence in Prague, what between inner lethargy and outer disturbances. This literary work will enable me, after these two years, to live, however modestly, on what I earn myself. But let it be as modest as you like, it will be incomparably better than the life which I am now leading in Prague, and that which awaits me there in future. You will object that I am mistaken in my abilities and in the possibility of making a living out of these abilities. That's certainly not out of the question. Only the answer to that is that I am thirty-one, and mistakes of that kind cannot be taken into account at that age, otherwise it would make any accounting impossible. A further answer to it is that I have already written a certain amount, little though it be, which has half succeeded in meeting with recognition, but the objection is finally answered by the fact that I am not in the least lazy, and have fairly few pretensions, and therefore, even if this hope should fail, can find other ways of earning my living, and in any case should not make any claims on you; for that would anyhow, both in its effects on me, as well as on you, make things still worse than my present life in Prague is, in fact it would be completely unbearable.

" My position therefore seems clear enough to me, and I am anxious to hear what you will have to say about it. For even if I am convinced that this is the only right way, and that if I miss putting this plan into action I shall miss something of decisive importance, yet it is naturally very important for me to know what you have to say to it all.

" With best love, your FRANZ."

But these plans were not to mature. The Great War broke out. A period began against the background of which all we had ever suffered hitherto retired by comparison into a land of fairy tales round which played a rosy glow of childhood.

Undaunted by all the excitement, Fränz worked at three MSS. simultaneously, *The Trial*, *The Penal Colony*, *Die Eisenbahn in Rüssland*. In October he took a week's leave, " to push the novel on a bit ". He prolonged his leave by a further week. " Fourteen days, good work in parts, complete understanding of my position." A letter arrived from F.'s girlfriend, which attempted to mediate between them. The relationship with F. had been dropped for two months by this time, although a correspondence was still kept up during this period with F.'s sister. To the answer to F.'s friend's letter, a copy of which he kept for himself, and in which he writes, " I don't wish to mention what your letter coincided with ", he adds the note, " Suicide, letter to Max with a lot of requests." And somewhat later, " Have been turning over the pages of my diary. Have got some kind of idea of the organisation of such a life."

It is astonishing that his creative powers did not fail in the midst of all these visitations. But on the contrary, they were just at their height at that period. On 13 December he finished his " Exegesis of the Legend "; that was how he himself described the chapter which I have published as the ninth—next to last—in the *Trial*—and writes about it in his diary, " Contentment and a feeling of happiness, which I feel particularly in face of the *Legend* ".[1] Already on 19 December he writes, " Yesterday I wrote *Der Dorfschullehrer* almost without knowing what I was doing ". He is referring to the story of *Der Riesenmaulwerf*. In the Christmas holidays he took a little trip with my wife and me to Kuttenberg, to look at the architectural monuments there, and to have a short rest—it was only four days—from the terrors and privations of the war which were already making themselves very much felt in the city. In a hotel in Kolin he read aloud to us the unfinished last chapter of his American novel, which inspired us with the brightest enthusiasm. (This trip was preceded by a trip to Hellerau with Otto Pick in the summer of the same year.) On the last day of December 1914, contrary to his usual custom, he held a review of his work : " Have been working since August, in general not little and not bad, but neither from the first nor the second point of view to the limit of my capacities, particularly as my capacities, judging by all the prospects—sleeplessness, headaches, weak heart—will not last very much

[1] *In the Eyes of the Law* (*Vor dem Gesetze*).

longer. Written, unfinished : *The Trial, Erinnerungen an die Kaldabahn, Der Dorfschullehrer*, the *Der Unterstaatsanwalt*, and short beginnings. Finished, only *In the Penal Colony*, and one chapter of *Der Verschollener*, both during my fortnight's holiday. I don't know why I am making this survey, it's not in my line at all."

The relationship with F. was far from being finished and done with. In the last months of 1914 it experienced a painful rebirth—it goes against the grain for me to go into details, it is enough, apart from the extensive correspondence—there are extant perhaps several hundred letters from Franz to F.—to mention the main stages, a meeting at Bodenbach, January 1915, and in Marienbad, July 1916, and to make clear the constant and increasingly important connection between this great experience and Kafka's creative work and religious development. His mood is one of despair. In his diary he writes : " Am I to lodge my complaint here, in order to find salvation here ? It won't come from this copy-book, it will come when I am in bed, and will lay me on my back, so that I lie beautiful and light and bluish white ; no other salvation will come." Or, " I think it is impossible we should ever become one, but don't dare to say it either to her, or, at the decisive moment, to myself ". Or, " The hardship of living together. Under the compulsion of strangeness, pity, cowardice, vanity, and only deep down in the ground a thin trickle of a brook worthy to be called love, not to be found when you look for it, but suddenly shining forth for the twinkling of an eye." Or one of these comparative lists which are much more likely to make a decision much harder than to prepare the way for one.

20 *August* 1916.

To remain chaste.	To get married.
Bachelor.	Married man.
I remain chaste.	Chaste ?
I preserve all my powers in coherence.	You will remain without your coherence ; you will become an idiot, will follow every wind, but will never get any forwarder. I draw from the blood circulation of human life all the power that is available for me.
Responsible only for myself.	The more infatuated with yourself. (Grillparzer, Flaubert).
No worries, concentration on work.	As I grow in strength I shall stand more. But there is a certain kernel of truth in this.

At the same time there is no lack of assertions, in which he pictures to himself a marriage with F. as something completely possible and desirable. Thus he writes to me from Marienbad, " But now I have seen the look of trust on a woman's face, and could not shut myself against it. Many a thing gets torn up that I wanted to preserve for ever (it isn't single details, but wholes), and from this tear there comes out, I know it, enough misery for more than one man's life ; but it is not something one has summoned up, but something laid upon one. I have no right to defend myself against it, because to receive just that look again, I should do that which happens voluntarily, with my own hand, were it not to happen." And, " Now it is all different and all right. Our compact is, in brief : Get married shortly after the war is over ; take two or three rooms in a Berlin suburb ; leave each one only his own economic worries ; F. will go on working as before, and I, well I, that I can't yet say. But if nevertheless you look at the menage carefully, you get the picture of two rooms, in Karlshorst, shall we say ; in one F. gets up early, runs off to work and falls dead tired into her bed in the evening ; in the other there is a sofa, on which lie I and feed myself on milk and honey. ' There he lies and takes his ease, the man whom morals do not tease ', as the saying goes. Nevertheless—now there is peace there, certainly, and therefore the possibility of living." *P.S.*—" Looking back on them, strong words, hardly to be held down for ever by a weak pen ".

In a certain sense F. remained still later, even after the final farewell, an ideal figure for Franz. Thus he writes to me from a sanatorium, when I wrote and told him about my lectures in Berlin : " Wasn't F. at your lectures ? To have been in Berlin and not to have seen F., it seems to me, privately, all wrong, although of course it would have been exactly the same had I been there. For F. I have the love an unfortunate commander has for a town he could never take, and which has nevertheless somehow become great—a happy mother of two children." Elsewhere he writes, " I loved a girl who loved me too, but I had to leave her . . . and so on ".

For five years Kafka's strivings to wrest a marriage with F. from himself and the opposing circumstances was the prevailing motive in his life, the thorn in his creative work and in his harassed religious questionings. He read a lot of Strindberg at this period—also the Bible, Dostoievski, Pascal, Herzen, and Kropotkin. On Herzen's *London Fog*, he passed the following judgement : " I had no idea what it was all about, and yet the complete, unknown man emerged, purposeful, self-torturing, in control of himself and then again falling to pieces ". Werfel used to read his poems aloud for him, from a drama called *Esther, Empress of Persia* for example. He took a lively interest in all the positive activities of his friends, as for instance in the courses of lectures Felix Weltsch was giving ; he always cheered them up, praised, criticised, encouraged, allowed none —except himself—to yield to despair, interested himself in my work in the school for refugee children from Galicia, often came to my lessons, made friends with the family of one of my little girl pupils. An understanding of the tenderest kind developed between him and the eldest daughter of this family. He also took part in debates between Jews from the East and Jews from the West—in silence, observing. At that time I used to spend a lot of time, together with my cabbalistic friend Georg Langer at the house of a miracle-working Rabbi, a refugee from Galicia who lived in dark, unfriendly, crowded rooms in the Prague suburb Žižkov. Unusual circumstances of life had brought me near to a kind of religious fanaticism. It is worthy of note that Franz, whom I took with me to one of the " Third Suppers " at the close of the Sabbath, with their whispering and Orthodox chants, remained, I must admit, very cool. He was undoubtedly moved by the first original echoes of an ancient folklore, but on the way home he said, " If you look at it properly, it was just as if we had been among a tribe of African savages. Sheerest superstition." There was nothing insulting, but certainly a sober rejection in these words. I understood him very well. Franz had his own personal mysticism, he couldn't take over from others a ready-made ritual.[1] He was often alone, and enjoyed being alone. The " most beautiful place in Prague " was the description he gave of the Chotek gardens, where he used to go again and again for lonely walks. " The birds were singing, the castle with its gallery, the ancient trees, with last year's leaves still hanging on them, the semi-darkness."

He also made some energetic attempts at this time to escape from the spell of the family circle, to become independent. For some time he didn't live with his people but in a room of his own. The first he took was in Bílek Street, February 1915, the second in Langen Street, Dlouhá, in the house " At the sign of the Golden Pike ", where in April 1915 he gave me unutterable pleasure and compelled my admiration by reading me the fifth and sixth chapters of *The Trial*. In February he wrote " The Dog Story ". He passes a very severe judgement on this story in the diary : " I have just been reading the beginning. It is ugly and gives one a headache. For all the truth it contains, it is bad, pedantic, mechanical, a fish just able to gasp on a sandbank. I am writing ' *Bouvard and Pécuchet* ' [2] at a very early age. If the two elements most clearly stamped on ' The Stoker ' and *In the Penal Colony* don't unite, I am finished. But is there any prospect at hand of such a union ? " By the two elements he means most probably the realistic-hopeful and the idealistic-severe tendencies in his writings.

[1] Yet the impression was strong and had its after-effects. The beginning of a Golem story seems to go back to this episode.

[2] i.e. a work displaying every sign of a work of an old man.

One journey that Franz made with his sister to Vienna, Budapest, and Nagy-Mihály to see his brother-in-law, who had been called up, brought him very near the front. Then Franz received his " calling-up papers ", but exempted as being employed in an indispensable Government office. Later, when he could see no way out of his difficulties any longer, he tried to have his exemption cancelled and go into the army. His illness brought this plan to nothing.

The award of the Fontane prize in October 1915 was a temporary consolation in the midst of these sorrows, and was accepted with a certain amount of satisfaction. If I am not mistaken, this is how it all happened ; that it was Sternheim who was really awarded the prize, but handed it down to the " young writer " for his short story, " The Stoker ", which had already been published in 1913. Poor consolation. For in the diary you find wild pen-and-ink drawings, complaints without end about sleeplessness and headaches, the beginning of the meditation on the fall of man, lines like : " The ragings of God against the human family " ; " Only the Old Testament sees—say nothing about it yet " ; ' Take me, take me, network that I am of madness and pain " ; and also the fragments from which I have reconstructed the poem, " In the troubled heart a clock strikes ". He reproaches himself, in his conduct towards F., with " the office-clerk's vices of weakness, meanness, indecision, counting the cost, caution ". And again, " the soul of a clerk, childishness, a will broken by my father ". " Improve it, work at it, it lies directly to your hand. That means then, don't spare yourself (at the cost moreover of the human life of F. whom you love), because you can't spare yourself ; this apparent sparing of yourself has now already almost ruined you. It is not only the question of sparing yourself as far as F., marriage, children, responsibility, etc., are concerned, but sparing yourself as far as the office in which you are stuck is concerned." And in his agony the following prayer is wrung from him, " Have mercy on me, I am sinful in every corner of my being. But I had not entirely despicable talents, little, tender capabilities, dissipated them, ill-advised person that I was, am now ready at the last gasp, at a time when outwardly everything might take a turn for the good for me. Don't thrust me among the lost souls."

Unmistakably two kinds of causes working together effected Kafka's engagement tragedy, exactly as they did the tragedy of his employment : those of a metaphysical, and those of an economic nature. As far as the latter are concerned, the fact cannot be overlooked that Franz's financial position was, in fact, extremely unfavourable if he followed the dictates of his pride, and refused to call on his parents' aid, and was not prepared to do violence to his gift of writing. Perhaps one can imagine a social and political order in which such a unique narrative talent and such a literary genius would not be damned to scribbling legal documents, and when he thinks of the marriage he wishes to make and the responsibility towards wife and children bound up with it, would not see himself faced with the abyss and flaming despair. " You belong to me ", he once wrote to F. (according to a copy of the letter in the diary), " I have taken you to myself. I can't believe that in any fairy story any woman was more often and more desperately fought for, than you were in me." Certainly Kafka would have had a hard time of it even in an ideal social order ; the metaphysical, erotic roots of his pain, the irremovable misery would then have come out more clearly. But in his soul the corresponding antidotes would have been found. Anyhow, as a result of our as yet still very primitively organised community, he foundered on obstacles which were removable (I call them in another passage " ignoble "), and therefore the great struggle in the metaphysical sense never found expression at the right level.

In the winter of 1916–1917, Franz lived in the Alchemists' Street. Legends are already growing up around the place where he stayed, and foreigners who come to Prague are shown the tiny little house and the room that " the author " used to live in—they are almost identical. The house consists of only the one room, together with a tiny kitchen and a loft. But Franz didn't choose this quarter at all from any mystic or romantic inclination, or at least any such inclination was not the deciding factor, except perhaps subconsciously, in the form of an old love for old Prague ; in the foreground was Franz's need for a quiet place to work in. His extraordinarily keen sensitivity to noise, with which he ever occasionally infected me, by suggestion—when we travelled together, for example —made the choice difficult. In the Alchemists' Street Franz felt comparatively happy, and was extremely grateful to his youngest sister who had discovered this refuge for him—as she did later in Zürau. On 11 February 1917, a Sunday, I wrote, " With Kafka in the Alchemists' Street. He read aloud beautifully. The monastic cell of a real writer." A letter to F., the copy of which has been preserved in the posthumous papers, gives an account of this lodging, in which was conceived *Der Kübelreiter*— the sole thing of beauty that came out of the coal shortage, with its quietly sad gaiety, its ironic treatment of human weakness, as though looking at them from above, its singing quality—and of Franz's next lodging in the Schönborn Mansions. At the same time the seriousness with which Franz approached the preparations for his marriage can be seen from this letter. It is a fact that in the following summer a flat was taken for the young couple, furniture was bought, and Franz had already begun the conventional round of calls on relatives and acquaintances and even went to Hungary, to Arad, with F., to pay a visit to her sister. Franz and the conventions ! It was a pitiful sight. At the same time he certainly made every effort to conform to the conventions that were held to be seemly. Another partner might, it is true, have freed him from this compulsion with a good hearty laugh. At the same time it is doubtful, too, whether Franz would have accepted or wanted this freedom. Comically enough the pair of them paid even me a formal call, on 9 July 1917—the sight of the two, both rather embarrassed, above all Franz, wearing an unaccustomed high stiff collar, had something moving in it, and at the same time something horrible. (On 23 July after this there was quite a large party at my place, at which were present in addition to Kafka, Adolf Schreiber, the musician, Werfel, Otto Gross and his wife. Gross unfolded a plan for a newspaper which very much interested Kafka—this is the last note I have on him before the catastrophe.) The letter to F. which deals with questions of the flat and the wedding follows below (the beginning refers to the flat in Dlouhá—the stay in Munich was the occasion for a reading, at which Kafka read, besides works of his own, also some poems from my " Promised Land ", and with his usual conscientiousness insisted afterwards on handing over a share of his fee to me).

" DEAREST,—Well, here is the history of my flat. A tremendous theme. I am terrified I shall not be able to master it. Too big for me. I shall be able to relate only a thousandth of it, of that thousandth only one-thousandth will come back to me when I begin writing, and only one-thousandth of that shall I be able to make clear to you, and so on. Nevertheless, it must be done, I want to have your advice. So read carefully and advise me well : How much sorrow I have had for two years you know ; little in comparison with the contemporary sorrow of the world, but sufficient for me. A comfortable, friendly room on a corner, two windows, a door leading on to a balcony. A view over lots of roofs and churches. Tolerable people, because after a little practice there was no need for me to see them any more. A noisy street, heavy lorries at dawn, to which however I had already almost got accustomed. A room, however, that I couldn't live in. It is true it lies at the end of a very long entrance hall, and to outward appearance is sufficiently shut off, but the house is a concrete one ; I hear, or rather heard, until well past ten in the evening the sighing of my neighbours, the talking of the people on the floor below, now and then a clatter from the kitchen. Moreover, just above the thin ceiling is the loft, and one cannot count the number of times, late in the afternoon, when I am just settling down to work, some servant girl hanging out her washing digs her heel purposely into my innocent skull. Now and then, too, someone would play the piano, and in summer, from the semi-circle of the other houses that cluster around, there would be singing, a violin, and a gramophone. Even an approximation to complete peace then, not before eleven at night. Well then, impossibility of finding peace, complete homelessness, breeding-grounds for every kind of madness, ever increasing weakness and hopelessness. How much more there is to say on this subject ! But let us get on ! In summer I once went flat-hunting with Ottla, I didn't any more believe in the possibility of real peace, but all the same I went in search of it. We looked at a few places on the Mala Strana, all the time I was thinking, if only there were some place in a quiet attic-corner in one of the old palaces, where one could at last stretch oneself in peace. Nothing ; we found nothing that would do. For a joke we asked in one of the little alleys. Yes, there would be a little house to let in November. Ottla, who is also, only in her own way, looking for peace, fell in love with the idea of taking the house. I with my native weakness advised her against it. That I could be there too, that hardly entered my head. So small, so dirty, so uninhabitable, with every conceivable inconvenience. But she insisted on it, and after the huge family that had inhabited it had moved out, had it painted, bought a few pieces of cane furniture (I know of nothing more comfortable in the way of chairs than a cane one), kept it, and keeps it, a secret from the family. At about that time I came back from Munich full of fresh courage, went into a flat agency, where almost the first thing they offered me was a flat in one of the most beautiful of the palaces. Two rooms and a hall, one half of which had been fitted up as a bathroom. Six hundred crowns a year. It was like a dream come true. I went to see it. The rooms were lofty and beautiful, red and gold, like something in Versailles. Four windows looking on to an entirely hidden quiet court-yard, one window looking over the garden. The garden ! When you come to the gate of the castle, you can hardly believe your eyes. Through the lofty semi-circle of the second door which is flanked by cartyatids, standing on stone steps, beautifully divided in a zig-zag to the great garden, you see a broad balustrade rising gradually and in sweeping curves to a gloriette. Well, the flat has one small fault. The former lessee, a young man living apart from his wife, had made his home in the flat, with his manservant, for a few months only, was then unexpectedly transferred (he is a civil servant), had to leave Prague, but had invested so much money in the flat in this short space of time that he was unwilling to give it up just like that. So he was hanging on to it and looking for someone who would at least in part cover his outlay—putting in electric light, fitting up a bathroom, building cupboards, putting in a telephone, and laying down a big carpet. I was not the man he was looking for. He wanted 650 crowns for it—certainly little enough. It was too much for me, also the over-lofty, chilly rooms were too magnificent for me ; finally I had no furniture after all, and there were other, smaller considerations to be taken into account as well. Now in the same castle, however, there was another flat to let, direct from the agent, on the second floor, the ceilings somewhat lower, looking on to the street, the Hradschin close up in front of the window. The furniture was more friendly, more human, modest ; a countess who had been here on a visit, probably a person with more modest pretensions, had lived in it ; it was still arranged as she had had it, with a maidenly air about it, its furniture consisting of a few old pieces thrown together. But there was some doubt as to whether the flat could be got. That threw me into despair at the time. And in this state I moved into Ottla's house, which just happened to be ready at the time. There was a lot wrong with it in the beginning. I haven't the time to go into the whole story. Now it suits me down to the ground. To sum up its advantages : the lovely way up to it, the quiet there—from my sole neighbour I am separated by only a very thin wall—but the neighbour is quiet enough, and generally stays there until midnight ; and then the benefit of the walk home : I have to make up my mind to stop. I then have the walk that cools my head. And the life there : it is something special to have one's own house, to shut in the face of the world the door not of your room, not of your flat, but of your own house ; to step out through the door of your lodgings straight into the snow of a quiet alley. All that for twenty crowns a month, provided with everything I need by my sister, " done " by the little flower-girl (Ottla's pupil) for as little as is necessary, everything lovely and in order. And just at this moment it turns out that the flat in the castle is at my disposal after all. The manager, whom I once did a favour, is very kindly disposed towards me. I get the flat on the street I told you about for 600—without the furniture on which I had counted, it is true. There are two rooms and a hall. There is electric light there, but no bathroom, certainly, not even a bath ; but I don't need one. Now in brief, the advantages of my present lodgings as compared with the flat in the castle : 1. The advantage of letting things be as they are ; 2. I am content now ; after all, why create for myself the possibility of regrets ; 3. Losing a house of one's own ; 4. Losing my nightly walk that is an aid to sleep ; 5. I should have to borrow furniture from the sister who is living with us now ; for the one room, which is enormously big, I should have really only a bed. The cost of moving ; 6. Now I live ten minutes nearer the office. The flat in the castle faces west, I fancy ; my room gets the morning sun. On the other hand, the advantages of the flat in the castle : 1. The advantage of change in general and change in particular ; 2. The advantage of a quiet lodging of one's own ; 3. In the flat I have now to work in, I am after all not entirely independent ; really I am taking it away from Ottla ; kind and self-sacrificing as she is towards me, one day when she is in a bad mood she will let me know it without wanting to. It's true she will certainly be sorry if I stop coming to the little house ; at bottom she is quite satisfied if she can be there occasionally in the afternoon and on Sundays till six o'clock ; 4. I shan't have my walk home, it is true ; going out at night will also be difficult, because the gate cannot be opened from the outside, but to balance that I can very well take a little walk at night in the part of the park which is otherwise reserved for the gentry. 5. After the war I shall try at any rate to get a year's leave, if I can, but that will surely not be possible—if I get any leave at all. Well in that case we two would have the most wonderful place to live in that I can imagine in Prague, all ready for you, only for a comparatively short time it's true, during which you would have to go without a kitchen of your own, and even without a bathroom. But anyhow it would be in my taste, and you could have a thorough rest for two or three months. The indescribable park, perhaps in spring, in summer (the gentry are away), or in autumn. But if I don't make sure of the flat now, immediately, either by moving in, or—mad extravagance, that is far beyond the capacity of a civil servant to grasp—by paying the rent only, 150 crowns a quarter, I shall hardly be able to get it later. To confess the truth, I have taken it already ; but the agent will certainly release me from my undertaking with pleasure, particularly as the whole affair, I can well understand, has not the tiniest fraction of the importance for him that it has for me. How little I have told you ! But give me your opinion, and soon."

His coughing blood, which began in August for the first time, Franz described as being psychic in origin. That is how I find it noted down without possibility of doubt in my diary in his own words. " 24 August 1917. Steps taken in the matter of Kafka's illness. He insists it is psychic, just like something to save him from marriage. He calls it his final defeat. And yet he has been sleeping well since. Has he found release ? Tormented soul ! " It is possible that the flat in the Schönborn Palace, which couldn't be heated, hastened the breaking out of the illness, and that therefore his father, who warned him against " extravagances " of this kind, and who always expressed his deep disapproval of them, once more appeared after all to be right in a certain sense. This aspect of his illness which Kafka probably never took into consideration might be taken straight out of one of his own short stories, from which, however, the only thing that emerges clearly is the close connection between his life and his creative function. If you go deeper, however, the illness was after all the result of years of stress, efforts to unfold his literary gifts to the full, despite all the hindrances of his profession, and his marriage plans, and of the bodily weakness bound up with all that, combined with " hygienic " treatment that only a much stronger body could have supported.

It took till 4 September before I could finally persuade Franz to call in a doctor. In such matters he was quite unbelievably pig-headed ; it took a great deal of patience and perseverance to handle him properly. My description of the decisive, wretched day runs :

" 4 September. In the afternoon went with Kafka to Professor Friedl Pick. It has taken all that time to carry it through.

" Catarrh in the lungs diagnosed. Must have three months' leave. There is a danger of T.B. My God ! Nothing so horrible can happen. Then the Sophie Island. Swimming-pool with Franz. He feels himself released and beaten at the same time. There is a part in him which resists, and considers marriage as a distraction from the one direction of his gaze —towards the absolute. Another part fights for marriage as in accordance with Nature. This struggle has worn him out. He considers his illness as a punishment, because he has often wished for a violent solution. But this solution is too drastic for him. He quotes against God, from the *Mastersingers*, ' I should have taken him for more of a gentleman '."

Then : " 10 December. Went with Kafka to see Professor Pick again. His revelation that he had been learning Hebrew, forty-five lessons in Rath's handbook ; never said anything to me about it. So he was trying me out when he asked me sometime ago, with every appearance of innocence, how do you count in Hebrew. This making a big secret of everything. There is something very great about it, but also something evil."

To go to a sanatorium for T.B. patients—Franz fought against the idea with all his might. It was not until he was older that he had to give in. You might find a certain self-contradiction in the fact that he refused to go and stay in any sanatorium now that it was advisable for him to do so, whereas in previous years he had gone for a rest to sanatoria like Erlenbach near Zürich, Jungborn in the Harz Mountains, Hartungen in Riva. But these had been centres of " Nature healing methods ", where Franz spent days, or even weeks, so to speak, profitably pandering to the " living-according-to-Nature " which he loved and also made fun of, but which at the very bottom, he welcomed so hopefully. The threat of institutions run according to orthodox medical principles was quite another thing ; and it was only to be expected from Franz's way of looking at things that he should resist such demands upon him as long as possible. Chance came to his aid this time. Franz's youngest sister took over the management of a small estate that belonged to her brother-in-law at Zürau (Post Flöhau, near Saaz). It was decided and finally agreed upon by all sides that Franz should spend his convalescent leave there. This leave was prolonged several times, once or twice Franz tried to take up his office work again but succeeded only for short spaces of time. At last it became inevitable that he should be retired. From his surroundings at Zürau, where Franz was for the first time brought into close contact with country life, farming, German peasants, grew the novel *The Castle*.

On 12 September I wrote in my diary, " Said good-bye to Kafka. It hurts me. I have not been without him for such a long time for years. He now thinks he can't marry F. because of his illness. Despairing letter from her, although she knows nothing about it yet. Two people come from the shop with handcarts to take his luggage. He says, ' They are coming for the coffin '."

Now I got very many letters from him ; they are too precious to be given piecemeal. I must hope I shall one day be able to publish them complete. They throw light on Kafka's studies of Kierkegaard, which grew deeper and deeper, and on his religious and ethical development. Other letters from Zürau—to Baum and Weltsch—have already appeared in my collected edition of Kafka. They give the picture, growing clearer and clearer, of a man who feels himself at home in the most primitive of country districts, and never wishes to return to the town. Characteristic of his mood and of the fundamental material of the novel *The Castle* are pages in the diary like these : " Was at Farmer Lüftner's. The great long room. The whole thing quite theatrical. There is he with his ' Ho ho ! ' and his ' Ha ha ', and banging on the table, and waving his arms and shrugging his shoulders and raising his glass of beer like somebody out of *Wallenstein*. Sitting next to him is his wife, an old woman whom he married when he was her serving-lad ten years before. His passion is to be out with a gun ; he neglects his farm. Two gigantic horses in the stable, Homeric forms, in a fleeting ray of sunshine that came through the stable window." Slowly Franz got better. Only when a letter came from F. he wouldn't eat for half a day, and didn't open the letter. I myself, caught up in terrible soul-storms, as well as in a heap of work, unfortunately never went to see Franz in Zürau. I met him only at the railway station of Michelob, where he travelled down to meet me, when I was giving a lecture somewhere near the place. Moreover, he used to come to Prague for a day or two from time to time, to settle things that could not be put off. Oskar Baum spent a week with him as his guest at Zürau ; the "village was then under deep snow ", Baum writes it in his *Memoirs* ; " In the long nights we talked right through till the morning, I got to know more about him than in the ten previous years, and the five that followed."

In September still, that is to say, soon after the diagnosis of the serious illness, F. came to see him. The diary reports : " F. was here ; travelled thirty hours to see me. I should have stopped her. As I imagine it to myself she is suffering the utmost unhappiness essentially through my fault. I myself can't make myself out ; I am quite unfeeling, and just as helpless, keep thinking of the disturbance of a few of my comforts, and the only thing I do by way of confessing, is to do a little play-acting. In small details, she is wrong, wrong in defending the rights she pretends to or perhaps really has, but on the whole she is an innocent woman condemned to be severely tortured ; I have committed the fault for which she is being tortured, and deserve the rack. The day ends with her departure (the carriage, with her and O. in it, goes round the pond, while I take a short cut straight across which brings me near her once more) and a headache (mortal remains of the actor)."

At the beginning of November I recorded a conversation with Franz. It had to do with my conflict with myself, but throws light on his own too.

" HE : That's the way it is always. The fault lies just in the fact that we think things over."

" I : Well, should one do things without thinking them over ?

" HE : That is, of course, not a law. But it is written : *Thou shalt not be able* to think things over. You can't do it by force. Thinking things over is the advice of the serpent. But it is also good and human. Without it one is lost."

At the end of December Franz came to Prague, met F. here, who, as the manageress of a big Berlin firm—tact, efficiency, generosity are among her excellent qualities—had to use her Christmas holidays to come and have the last talk with him. The tragic drama was nearing its end. On the evening of 25 December, Franz and F. were the guests of my wife and myself. " Both unhappy, don't talk." On 26 December I wrote, " Kafka came at half past seven in the morning, wants me to give him my morning. Café Paris. But it isn't to get advice that he wants me for, his firmness of purpose is admirable. Yesterday he told F. everything quite clearly. We spoke about everything but that. Kafka on Tolstoy's *Resurrection* : ' You cannot write about salvation, you can only live it.' In the afternoon, an excursion with Baum and Weltsch. So three married couples, alongside Kafka and F. Kafka unhappy. He said to me, ' What I have to do, I can do only alone. Become clear about the ultimate things. The Western Jew is not clear about them, and therefore has no right to marry. There are no marriages for them. Unless he is the kind that is not interested in such things—business men for example '."

The next morning Franz came to my office to see me. To rest for one moment he said. He had just been to the station to see F. off. His face was pale, hard, and severe. But suddenly he began to cry. It was the only time I saw him cry. I shall never forget the scene, it is one of the most terrible I have ever experienced. I was not sitting alone in my

office ; right close up to my desk was the desk of a colleague—we worked
in the legal section of the G.P.O. This particular section was housed on
the top floor of a block of flats, not in the main office building of the
G.P.O. The way in which the office had succeeded in turning a friendly
four-roomed flat, with kitchen and bathroom into proper, dusty, ugly,
impersonal office premises, into something bad-temperedly unreal, had
something uncanny about it. Private visitors such as I sometimes had, I
generally received—and this too with a guilty conscience—in the kitchen,
which had been half pulled down and turned into a lumber room for
legal documents. But Kafka had come straight into the room I worked
in, to see me, in the middle of all the office-work, sat near my desk on a
small chair which stood there ready for bearers of petitions, pensioners,
and debtors. And in this place he was crying, in this place he said between
his sobs : " Is it not terrible that such a thing must happen ? " The tears
were streaming down his cheeks. I have never except this once seen him
upset quite without control of himself.

A few days later he returned to Zürau. He showed me still a very
unhappy letter from F. His attitude towards her, however, was quite
firm, he had given up not only her, but *any* possibility of married bliss.
The pain he inflicted on himself gave him the strength to conquer his
natural weakness even where others were concerned, and not to turn
back when he had once realised the inevitability of the bitter decision.

Some fifteen months later I received the news that F. had got married.
I broke the news gently to Franz. He was moved, full of the most honest
good wishes for the new plighted troth, which then to his great joy
duly turned into marriage. " It is a good thing that some things which
are insoluble seem to find a solution after all ", was how I summed up
the story for myself, knowing full well that on Franz's side at least a road
to salvation had far from been thrown open by the disappearance of this
one overshadowing problem.

VI

RELIGIOUS DEVELOPMENT

KAFKA'S failure to find a way out was, from now on, chiefly due to his illness which, rising out of the crises of his soul, or at least harmfully stimulated by them, had developed into an evil that had its own independent, injurious, nay devastating, effect, and to which Franz finally succumbed. Franz bore his sufferings heroically, generally even with cheerful equanimity. Only once, in his later years, did I ever hear him complain about pain. I went to see him after he had had a severe bout of fever. He was lying in bed ; while he was speaking he pulled a face : "It takes such a long time before one is crushed up quite small, and squeezed through this last narrow hole ". As he was saying this he was clenching his hand as if he were crumpling a handkerchief up in it.

Until the summer of 1918, Franz stayed, with short interruptions, in Zürau. Then he came to Prague, worked for some time again in the Civil Service, but devoted his afternoons to gardening at the Pomologic Institute in Troja, a suburb of Prague. I often used to go and call for him there, and take him for long walks. We had two chief topics—the war, and learning Hebrew. At that time, too, I was asking his advice on a literary affair. Kafka's sense of justice, his love of the truth, his simple honesty that never had the least pose about it were unsurpassable. "One must limit oneself to what one is absolutely master of" is one of his sayings that I have preserved from those days. Sometimes, I must admit, this led in his case to a state in which he curled up painfully in himself. He wanted to withdraw from everything, finally even to give up meeting me.

On 1 July 1918, I have a note on his views : "Country as opposed to town. And yet he feels better in Prague, because in Zürau he was lying about doing nothing. Here he studies Hebrew and gardening. The positive things in his life. Wants to keep these quite pure—they are the 'country things'. Would like to withdraw from everything else." "3 July. Sleepless night because of Kafka. Feel I am deserted, but respect his decision. There has never been any quarrel. His fine way of seeing what is positive in everybody—even in his opponents—what they are right in, what they can do nothing else about—Hans Blüher, for example—often comforted me, gave me a basis. His confidence that a pure intention, an objective piece of work is never meaningless, that nothing good can ever go lost—on that I leant for support." This

[132]

" obituary ", however, is immediately followed by the correction, " A few days later he came along to me. Then often on the Sophie Island, the swimming-baths with him. Troja, too."

The following extract from one of his letters gives an account of the severity with which he conducted his own life and judged everything at this period. I had passed on to him a request from an actress who wanted to give a reading from his books in Frankfurt. He wrote back to me, from Zürau, " I am not sending anything to Frankfurt ; I don't feel it is a matter that I should bother about. If I send anything I shall be doing it out of vanity ; if I don't send anything, it will also be out of vanity, but not out of vanity alone, that is to say, out of something better. The pieces I could send mean really nothing to me, I respect only the moment in which I wrote them ; and now an actress, who can find something much more effective to show herself off, is to drag them out of the abyss into which they are sooner or later falling, and give them a moment of glory for one evening ? That would be senseless trouble."

But he didn't always dismiss all his literary work so contemptuously. He began to arrange the stories which were to be put together to form the volume *The Country Doctor*. This time he even insisted on having them published. That can be seen from the following lines—also addressed to me from Zürau : " Thanks for speaking to Wolff's for me. Since I have decided to dedicate the book to my father, I lay great importance on its coming out soon. Not as though I could reconcile my father by doing so, the roots of this enmity are ineradicable in this case ; but I should, all the same, have at least travelled along the map with my finger even if I haven't emigrated to Palestine."

One sees from these few lines how strongly Kafka's yearning to be made a proper member of the family, for peace with his father, links up with incorporation in the people's way of life (Palestine) which is after Nature's plan and morally right—and in fact these motives, which are nothing else than a making concrete of Kafka's fundamental problem— how is a properly fulfilled life for everybody, the whole of mankind, to be realised ?—make themselves felt with ever increasing force in the last years of Kafka's life.

What I emphasise, and what I believe distinguishes my exposition of Kafka from all the others—e.g. Schoeps, Vietta, and Stumpf—is the fact that I consider that the positive side of him, his love of life, of the earth, earthy, and his religion in the sense of a properly fulfilled life, is his decisive message, and not self-abnegation, turning his back on life, despair —the " tragic position ".

The three quotations which I have placed at the head of this mono- graph speak a clear language. I beg you to read them again before going on with the text. Without these guiding sentences one cannot, so I think, ever understand Kafka's religious position. The hopefulness that lies in these and similar sayings of Kafka's must not be magicked away. Only by overlooking propositions like this, with their positive outlook, could one arrive at the point of placing Kafka in line with the " Theology of the Crisis "—with that religious tendency that sees between God and man, between man and the good deeds that are to be achieved by human strength, an abyss gape that can never be bridged. It is significant that Franz, in a letter to me, draws attention to just those passages in Kierkegaard which explain not the powerlessness but the good moral strength and effective possibilities of mankind. Kafka quotes Kierkegaard with the introductory words, " And the following passage is *not* from the Talmud ", which, when placed alongside my letter, is as much as to say, " It corresponds with Jewish modes of thought ; although it is to be found not in the Talmud but in Kierkegaard's books ". He quotes the following great sentence : " As soon as a man appears who brings something of the primitive along with him, so that he doesn't say, ' You must take the world as you find it ', but rather ' Let the world be what it likes, I take my stand on a primitiveness which I have no intention of changing to meet with the approval of the world '. At that moment, as these words are heard, a metamorphosis takes place in the whole of Nature. Just as in a fairy story, when the right word is pronounced, the castle that has been lying under a spell for a hundred years opens and everything comes to life, in the same way existence becomes all attention. The angels have something to do, and watch curiously to see what will come of it, because that is their business. On the other side, dark, uncanny demons, who have been sitting around doing nothing and chewing at their nails for a long time, jump up and stretch their limbs, because, they say, here is something for us, and so on."

While I lay special worth on the hopeful side of Kafka's work, that rejoices in activity, that is to say on the fundamental recognition of the fact that man, with his spark of reason, will, and ethical perception is not altogether the plaything of super-mighty powers, who judge according to other laws than his, which he does not understand and never can understand, faced with which he is lost, and only thrown unconditionally on God's mercy—the old problem of Job—while underlining then the position of human freedom in the case of Kafka, I do not of course wish to forget that this attitude of Kafka's is only an occasional flash, and that passages which describe man as powerless, crowd in on the reader in an overwhelming majority. But the propositions of freedom and hope *are there, too* ! And if only *one* such proposition is found, in a religious thinker, it has the remarkable quality of decisively changing the whole picture of him. That's all I want to say, no more. These dispositions towards a more optimistic interpretation must not be neglected if one wants to read Kafka properly. In fact I think that just these gentle dispositions, wrung from all the endless bad moods and failures of a horribly difficult life, dispositions towards a " Fight for the good against anything and everything ", form the kernel, the best and the most characteristic part of Kafka's attitude as a thinker. *Just because the dispositions to faith were won from such a radical scepticism, they are in their truthfulness, refined by the ultimate tests, infinitely valuable and powerful.*

" Man cannot live without a permanent faith in something indestructible in himself ", says Kafka. And adds, " At the same time this indestructible part and his faith in it may remain permanently concealed from him ". Very significant is the following minor proposition which rejects the theism of the ordinary religious observance : " One of the forms in which this concealment may be expressed is the belief in a personal God ". One might well say that scepticism and faith cannot be more intimately wedded than in this aphorism.

Kafka disputes with God as Job once did. He disputes about original sin, and Paradise Lost. He seeks, but fails to find the definitive word. He seeks a faith " like a guillotine, as heavy, and as light ". But one thing he has become assured of, in any case : quite independently of how we may judge God's attitude towards us—the attitude and the task of mankind is clear, it is activity in the service of the Good so far as it is discernible by us. " Death is in front of us, rather like a picture of the battle of Alexander on the wall in the classroom. The point is to blur or even wipe out the picture *by our deeds while we are still in this life.*"

Compare with this an entry in the diary dated 11/11/1911—to my feeling one of the most moving entries : " As soon as I perceive in any way that I have allowed evil conditions, for the removal of which I am really the right person, to go on their own sweet way—for example the outwardly satisfied, but from my point of view desperate, life of Mrs. N.— for a moment I lose the feel of the muscles of my arms ". There is a similar passage, May 1914, which reveals, however, a stronger emphasis on the limitlessness and complicated nature of all mortal things, which indeed so endlessly lead the fight for the Good into false paths— (one could say, every great writer has made some facet of life clear, that no one had seen so clearly before him. And what has become clear through Kafka ? The unclearness of Life !) :

" If I am not very much mistaken, I am getting nearer. It is as though there were a spiritual fight in a clearing in some wood. I penetrate into the wood, don't find anything, and through weakness, hasten out of it again ; often when I am leaving the wood, I hear, or think I hear, the clash of the weapons of those fighters. Perhaps the fighters' looks seek me through the darkness of the wood, but I know only so little and such deceptive things about them."

Man's bewilderment is great. And yet, and yet—we let the "chariot", God's chariot, and the chariot of the good life, pass us by without getting in; one misses it only when one does not take things seriously. " Hold fast ! "—says that meditation which I believe to be the conclusive one . . . " then you too will see the unchangeable, dark distance, out of which nothing can come except one day the chariot ; it rolls up, gets bigger and bigger, fills the whole world at the moment it reaches you— and you sink into it like a child sinking into the upholstery of a carriage that drives through storm and night."

Kafka's fundamental outlook may be summarised in some such formula as this; almost everything is uncertain, but once one has a certain degree of understanding one never loses the way any more. It is Plato's doctrine in its purest form. For Plato, too, assures us in *Phaedrus*, that for those who have once trodden the upper path, it is not ordained that they shall get on to the lower one.

For all his mourning over the imperfection and intransparency of human actions, Kafka was convinced that there were truths which could not be assailed. He did not express this in words, but he did so by his whole behaviour all his life. It was for that reason that in spite of all the depression he exuded, one felt infinitely well in his company. The " Indestructible " made its presence felt, Kafka's unobtrusively quiet but firm behaviour was at the same time a pledge for the everlasting laws of love, reason, and kindness. He was admittedly limitlessly sceptical and ironic. But there was, for instance, for him no scepticism about the substance and heart of Goethe. Well then, after all not " limitlessly sceptical ? " No, the limit was there—a very distant limit, but a limit nevertheless.

Belief in an absolute world—but we go astray, we are too weak, we do not grasp it. Next to his belief in the Absolute stands for Kafka his consciousness of human insufficiency. This feeling of weakness Schoeps explains by the special situation of the Jew to-day, who does not follow the traditional law of his religion. There is also an explanation from the ⌐atholic side ; the Jew who does not accept Christ. But as a motive in ⌐s feeling of weakness, we must not forget Kafka's many private, accidental failings and sufferings, beginning with his youthful impressions and the ' Education that went wrong ' ; they all condition the feeling of God's ' farness ' which expresses itself so insistently in his works. Through this one grasps real life and truth better than through theological interpretations. " To be near God " and " to live rightly " were identical for Kafka. As a member of a race without a country one cannot live properly. This almost realistically Jewish interpretation of Kafka, in which Zionism is accepted as a way of life of almost religious relevance, I shall endeavour to develop later on.

But let us first establish the General Religious side.

The Absolute is there—but it is incommensurable with the life of m an —this would seem to be a fundamental experience of Kafka's. From he depth of his experiences it takes on ever new variations ; in the bitterest irony, in despair, in unexampled self-abasement, and in a tender hope that sings through all his savage scepticism, not often, but all the more unmistakably, here and there. The chief theme remains the enormous danger that we may lose the right way, a danger so grotesquely out of proportion that it is really only an accident—" *gratia praeveniens* "—that can bring us to the point of entering into " The Law ", i.e. the right and perfect life, into " Tao ". How much more probable it is, on the contrary, that we miss the way altogether. " Once follow the false stroke of the bell in the night, one can never put it right again." The eternal misunderstanding between God and man induces Kafka to represent this disproportion again and again in the picture of two worlds which can never, never understand one another—hence the infinite separation between dumb animals and men is one of his chief themes in the numerous animal stories which his works contain, not by accident. The same is true of the partition wall between Father and Son. This writer's gaze rests with the endless pity of understanding on everything that expresses incommensurability, and brings it into silent relation with the most fatal and greatest of all misunderstandings, the failure of man in the sight of God.

This perception undoubtedly has its kernel in the feeling that there is a world of the Absolute, Freedom from sin, Perfection—that is that which the faithful call " God ". This feeling for the " Indestructible " was for Kafka an immediate certainty, at the same time—equipped as he was with the sharpest of eyes of the soul—he did not overlook a single one of the countless, wretched backslidings, not one of the sins, not one of the absurdities with which men embitter each other's lives, make each other's lives impossible indeed, and which cause them to wander farther and farther away from the fountain of life. A good life is prescribed for us, but we are incapable, through faults in our innermost being, of comprehending this life. For this reason the divine world becomes for us a transcendental territory, and in the truest sense of the words, strange, uncanny. To our ears the will of God sounds illogical, that is to say opposed to our human logic in a grotesque fashion. Since the book of Job in the

Bible, God has never been so savagely wrought with as in Kafka's *The Trial*, and *The Castle*, or in his *In the Penal Colony*, in which justice is presented in the image of a machine thought out with refined cruelty, an inhuman, almost devilish machine, and a crank who worships this machine. Just the same in the Book of Job, God does what seems absurd and unjust to man. But it is *only* to man that this seems so, and the final conclusion arrived at in Job as in Kafka is the confirmation of the fact that the yardstick by which man works is not that by which measurements are taken in the world of the Absolute. Is that agnosticism ? No ; for the fundamental feeling remains that in some mysterious way man is nevertheless connected with the transcendental kingdom of God. Only the usual, flat, rationally understandable kind of connection it just isn't. And the terrible wound of doubt that Kafka's ever-fresh wit, and Kafka's ever freshly creating, bizarre fancy, deal our moral system, cannot be healed by phrases, by sanctimoniously lifting up one's eyes, and patching things up with evil, not by belletristic anointings, but only by a tremendous, mounting feeling for the positive that dares bid defiance to all this undisguised negation. To have registered the negative and fearfully defective sides of Nature without veiling them in any way, and yet at the same time to have seen continually from the depths of his heart the " World of Ideas ", in the Platonic sense—that was the distinguishing feature of Kafka's life and of his works, that was the thing that proclaimed itself to his friends, without a word being said about it, as a kind of revelation, peace, certainty, in the midst of the storm of suffering and uncertainty.

Perhaps there have been men who have had a deeper, that is to say, a less questioning faith than Kafka's—perhaps also there have been men with even more biting scepticism—that I don't know. But what I do know is the unique fact that in Kafka these two contradictory qualities blossomed out into a synthesis of the highest order. One might gather its importance into this sentence : Of all believers he was the freest from illusions, and among all those who see the world as it is, without illusions, he was the most unshakeable believer.

It is the old question of Job. But Kafka stands almost completely on the side of man. That is how it is in the story, " In the Eyes of the Law ". The doorkeeper has deceived the man who demands admission, or he is too simple. To close the argument, K., to whom the legend is related, says, " Lies are being made the order of the world ". It is true that that is also not the last word. The priest argues against it, protests by word and deed. Thus the justice of the highest court—in his novel *The Trial*—the possibility of a good life in accordance with the divine command, "The Law" in fact, is not denied—but this possibility is not a certainty.

Everything remains hanging in the air. Darkness and light hold the scales against one another. In what time is this "timeless" novel set? One minute before the creation of the world. Will it succeed, or not? A terrible fear of doubt, of uncertainty, fills one's heart.

What is the reason? Why man does not achieve the real, the true, that, with the best will in the world, he wanders from the path like that country doctor that followed the "false stroke of the bell in the night"? Kafka, by the very nature of his being, was not inclined to give any promises, or any directions for the happy life. He admired everyone who could—he himself remained in suspense. But just this suspense would have been empty and bare, had he not felt the Absolute as something inexpressible (ἄρρητον) in himself. In his uncertainty one felt a distant certainty, through which alone this uncertainty is made possible and preserved. I have already said that this positive trait appears perhaps less strongly in his writings—and that is why they have been found depressing by many readers—than it was to be felt in his personal calm and serenity, in the gentle, considered, never hasty, character of his being. But he also who reads Kafka's works with care, must again and again catch a glimpse, through the dark husk of this kernel that gleams, or rather beams gently through. On the top lie distraction, and despair in that which is related—but the ease and minuteness of detail with which it is related, the "copy fever" which is in love with detail, that is, with real life, and with descriptions true to Nature, the humour in the constrictive structure of his sentences, which often has the effect of a short circuit, in so many tricks of style—the debtors "have become extravagant, and are giving a party in the garden of some inn, and others are breaking their flight to America for a little while to attend the party"—all this points, already *through the form alone*, to the "indestructible" in Kafka and in the human-being-in-general that he recognises.

When Kafka read aloud himself, this humour became particularly clear. Thus, for example, we friends of his laughed quite immoderately when he first let us hear the first chapter of *The Trial*. And he himself laughed so much that there were moments when he couldn't read any further. Astonishing enough, when you think of the fearful earnestness of this chapter. But that is how it was.

Certainly it was not entirely good, comfortable laughter. But the ingredients of a good laugh were also there—alongside the hundred ingredients of uncanniness, which I shall not try to minimise. I am only pointing out the fact that is otherwise so easily forgotten in studies of Kafka—the streak of joy in the world and in life.

What he reproached himself with was, in fact, just that his belief in life wavered, that life was not strong enough in him. And he admired the things of the country, as is expressed as early as in his (unpublished) youthful letter to Oskar Pollak : " Have you already noticed how the soil comes up to meet the cow as she is grazing, how intimately it comes up to meet her ? Have you already noticed how heavy, rich arable earth crumbles at the touch of fingers which are all too fine, how solemnly it crumbles ? " It is still more clearly expressed in the diary he kept of his stay in Zürau, which says, among other things, " General impressions of the farmers : Noblemen, who have found salvation in their farming, where they have arranged their work so cleverly and humbly, that it fits without omission into the whole, and will keep them safe from every wavering and sea-sickness, until their happy death. Real citizens of the Earth." But naturally his admiration did not stay confined to country folk alone. He writes in just the same style, 20/10/1913, in his diary, about a completely urban author, who was sure of his path : " Have just been reading the case of Jacobsohn. This strength to live, to make decisions, to set one's foot with joy in the right spot. He sits in himself as a first-class oarsman sits in his own boat, and would sit in any boat."

The scale of values that Kafka applied becomes clear from notes such as that. He loved an efficient vitality but only one which stood at the service of what is good and constructive. (A twofold demand hard to satisfy !) He always found fault with himself for " never having learnt anything useful ". He complains in his diary, 25/10/1921, that " the current of life has never caught me up, and that I never broke away from Prague, was never put on to any game or trade ". He often reproaches himself with coldness, incapacity for life, lifelessness, as we often find in his letters, and in the last chapter of *The Trial*. The two black mysterious dwarfs only carry out a sentence that has already been carried out. As they lead K. away, they form together with him " one unit, such as almost only lifeless matter can form ". He is dead already : that is to say, dead to real life. That is the real reason why the ghostly appearance of Miss Bürstner has such a paralysing effect on him. He wants to see her, not because he promises himself any help from doing so, but " in order not to forget the warning that she holds for him ". K. had not married, remained a bachelor, had allowed himself to be terrified by the reality of life, had not defended himself against it—that is his secret guilt, which had already, before his condemnation, shut him out from the circle of life. " There would be nothing heroic about it if he did resist ", is therefore the final conclusion ; " If he were now to make difficulties for his masters—the dwarfs—if he tried now by defending himself to enjoy the last appearance of life ". K. died of weakness in living, is already dead from the beginning of the book—from the moment of the arrest, which Kafka must have written in a kind of trance, in a moment of clairvoyance, or did there exist, then, in 1914, the tight-fitting black uniforms with buckles, pockets, buttons, and belt ?—admittedly weakness is a relative idea, and if you translate the novel back into the autobiographical, from which it came, then one must not forget that Kafka's life can only be considered as tainted with weakness when measured by the heroically moral, in fact monumental demands he made on himself. But what would not be weakness in this case ? A feeling of this comes to life in the unbearably moving passage at the end of *The Trial*, where " the responsibility for this last misdoing " is thrust off, where K. rears up, reaches after a far-away, unknown, indistinct person. " Who was it ? A friend ? A good man ? A man who wanted to help ? Was it an individual ? Was it everybody ? Was there still help ? Were there objections one had forgotten to raise ? Surely there were some. Logic is, of course, irresistible, but it cannot withstand a man who wishes to live. Where was the judge he had never seen ? Where was the high court before which he had never appeared ? "

The old problem of Job.

Kafka's fundamental principle : pity for mankind that finds it so hard a task to do what is right. Pity, half-smiling, half-weeping pity. Not the fulminating excommunication of the " Theology of the Crisis " which knows so exactly where mankind has gone wrong.

Kafka's demands on himself were the most severe. Almost never did he believe he had come up to them. On the other hand, he was no " Cultural Critic " in the accepted sense of the word. For very much of what went on around him, many quite ordinary people he came into touch with seemed to him self-contained, admirable for their achievements and their strength, in fact absolutely blessed by God. In this there was a certain amount of truth, inasmuch as no one was so burningly conscious of the " distance from God " as he was. But in this consciousness of the distance, Kafka, in his humility, saw no virtue, but only uncertainty, that is, weakness. But as it was a preliminary condition of all life to feel the distance from God—from the perfection of a right way of life—clearly and without any veiling of ritual or mysticism, his praise and his admiration of the everyday man—the " Pedestrian " as Kierkegaard describes him—often involved an extremely tender, unintentional, playful and at the same time touching irony. He gave the preference fictively to the victors of everyday life, simply out of the kindness of the superfluity of his wealth : " They know about the abyss as well as I do—and yet they balance gaily over it ". But did they really know ? The joking hypothesis of the premise loosened up the personal tragedy of his life—was one of the roots of his entirely unique humour.

So Kafka's attitude is related to Job's attitude, and yet in many points is a quite different one. I cannot, as Schoeps and Margarethe Susmann do, trace this difference back in essentials to the historical difference between the stage of development of the Jewish race at that time and now.

In the first place the fact that Job from the very beginning appears a perfectly just man to others as well as to himself, whereas Kafka—with the reservations I have just made above—considers himself as a particularly imperfect one, demands a different approach to the problem.

In the question and charge laid against God, they are, it is true, at one with each other. It is the experience of incommensurability that is common to them both. The world of God's justice, and the world of human ethics gape wide asunder—the space for Kierkegaard's " Fear and trembling " is created. Or as Kafka once expresses it in his diary : " Nothing is more completely and wantonly wicked than to have tubercular children. Flaubert's father was tubercular. The choice : either the child's lungs go for a penny whistle—very fine expression for the music the doctor puts his ear to the patient's chest to listen for—or it becomes a Flaubert. The trembling of the father while counsel is taken in empty space." Plumb the terrible hopelessness that lies in the phrase, " counsel is taken in empty space ". It reminds one of that old demoniac hymn, which Kafka surely did not know, " *sederunt principes* ". In the same way, Job does not mince matters ; when he strives with God no expression is too strong for reviling God.

Job ix. 11–19. " Lo, he goeth by me, and I see him not : he passeth on also, but I perceive him not.

" Behold, he taketh away, who can hinder him ? Who will say unto him, What dost thou ?

" If God will not withdraw his anger, the proud helpers do stoop under him.

" How much less shall I answer him, and choose out my words to reason with him ?

" Whom, though I were righteous, yet would I not answer, but I would make supplication to my judge.

" If I had called, and he had answered me ; yet would I not believe that he had hearkened unto my voice.

" For he breaketh me with a tempest, and multiplieth my wounds without cause.

" He will not suffer me to take my breath, but filleth me with bitterness.

" If I speak of strength, lo, he is strong : and if of judgement, who shall set me a time to plead ? "

That is exactly the same judge, to whom K., in *The Trial*, cannot fight his way : or again, the gentlemen of the Castle, who don't allow themselves to be spoken to, who always put forward a screen of courts of appeal which have no responsibility and which do very wicked things.

In the Book of Job :

" If the scourge slay suddenly, he will laugh at the trial of the innocent.

" The earth is given into the hand of the wicked : he covereth the faces of the judges thereof ; if not, where, and who is he ?

" If I wash myself with snow water, and make my hands never so clean ;

" Yet shalt thou plunge me in the ditch, and mine own clothes shall abhor me.

" For he is not a man, as I am, that I should answer him, and we should come together in judgement.

" Neither is there any daysman betwixt us, that might lay his hand upon us both.

" Let him take his rod away from me, and let not his fear terrify me :

" Then would I speak, and not fear him ; but it is not so with me."

The solution in the Book of Job comes about later through God's answer out of the whirlwind, " Where wast thou when I laid the foundations of the Earth ? " But thereby only the heteronomy between God and man is strengthened. Thereby Divine right would be differentiated from human right *toto coelo*. To cap everything the book of Job ends with a hymn-like description of two beasts, two monsters, " Behemoth and that Leviathan " whose beauty, so completely removed from humanity, is praised. " He maketh a path to shine after him ; one would think the deep to be hoary—He is a king over all the children of pride." Really magnificent. But the paradox that God's yardstick is not man's remains unanswered. By human standards, God appears to be unjust— the wound remains. Job, it is true, finds some way of accommodating himself with this " Beyond Good and Evil ".

Not so Kafka. His charge, at the same time, goes one step further than Job's, although one might think that were hardly possible. This is the step : " Behemoth and that Leviathan " have no ethics that man can fathom, but they are praised in an aesthetic sense, as God's works, magnificent to look at in their strength. Now with Kafka the " Court " is, in addition, dirty, ridiculous, despicable, corrupt ; it sits in rooms in a suburb, works in a stupidly bureaucratic way, is treated in fact as aesthetically inferior. The intention of both writers is, of course, the same. The heteronomy of God is to be described—something that cannot be measured by men's standards. So far efforts have been made to describe this heteronomy solely by an endless exaggeration in the direction of the positive side : more light than one can imagine, greater, stronger than is bearable by human powers of comprehension. Kafka makes comprehensible the difference in kind of the perfect world, by fitting it out with negative characteristics. Already, with Job, the world of God—as that of his monsters—is radically opposed to the world of man, but it is at least on the grand scale. With Kafka it is seen besides to be petty, rough, trashy—this too is only a symbol for its being different, its being opposed. The world of perfection seems so disgusting to man; man is just forming a wrong judgement, that is all. This fact is thereby expressed with the boldest consistency—and the world of perfection remains, of course, for all this deliberately abusive picture of it, just as unaffected, just as fundamentally incapable of being affected, with Kafka as with Job.

But Job comforts himself with the idea that God and man cannot be brought to the same levels. Kafka, however, does not comfort himself. And that shuts him out of the line Job-Kierkegaard—Theology of the Crisis. That brings him back to the Jewish creed, in one sentence from which, " Our God is one God ", I see the strongest spell against all attempts to hypothecate for God fundamentally different ethical laws than for mankind. God, the world of perfection, of the Platonic " Highest Good ", is under the same laws as we are, our morality runs towards this goal, without, it is true, our being able to comprehend the goal ; but the path that leads to it we can comprehend, and we refuse to recognise any heathen-divine Nature-ethic, which would really be heteronomous to it. In that probably lies the deepest ground for the commandment in the Bible that we may not make ourselves any image of God. The theology of the crisis—in fact, Job already—Kierkegaard's Abraham-conception already—easily fall victim to the danger of deducing an unmoral or nature-moral God from the difference in kind between God and man, between the perfect and the finite, to imagine God as a negro fetish that bares its teeth. But, " Thou shalt not make any graven image ". Even Behemoth and that Leviathan do not say the last word on the nature of God. God *did* create man " in His own image "—the humane teaching of the Old Testament to which the great Thomas of Aquinas found the way back after the pessimistic errors of Augustine : " *Signatum est super nos lumen vultus Tui, Domine* ". Thus, too, Kafka sees no heteronomy between God and man, but only indistinctness, an admittedly almost desperate complication, caused by intermediate courts full of malice and poison, which thrust their way bureaucratically between, and continually hinder the Good.

In spite of all these intermediate courts which take up so much room in his writings, in fact sometimes rob life of all its pleasure, he writes sentences like the following, which are full of hope and love, full of a comfort born at a heavy cost through a thousand sufferings :

"It is not a denial of the premonition of a final delivery when the imprisonment remains still unchanged the next day, or is even made more severe, or even if it is expressly stated that it will never come to an end. All that *can* be, much rather, the necessary basis for a final delivery."

"He is of the opinion one has only once to find the way over to the Good, and one is immediately saved, without paying any attention to the past, and even without paying any attention to the future."

Kafka saw the world of the Absolute before him, not beyond redemption, and not barred to us. Hope—for us, too ! That he once expressed the opposite opinion is not conclusive enough to counterbalance the many "entries" into the Absolute which he recognised over and over again, and which I have taken it on me to describe in this biography as possibilities, which frequently recurred, of the right profession, the right marriage, and so on. For it seems to me that just this is the most important point on the presentation of a man who is motivated by religion ; to point out the cramp-irons that this man recognises between the visibly finite world and the perfect world that lies beyond, to show where they are to be found, whether he has perhaps denied them altogether, and avoided them, or has only accidentally missed them, but in principle knows them and has striven to get at them, to experience them.

On 15 March 1922, Franz read me the beginning of *The Castle*.[1]

In *The Castle* an exhaustive description is given of how a certain type of man reacts to the world, and in so far as every man feels an element of this type in himself—exactly in the same way that Faust, or Don Quixote, or Julien Sorel is hidden in each of us, whether it be as a predisposition, as a yearning, or as a component part of the ego—so Kafka's *Castle*, for all the individuality of the character it describes, is a book in which everyone recognises his own experiences. Kafka's hero, whom he calls simply K., in autobiographical fashion, passes through life alone. He is

[1] He used to come to Prague, at this time, only temporarily and for short periods. In 1919 he lived for a few months in Schelesen near Liboch, at Stüdl's boarding-house ; alone at first, then in winter with me. A second unhappy tale of love and betrothal began there, but came to a speedy end. He wrote the " Letter to My Father ". His stay in Meran falls in the year 1920, as well as a love affair that went very hopefully for a short time. Many letters from this period are extant. That winter he tried to find in the Tatra Mountains, in a sanatorium at Tatranské Matliary, a cure for his illness, which was becoming more and more acute, and sometimes led to the severest crises. There he found a friend in Dr. Robert Klopstock, a fellow-patient and a doctor. He coughed a great deal, suffered from high temperature and shortness of breath—Kafka, whose beautifully constructed phrases and magnificent sentences are distinguished by such long breaths. In the same way cruel Nature let Beethoven and Smetana grow deaf, and many a painter go blind—just the organ which has been best developed is destroyed. Of the exact period in which Kafka wrote *The Castle*, I cannot inform my readers. Only the date of its first reading aloud is fixed on the evidence of my diary—it is probably not far from the beginning of his writing it.

the loneliness-component in us, which this novel works out in more-than-life-size, terrifying clarity. But at the same time it is a very special nuance of loneliness that is treated—and this, too, we know deep down in ourselves, feel it sometimes in quiet moments rising to the surface. K., namely, is a man of good will through and through ; he doesn't wish for his loneliness, and is not proud of it, but would gladly be an active member of human society, would like to play his part in an honest way, would like to fit in ; he strives after a useful career, wants to marry, wants to found a family. But everything goes wrong with him. One notices more and more clearly that the chilly layer of isolation that surrounds K. is nothing accidental—it is also no accident that the old-established inhabitants of the village in which K. had wrought a dwelling-place for himself shut themselves up against him, and that in his efforts to find contacts he hits upon just that family of farmers which is spurned by all the others. But the riddle as to why K. cannot make himself at home is not solved. He is a stranger, and has struck a village in which strangers are looked upon with suspicion. More is not said. One feels at once that this is the general feeling of strangeness among men, only it has just been made concrete in this one special case. "Nobody can be the companion of anyone here." One can take this making-concrete a step further. It is the special feeling of a Jew who would like to take root in foreign surroundings, who tries with all the powers of his soul to get nearer to the strangers, to become one of them exactly—but who does not succeed in thus welding himself.

The word Jew does not appear in *The Castle*. Yet, tangibly, Kafka in *The Castle*, straight from his Jewish soul, in a simple story, has said more about the situation of Jewry as a whole to-day than can be read in a hundred learned treatises. At the same time this specifically Jewish interpretation goes hand in hand with what is common to humanity, without either excluding or even disturbing the other. The general religious interpretation I have endeavoured to give in the appendix to the published version of the novel. Here are a few pointers on the relation between the novel and the lot of the Jews.

The first meeting with the farmers is immediately characteristic. K. has got lost in this village that is strange to him. He is tired. He sees an old peasant. "May I come in for a while ?" asks K. The peasant mumbles something indistinctly. Immediately K. takes this as an invitation and enters the cottage. Later it turns out that the person who let him in is weak in the head. The remarkable legal claim on which the Jews in the dispersal built up their "right to settle" occurs to one as a parallel, when one has entered into the spirit of this half-accidental "Tolerance" which K. claims. It is very much the same a few pages before that. K. has asked the extremely unfriendly schoolmaster whether he could come and see him some time. The schoolmaster's answer is, " I live in Swan Street, at the butcher's ". The author comments, " That was, it is true, rather giving an address than an invitation ", but nevertheless K. says, " Very well, I shall come ". Already in this little introductory scene one sees the position of the " gentiles " with their calm rejection, and that of the Jew with his obligatory friendliness, pushfulness, indeed importunity described with shatteringly objective melancholy. This is a peculiarity of Kafka's style : melancholy which seems to force itself out from an objective—not a subjective—arbitrariness.

But let us get on ! In the cottage K. is shown immediately that he is not at all welcome to the people in it : that he is disturbing them in the middle of very intimate household tasks—washing the floors and the clothes, feeding a baby. At a pinch, they allow him to sleep there a little. Then he is bowed out. A " silent, slow-thinking man, broad built, and with a broad face too ", comes up to him. " You can't stay here." The Jew is not always thrown out rudely or on legal quibbles. But the thing goes with the inevitability of a law of Nature, without passion, under compulsion. " We don't want any lodgers." K. appeals to the fact that they had invited him, that he is going to have a proper post here as a land surveyor. Whether there is any truth in this story of an invitation, or whether K. only imagines it, that is the point on which the whole novel really turns—here again the parallel with the Jewish problem is easy to complete. Now, in this first chapter the simple man of the people gives the provisional answer which more or less corresponds to the attitude of instinctive anti-semitism : " (Whether they want you) . . . that I don't know. If you've been asked to come, then you're probably needed, that is an exception, but we, we poor people, stick to the rule, and that you can't blame us for." K. tries still to get quickly into conversation with a girl who is in the room, but " at once K. had one of the men on each side of him, dragging him towards the door, silently, but with all their strength, as though there was no other way of making him understand. The old man was pleased about something or other as this took place, and clapped his hands. Even the washerwoman was laughing with the children, who were suddenly yelling like mad things." The scene, which is the eternal fate of Jews, sounds like a very impartial re-writing of the saying, " It doesn't matter, the Jew will be burnt." Arguments have no place in the debate about Jews which the world conducts with us : " Silently, as if there was no other way of making him understand."

The hostile village splits itself up for Kafka into two strata—the village—and the castle that dominates it. In order to settle in the village, he needed permission from the castle. But the castle barred itself against him, in the same way that the peasants turned their backs on him. The castle, in the peculiar symbolic language of the novel, stands for the divine guidance, the village and its peasants stand for " Mother Earth ". For women attract K.—through them he hopes to get an entrance into the families and to find firm ground under his feet. In just the same way his work is a connection with the earth, a taking-root. As soon as the prospect of a girl from the place and of a job opens up for him, he thinks he has won the game, and he lulls himself with the dream that he will be able to walk about among the people of the village " indistinguishable " from them. The whole passage breathes the illusionary spirit of the psychology of assimilation : " Only as a village labourer, removed as far away as possible from the gentlemen of the castle would he be in a position of achieve anything in the castle. These people who were still so suspicious to him would begin to speak to him when he had become, not of course their friend, but still their fellow-citizen, and once he was undistinguishable from Gerstäcker or Lasemann—and that would have to happen very quickly, everything depended on that—then all paths would be opened to him at one stroke, and so on." K.'s reflections follow the familiar lines : to reach God through the community, out of the coalescence with a natural form of life to draw religious strength. But K. might very well be able to explain this mystery rationally—to live it to the depths (in these strange surroundings) he was not able. " I have been here quite a long time and am already feeling a little deserted ", he complains to the schoolmaster. " To the peasants I don't belong and to the castle I don't either, I suppose." " Between the peasants and the castle there is no difference," the schoolmaster corrects him. And that, too, again sounds like a paraphrase of a well-known saying, a saying of the Psalms, " How can we sing the Lord's song in a strange land " !

The difference between K. and the natives in the passage given below display the familiar features. On all sides the Jew comes up against the old customs—he becomes a nuisance without wishing to be one—at the same time he has the feeling he knows everything better than the people on the spot, he would like to make the whole thing simple, more practical than they do, but they, in their incredible selfwill remain unapproachable. In numerous scenes Kafka shows with superior irony what unsuspected powers of resistance the outmoded and distorted arrangements of the village and the castle develop to oppose the intruder. " You are not from the village, you are nothing. But unfortunately you are something after all, a stranger, a person who is superfluous, and always in the way, a person for whose sake one has continual vexation, a person whose intentions are obscure—for all that I don't in fact at bottom reproach you. You are what you are. I have seen too much in my life already not to be able to bear the sight of this, too. But now just think what you are really asking for. . . . You have been in the place a day or two, and already you think you know everything better than the people who live here. I am not saying that it isn't possible once in a while to get something done even in the teeth of every rule and tradition, but then it certainly doesn't come about in the way you are going on, by saying no all the time, and sticking to your own opinions and flouting the most well-meant advice."

It is the same thing with the chairman of the parish council, who expresses his fundamental dislike of K. in a slightly different tone, but just as conclusively. "You were engaged as a surveyor, but we have no work for you here. . . . Nobody is keeping you here, but, after all, that is not throwing you out. . . . Who would dare to throw you out, Mr. Surveyor, the lack of clarity of the preliminary questions is already enough to hide from you the polite way you are being treated."

In the long history of the sufferings of Jewry, we have heard all these notes before. K. comes to grief in the most pitifully ridiculous way, despite the fact that he went at everything so earnestly and conscientiously. He remains alone. Over all the painful situations this novel takes us through, over all the undeserved misery hangs, invisibly visible, the motto, " This is not the way to do things. A new, a quite different way of taking root must be sought."

In a still unpublished fragment from the year 1914, Kafka describes this fundamental feeling still more sharply. " I came once in summer, towards evening, to a village where I had never been before ", is the opening sentence of a short story that covers 14 quarto pages, but is then, alas ! broken off. " On every side in front of the farmhouses one saw old and lofty trees. It was after a shower ; the air blew fresh, I was so well pleased with everything." A door in the wall is opened. The children of the tenant-farmer were peeping out to see who was passing by so late in the night. The narrator is startled, but is given information by a passer-by. " To a stranger everything may easily seem odd ", he apologised, with a smile. The narrator would like to stay the night in the village, looks for an inn, is under observation. The man he first spoke to says to his wife, " I just want to see what this man is going to do here. He is a stranger. He is fussing around here in a quite unnecessary way. Just watch ! " And Kafka goes on : " He was talking about me as if I were deaf, or didn't understand his language ". An uncanny conversation follows with the married couple. The stranger is given a night's lodging in their house. Everything takes place in an atmosphere of half, or complete, unexpressed hostility. " If putting me up gives you even the faintest trouble, then tell me so frankly, I am not at all insistent on the point. I shall go to the inn ; it's all the same to me." " He talks such a lot ", said the woman softly. " It could only be meant as an insult ; well, they answer my politeness with insults then ; but she is an old woman, I can't defend myself. And it was just this defencelessness perhaps that was the reason why this remark of the woman's which I could not answer back, had a much greater effect on me that it deserved. I felt some kind of justification for some kind of fault found with me, not for the reason that I had spoken too much, for really I had said only what was absolutely necessary, but for some separate reasons which touched my existence very nearly." Finally there is a description of how the stranger, without wanting to, disturbs the children in their sleep by his clumsiness and misunderstanding, turns the whole house upside down.

The negative aspect of the Jewish problem, the indefensibility of the Jewish position is also demonstrated in the story, *Josefine, die Sängerin, oder das Volk der Mäuse*, the last finished work of Kafka's, and one which he himself destined for the printing press. To what particular people this picture of the baited, helpless host of mice most nearly refers need not be expressly stated. How the vanity of the star, of the literary man, of the leading " Personality " asserts itself even in the midst of the deepest anguish of the people : this extremely ironical presentation of the protagonist who believes the world has waited for him alone, for his word of salvation that he, and only he, could utter, unhappily applies also to a phenomenon which is particularly common just in the Jewish Party and the Jewish literary world—the man who thinks that he alone was chosen, and with sneering superiority dismisses as unimportant, or hardly takes any notice of, anything that anybody else advises, does, or says. (*N.B.* Kafka himself is an example of the opposite type, that is, modest, and humble, and has none of those " gestures of a saviour " about him. He went, or so I think, almost too far in this direction. It is open to argument how far the unfavourable conditions of his life were responsible for his occasional self-depreciation and whether without it he would not have risen to the rank of a great, historically effective prophet of true religiosity.) Don't misunderstand me ! The position of the helpless mice is simultaneously that of weak humanity in the battle against the demons of Evil. The vain prophet is to be found among other peoples too. And only in so far as the position of helplessness, as well as of the irresponsible, conscienceless " famous man " stands, in the case of the Jews, under the dazzling searchlight of the distress of the Jewish masses and of the Jewish soul, is it an especially sharp portrait in miniature, a symbol of the general sufferings of mankind presented in the form of a caricature.

In *Josephine*, however, the road leading to a positive solution is indicated, and it seems to me not a matter of indifference that this happens just in the last work Kafka finished. Josephine the singer defies, hides away from her people, that has so warmly admired her art, indeed has regarded it as indispensable, and now the story says, " But the people, quietly, without showing any disappointment, imperiously, a mass relying on itself, which even if appearances speak against it, *can absolutely only make gifts, never receive them, not even from Josephine, goes on in its own way.* For Josephine, however, there can be only the downward path. The day will soon come when her last squeak has sounded and is heard no more. *She is a tiny episode in the eternal history of our people, and our people will get over the loss.*" The incorporation of the individual in the fate of his people, his active participation is demanded. The reader of this biography will find sufficient points to show how Kafka, in his special, Jewish case, tried to find the link with the people. The last chapter also adds a few indications of this. Of course Kafka did not believe that a geographical change of address was sufficient ; he regarded a change of heart as equally to be demanded. Both must be changed, both were equally necessary. Order in one's soul—as well as a normalisation of the outward conditions of life.

Now one might ask why Kafka expressed this only in his diaries and letters, and never expressly in his literary works, why, as a writer, he expressed himself solely, allegorically or symbolically, in parables.

First one must recognise the peculiarity of Kafka's way of thinking, which went on in images, and not in discourse. Even in conversation, in a debate, the image prevails. In the diary, too, the inexpressibly lovely lyric passages—one of many : " Dreams come along, they come up the river, on a ladder they climb the quayside. One stops, one talks to them they know so much, only, where they come from, that they don't know . . . why do you raise your arms instead of folding them round us ? "

Furthermore, one must not confuse " allegory " and " symbol ". Allegorical Kafka never is, but symbolical he is in the highest sense. An allegory is created when one " says something else " for something. This " something else " in itself is of little importance. The anchor, which stands for hope, in its character as an anchor, does not interest us in the least. It is all the same what colour, what shape or what size it is. That is why, as a pure hieroglyphic sign, it stands so unequivocally, and sharply silhouetted, for " Hope ". But Andersen's " Tin Soldier ", who expresses, perhaps, a good, patient, loving heart, and many other things as well, running into infinity, touches us also through the personal story of himself, the tin soldier, in all its detail. The tin soldier is no more an allegory, but a symbol. The symbol stands on both levels at the same time, on the level which it describes by suggestion, and on the objective, real level. It unites the two levels in a peculiar way, and, which the Greek word also expressed, throws them together mixed up with one another—and this in such a way that, the deeper one penetrates into the individual case, with all its details about the tin soldier, the clearer one sees the universal. The " Marchioness of O " deals with faith between parents and child, but behind it, on the high level stands the question of faith in general, faith in the order of the world. Why then did the writer not say straight out the universal that he wanted to say ? Because it cannot be said to the end, because it stretches into infinity. In the special case which he relates the writer gives only the starting point of an infinite process. Allegory takes the opposite path, presents the end of such a process, presents it in clear outline as a plaything—the mark of a tired soul. Symbol on the other hand is the bursting forth of a soul, is a matter of the tensive power which allows the individual case to send a ray into the infinite—and at the same time, according to the point at which one takes a cross-section of the ray, one finds the affairs of the individual, of the people, or of mankind dealt with. And all this, too, simultaneously, with the same words, and in one single situation.

Behind all Kafka's scenes this infinite vista opens out. But the scene itself, too, the plain narrative, from which the ray shines, is full of love of Nature and faithful to Nature, of fine observation that is never boring —read at this point, shall we say—but there are thousands of examples— the scenes of office life, which have been so thoroughly experienced, or of the rivalry between the clerks in *The Trial*. Only a man who loves life on the deepest foundation tells a tale in such a way. There is not a word that the presentation does not lend new colour to, not a word that is meaningless—this special mastery of style is not merely aesthetic, it is a moral phenomenon, it is a result of Kafka's peculiar honesty. This would already be a great thing were it only a question of a simple realistic presentation. But the happenings he describes mean, with Kafka, himself in the first place, but they mean also at the same time *not only* himself. A ray shines out from every detail, pointing to the eternal, the transcendental, the world of ideas. In every great work of art one finds the eternal shining through the mortal forms. In the case of Kafka, however, it has, apart from that, become a formal principle of his writing ; one simply cannot any longer separate content from structure, so intimately have they united.

VII

The Last Years

"THERE is no one here that understands me as a whole. To have one person that had this understanding, a woman for example, that would be to have a foothold on every side, it would mean to have God "—this is what Kafka wrote in his diary in 1915. It seems that this happiness did come his way at the end of his life, and that the outcome of his fate was more positive and more full of life than its whole previous development.

In the summer of 1923, Franz was staying with his sister and her children in Müritz, the Baltic seaside resort. There he chanced upon a holiday colony of the Berlin Jewish People's Home, which, founded by Dr. Lehmann, had filled him, as well as myself, with hope. Right at the beginning of the work, which has now spread widely and nobly in Palestine, he took a lively interest in it, and had at one time persuaded his fiancée F. in Berlin to take part as a voluntary helper in the work of this Home. Now, many years later, on the beach he meets children from this home, plays with them, gets to know their teacher, goes to social evenings with them. Once he notices a girl in the Home's kitchen. She is busy scaling fish. "Such gentle hands, and such bloody work ", he said with disapproval. The girl was ashamed, and had some other work allotted to her.

That was the beginning of his friendship with Dora Diamant, his life's companion.

Dora Diamant, who must have been nineteen or twenty at that time, came from a very much looked up to Polish Orthodox Jewish family. For all the respect she bore her father whom she loved, she couldn't stand the constraint, the narrowness of the tradition—a similar case to that of the actor Löwy, who combined a great respect for his parents with the realisation that he could not continue to follow in their footsteps. Dora escaped from the little Polish town, and found jobs first in Breslau, then in Berlin, and came to Müritz in the employ of the Home. She was an excellent Hebrew scholar. Kafka was studying Hebrew with special zeal at that time—of the papers he left behind, the papers filled with Hebrew exercises are not much less than those covered with literary works in German.

One of the first conversations between the two ended in Dora reading aloud a chapter from Isaiah in the original Hebrew. Franz recognised her dramatic talent ; on his advice, and under his direction, she later educated herself in this art.

Franz came back from his summer holiday full of high courage. His decision to cut all ties, get to Berlin, and live with Dora stood firm—and this time he carried it out inflexibly. At the end of July he left Prague, after offering successful resistance to all his family's objections. From Berlin he wrote to me for the first time that he felt happy, and that he was even sleeping well—an unheard of novelty in these last years. He was living with Dora in the suburb of Steglitz, first of all at 8 Miquel-strasse, at Hermann's. There was written the comparatively happy story *Eine kleine Frau*. The " Little Woman-Judge " who lives her life in constant anger with her own " Ego " who is really a stranger to her, is none other than their landlady. She must have put a lot of difficulties in the way of the young couple. Six weeks later, therefore, we find them in 13 Grunewald Street with Dr. Rethberg, a lady doctor, in a villa about whose loveliness Franz used to rave, although he had only two modest rooms in it. There I went to see him as often as I came to Berlin—three times it must have been in all. I found an idyll ; at last I saw my friend in good spirits ; his bodily health had got worse, it is true. Yet for the time it was not even dangerous. Franz spoke about the demons which had at last let go of him. " I have slipped away from them. This moving to Berlin was magnificent, now they are looking for me and can't find me, at least for the moment." He had finally achieved the ideal of an independent life, a home of his own, he was no longer a son living with his parents, but to a certain extent himself a paterfamilias. It is obvious that Kafka was not at all striving after a paradox, an ideal in principle inachievable—like Kierkegaard, like the " Theology of Crisis ", but—and this is the decisive factor—that he wanted an intelligently fulfilled, good and proper life, that he stood more perhaps on the side of Martin Buber, who, in rejecting Kierkegaard, the solitary from principle, says of living together with a wife, " Marriage is the exemplary bond, as no other bond does, it carries us into the great bondage and only as bondsmen can we enter into the freedom of the children of God—yes, woman stands in dangerous rapport with the finite, and indeed, the finite is the danger, for there is no greater threat to us than that of remaining tied to it, but just on this danger is our hope of salvation forged, for it is only over the finite fulfilled that our human path leads to the infinite " (Buber, *The Question for the Individual*, 1936). In this sense I saw Kafka on the right road, and truly happy with his life-companion in the last year of his life, which, despite his frightful illness, perfected him. He was working with pleasure, read " A Little Woman " aloud for me, wrote " The Burrow " from which he also read some passages aloud to me. When I introduced him to the manager of the publishing firm " Die Schmiede ", he agreed, without much need of long arguments to persuade him, to the publication of four short stories as a title for which he took the name of one of them, *A Hunger-Artist*. From all these circumstantial indications of his interest in life, I then later gathered the courage to regard as no longer valid his written instructions to me—written long before this period—which forbade the publication of any of his posthumous papers.

It was not only to me that Franz seemed to have found salvation in his whole existence, to have become a new man—from his letters you can see his good spirits and the firmness he had finally won. Take, for example, the following letter to his sister :

" DEAR VALLI,—The table is standing by the fire. I have just moved from the fireplace because it's too warm there, even for my back which is always cold. My oil-lamp burns wonderfully, a masterpiece of lamp-making, and of shopping—it has been borrowed together and bought together out of little odd bits—not of course by me—how could I manage a thing like that ! You can light it without taking the lamp glass and the globe off ; really there is only one thing wrong with it, it won't burn without oil ; but after all the rest of us don't do that—and so I am sitting down, and taking out your dear letter, now so old, The clock is ticking, I have got used even to the ticking of the clock, don't hear it very often, besides, and that generally when I am doing something particularly not worth while. In fact the clock has certain personal relations with me like many things in the room, save that now, particularly since I gave notice— or, more accurately, since I was given notice, which is a good thing from every angle, and, moreover, a complicated affair it would take pages to describe—they seem to be beginning to turn their backs on me, above all the calendar, about the mottoes on which I have already written to father and mother. Lately it is as if it has been metamorphosed. Either it is absolutely uncommunicative—for example, you want its advice, you go up to it, but the only thing it says is, ' Feast of the Reformation '—which probably has a deeper significance, but who can discover it ?—or on the contrary, it is nastily ironic. Lately, for example, I was reading something and hit upon an idea as I was doing so that seemed to me very good, or rather full of significance, so much so that I wanted to ask the calendar's opinion on it—it's only on such accidental occasions that it answers, in the course of its day, not like, say, by tearing off a page of the calendar punctually at a fixed time—' Even a blind dog finds something sometimes ' it said. Another time I was horrified at the coal-bill, whereupon it told me, ' Happiness and contentment are the joy of life ', in which there is admittedly together with the irony an offensive insensitivity : it is impatient, it can't wait any longer for the day I leave ; but perhaps it is only that it wishes to make parting easy for me. Perhaps under the page giving the date of the day I leave there will be a page which I shall no longer see on which is written, ' God has told each loving heart, the day will come when we must part '. No, one should not write down everything one thinks about one's calendar, ' He is only a man, like yourself, after all '.

" If I tried to write you about everything I come into contact with in this way, I should of course never come to the end, and it would give the appearance that I am leading a busy social life, but in reality it is very quiet where I am, but yet never too quiet. Of the excitements of Berlin, bad and good, I know very little ; of the former more, of course. By the way, does P. know what you say in Berlin when you are asked, ' How are you ' ! Oh, of course he'll know it. You all know more about Berlin than I do. Well at the risking of repeating an old, old joke, factually it is after all always topical, the answer is ' Mouldy × the index figure '. And this one—a man is talking enthusiastically about the physical culture festival at Leipzig : ' What a tremendous sight when the 750,000 athletes march in ! ' The other answers, counting up carefully, ' Well, that's nothing, after all—three and a half peace-time athletes '.[1]

" How are things—this is no longer a joke any more, but I hope not something sad either—in the Jewish school. Have you read the paper by the young teacher in ' Self-defence ' ?[2] Very well-intentioned, and zealous. I have again heard that A. is doing very well, and Miss M., they say, has reformed the whole of gymnastics in Palestine. You must not be too annoyed at old A.'s head for business. After all, it was already a tremendous thing to take the whole family on his back and cart them over the sea to Palestine. That so many of his kind do it is no less a miracle of the waters than Moses in the Red Sea.

" I thank M. and L. ever so much for their letters. Remarkable how their handwritings, if you compare them, convey not perhaps the differences in their characters, but almost their corporal differences ; at least so it seems to me in this last couple of letters. M. asks what about her life interests me most. Well, what she is reading ; if she still dances. Here, in the Jewish People's Home, all the girls learn rhythmic dancing, free of charge, of course—and if she still wears glasses. I am to send Anny G.'s love to L. A dear, lovely, clever child L., that is to say, but so is Anny— she is learning Hebrew hard, can almost read already, and sing a new song. Is L. making progress, too ?

" But now it is high time to go to bed. Well, I have been with you

---

[1] A reference to the inflation of the mark which had accustomed Berliners to divide all figures by a huge divisor, according to the index figure posted each day.

[2] *Selbstwehr*—the organ of the Zionist Movement in Prague.

almost a whole evening, and it is so far from Stockhaus Lane, to Miquel
St.—Love . . ."

The frightful winter of the inflation period has begun. It is that which
has really properly killed Franz, so I think. Every time Franz goes from
our quiet suburb to Berlin, he comes home " as if he were coming back
from the field of battle "—so Dora tells me. The sufferings of the poor
touch him to the heart ; he comes back " ash-grey ". " He lives with
such intensity ", says Dora, " that he has died a thousand deaths in his
life." But it is not sheer pity ; he himself must also endure great privations, because he stubbornly insists on managing on his tiny pension.
Only in the worst case and under great pressure will he accept money
and parcels of food from his family. For by doing so he feels the independence he has so hardly won is threatened. Hardly has he earned a
few pence through his contract with the " Schmiede " Publishing House,
and he thinks about paying back his " family debts ", and expensive
birthday presents—from the family who is worrying desperately about
him he keeps the true state of his affairs back as long as he can. There is a
shortage of coal. Butter he gets from Prague. When he heard that his
sister was a member of a Prague Jewish Women's Club which was sending gift parcels to Berlin, he gave her the addresses of people he knew who
were without means. " Not to let anything slip—for the money for
sending things like this generally runs out pretty quickly. I am sending
the addresses straight away ; could send many more of course, the supply
will not run dry." Against some of the addresses he put the note
" Koscher ". Then he happened to catch sight of one of these parcels,
and criticised it, saying " There it lay in front of us, deadly serious,
without the faintest smile in the shape of a slab of chocolate, an apple,
or something of that sort, as much as to say, ' Now live a few days longer
on groats, rice, flour, sugar, and coffee, then die as best you can, we can't
do any more for you '." Thus it was never possible to satisfy his fine
feelings.

So long as his health lasted he used to attend the High School for
Science of the Jews in Artillery St. He attended Prof. Torczyner and
Prof. Guttmann's introductory lectures on the Talmud. He read the
easier Hebrew texts. It was only for the sake of these courses that he
came regularly from his suburb into Berlin.

Between Christmas and the New Year he went through several severe
attacks of fever, but recovered again. In February he moved to Zehlen-
dorf, and his landlady this time was the widow of Carl Busse the author.
He lived a retired life. Very seldom visitors came from Berlin—Dr.
Rudolf Kayser, Ernst Blass.

The rise in the cost of living began to worry him. " If you cut

yourself down to lodgings—over-magnificent lodgings, I admit, I shall
give one room up next month—and food—excellent, I admit, conjured
up out of two methylated spirit stoves and a haybox—which may perhaps
also be an unwarrantable extravagance in comparison with the man my
former landlady was always telling me about who cooked everything
without exception in his bed—if you live in such simplicity you can just
get along, also only with the help of your father and mother and sisters,
it is true, but if anything out of the way happens, then you see suddenly
that everything is impossible. Once I called in a doctor, Mrs. L. recommended me a relative of hers, a famous professor, but luckily he didn't
come himself, but sent only an assistant, a young man, not yet thirty ; he
couldn't find anything more than a temperature, also ordered nothing for
the time being except to stay in bed and wait. For this visit he asked 20
marks, that is, 160 Czech crowns. The worst thing is, however, that this
price is not only somehow justified according to the scale of fees—nobody
ever asks more than his proper fee here—but that it also fully corresponds
with the rest of the prices ; everything is so dear, you must earn gold
marks if you want to live here ; I am already sometimes beginning to
think I must give up the struggle against Berlin prices, and to think of
Schelesen, Vienna, and Lake Garda."

When one went to see Franz, he mentioned his troubles only in a
jocular way. Thus he once worked out for me a plan for taking, together
with Dora, who was such an excellent cook, some small restaurant where
he would make himself useful as a waiter.

In the end it was impossible to shut one's eyes to the fact that Franz's
bodily health—despite his spiritual equilibrium, which continued—was
getting worse. One of his sisters went to see him ; then I came back from
Berlin and warned an uncle of his, a doctor, who went to Berlin and
confirmed my worst fears. On 14 March 1924 I was in Berlin for the
first night of Janáček (Jenufa) at the State Opera of Berlin, and on the 17
I brought Franz back to Prague. Dora and Dr. Klopstock had brought
him as far as the station. A few days later Dora followed him.

Now that Franz was living with his father and mother again, he felt
it, in spite of all the tender care that surrounded him, as the shipwreck of
all his plans for being independent, as a defeat. Now he wanted me to go
and see him every day. Other times he had never spoken so energetically,
had always been extremely considerate towards the piles of work that
overwhelmed me. This time he spoke as if he knew we should not have
one another much longer. " Come to-morrow again at this time," he
said with a certain amount of sternness almost.

As he grew worse and worse, he had to be taken to a sanatorium.

" All my terrors surpassed on the 10 April," stands the entry in my diary, " by the news that Kafka has been sent back from the Wiener Wald (Vienna Forest) Sanatorium, to the Vienna clinic—tuberculosis of the larynx discovered. The most fearful day of disaster."

The only car to be had for the journey from the sanatorium to Vienna was an open one. It rained and blew. The whole journey through Dora stood up in the car, trying to protect Franz with her body against the bad weather.

Robert Klopstock, too, proved his great love and loyalty. He broke off his studies in Berlin—which were later to lead to important research results in the field of the treatment of the lungs—and devoted himself exclusively from that moment on until Kafka's death, to looking after his precious patient. These two, Dora and Dr. Klopstock, now referred to themselves playfully as Franz's " little family ", it was an intimate living together in the face of death. Franz himself knew he was desperately ill, but was, as I was able to experience when I went to see him once, full of hope and courage. He seemed to be unaware of the imminent danger.

In the Vienna clinic—under Professor Hajek—he was not getting on well. All efforts to get more considerate treatment for him—a separate room, for example—were in vain. For a few days he even had to lie in a bed next to a dying man, and he told me afterwards, with great admiration, of the patience of the priest who waited on at the dying man's side with words of comfort, until the last moment, when all the doctors " had run away long ago ". I wrote letters to influential people in Vienna, Werfel intervened energetically on Franz's behalf, but the Professor just as energetically explained that he could not look upon Kafka as anyone else but the patient in room Number so-and-so.

Dora and Robert Klopstock finally succeeded in having Franz transferred at the end of April to the friendly, light sanatorium in Kierling, near Klosterneuburg. Here is an extract from a letter of Werfel's to me : " Professor Hajek maintained the only chance for Kafka was to stay in the hospital, because there all the medicines and treatments were ready to hand. He put up a direct struggle against letting him go." In Kierling, in a lovely room, filled with flowers, and looking on to the green country, cared for in every way by his two faithful friends, Kafka spent the last weeks of his life—so far as the pains he suffered allowed it, patiently and cheerfully.

Professor Neumann and the university lecturer, Dr. Oskar Beck, came from the hospital to Kierling. I shall quote a few lines from a letter the latter wrote to Dr. Felix Weltsch, on 3 May : " Yesterday I was called to Kierling by Miss Diamant. Dr. Kafka was having very sharp pain in the larynx, particularly when he coughed. When he tries to take some nourishment the pains increase to such an extent that swallowing becomes almost impossible. I was able to confirm that there is a decaying tubercular action which includes also a part of the epiglottis. In such a case an operation cannot even be thought of, and I have given the patient alcohol-injections in the *nervus laryngeus superior*. To-day Miss Diamant rang me up again to tell me that the success of this treatment was only temporary and the pains had come back again with all their former intensity. I advised Miss Diamant to take Dr. Kafka to Prague, since Professor Neumann, too, estimated his expectation of life at about three months. Miss Diamant rejected this advice, as she thinks that through this the patient would come to realise the seriousness of his illness.

" It is your duty to give his relations a full account of the seriousness of the situation. Psychologically I can quite understand that Miss Diamant, who is looking after the patient's interests in a self-sacrificing and touching fashion, feels she ought to call a number of specialists to Kierling for a consultation. I had, therefore, to make it clear to her that Dr. Kafka was in such a state, both with regard to his lungs and with regard to his larynx, that no specialist could help him any more, and the only thing one can do is to relieve the pain by administering morphia or pantopon."

In the last few weeks he was ordered to speak as little as possible. He used therefore to communicate with us by writing messages on slips of paper, a few of which are in my possession. On one of them he writes, "The story is going to have a new title, ' Josephine the Songstress—or The Mice-Nation '. Sub-titles like this are not very pretty, it is true, but in this case it has perhaps a special meaning. It has a kind of balance." He thinks of his father a great deal, of hearty eating and drinking. He tells Dora, " When I was a little boy, when I couldn't yet swim, I used to go sometimes with my father, who also can't swim, to the place reserved for non-swimmers. Then we used to sit together naked at the buffet, each with a sausage and a pint of beer. Father generally brought his own sausages with him, because the sausages at the swimming-pool were too dear. Just try and imagine the picture properly—this enormous man, holding a little, nervous bag of bones by the hand, how we used to undress, for example, in the little dark cabin ; how he would then drag me out, because I was ashamed ; how he tried then to teach me the little bit of swimming he pretended he knew, and so on. But the beer afterwards ! " Although he was a teetotaller and a vegetarian, he knew how to appreciate the pleasures of beer, wine and meat, used to take a sniff at drinks sometimes, and praise their wonderful aroma—one wasn't quite sure whether ironically or honestly ; quite towards the end he certainly did drink beer and wine again, once or twice, and was enchanted. " Don't

you have the feeling that Leonhard has a glass of Pschorr in front of him
when he was dictating " he writes on one of his conversational slips
(making a reference to some Leonhard or other which is not clear to me).
Pictures of vital strength are in the majority : " My cousin, he was a
magnificent man. When this cousin Robert, he was then about forty
already, used to come, towards the evening—he couldn't come earlier
because he was a lawyer, had a lot to do, what with his work and his
pleasures—well when he used to come, about five o'clock in the afternoon, to the swimming-pool on the Sophie island, threw off his clothes
with a few flicks of the hand, jumped into the water and threshed around
in it with the strength of a beautiful wild animal, gleaming from the
water, with his eyes sparkling, and then was off again like a shot towards
the weir—that was magnificent. And half a year later he was dead,
tortured to death by doctors. A mysterious disease of the spleen which
they were treating principally with injections of milk, in the consciousness that it was no use." He writes a lot, too, about his condition, about
needs of the moment, pills, bandages. He asks for " a top hat like this
made of water". In between words like " Songs of the Kings ", " Into
the depths, in the deep harbours ". He is tired, full of impatience. And
then again : " Max has his birthday on 27 May ". " Often offer the
nurse wine." " Here it is nice to give people a drop of wine, because
everyone is a little bit of a connoisseur, after all." "That is a pleasure, to
give someone something that gives him pleasure certainly and honestly
in the moment you give it him." " One must take care that the lowest
flowers over there, where they have been crushed into the vases, don't
suffer. How can one do that ? Perhaps bowls are really the best." On
Sunday 11 May I went to Vienna to see Franz once again. My journey
was preceded by a curious scene. When I got to my editorial offices
Saturday afternoon, they shouted to me, " Telephone ! Immediately !
There's a woman just calling you up from Vienna ! " Without waiting
to take my overcoat off I dashed into the telephone booth. It was Dora,
who greeted me with the words, " You rang me up ". I : " No, I've just
arrived this moment." DORA : " Prague rang up, the *Prager Tagblatt*
was speaking, that's why I asked for *you*." In spite of all my efforts to
clear it up, the affair is still unexplained, because while it is true the *Prager
Tagblatt* often rings up Vienna, it never rings up Kierling. Further, none
of Kafka's sisters had rung Kierling that day. In a remarkable fashion,
the whole journey after that lay under the shadow of death. Just as I was
about to leave the house I was told that a young man in the flat below
ours was lying on his death-bed. In the train a woman dressed in black
spoke to me, whom I didn't recognise immediately. It was the widow of
the Minister, Tusar, and she told me all about her husband's death and

her own unhappiness. In Vienna I spoke to no one, but went straight from the station to the hotel, and from the hotel to the station. Early in the morning I took the first train to Klosterneuburg, and from there to Kierling. I stayed till the evening, travelled to Vienna, and the next morning back to Prague. In the forenoon Franz had been quite fresh ; despite all the doctors' testimony, his position didn't seem hopeless to me. We spoke about our next meeting ; I was planning a journey to Italy which was to take in Vienna again. The first thing Dora told me, and Franz bore her out—he was not allowed to speak a lot—was the remarkable story of his wooing. He wanted to marry Dora, and had sent her pious father a letter in which he had explained that, although he was not a practising Jew in her father's sense, he was nevertheless a " repentant one, seeking conversion ", and therefore might perhaps hope to be accepted into the family of such a pious man. The father set off with the letter to consult the man he honoured most, whose authority counted more than anything else for him, to " Gerer Rebbe ". The Rabbi read the letter, put it on one side, and said nothing more than the single syllable, " No ". Gave no further explanation. He never used to give explanations. The miracle-working Rabbi's " No " was justified by Franz's death, which followed very soon afterwards, and Franz, too, took his letter from Dora's father, which had arrived just before I did, and more or less formed the topic of the day for the " Little Family ", as a bad omen. He smiled, and yet he was affected by it ; we made efforts to put other thoughts into his head. But shortly afterwards Dora took me to one side and whispered to me that that night an owl had appeared at Franz's window. The bird of death.

But Franz wanted to live ; he followed the doctor's instructions with an exactitude I had never observed in him before, and without protest. Had he got to know Dora sooner, his will to live would have become stronger sooner, and in time. That is my impression. The two suited one another quite marvellously. The rich treasure of Polish-Jewish religious tradition that Dora was mistress of was a constant source of delight to Franz ; at the same time the young girl, who knew nothing about many of the great achievements of Western culture, loved and honoured the great teacher no less than his dreamlike, curious phantasies, which she entered into easily and like a game. They often joked together like children. I remember, for example, how they used to dip their hands together in the same wash-basin and call it our " family bath ". Dora's care for the invalid was touching ; touching too was the late awakening of all his vital energies. Dora told me how Franz cried for joy when Professor Tschiassny—when he was in the last stage already—told him things looked a little better with his throat. He embraced her again and again, and said he had never wished for life and health so much as now. Let me contrast this with the journey we made together to Schelesen in November 1919, from which I remember two things. Kafka was talking about Hamsun's *The Blessings of the Earth*, and explained in detail how in this novel, partly even against the author's will, everything evil comes from the women in it—further, as the train stopped somewhere, in tones of the deepest despair, " How many stations there are on the journey to death, how slowly it passes ! " And now, in *articulo mortis*, he would have known how to live and wanted to live.

Franz Kafka died on 3 June, on a Tuesday. The body was brought to Prague in a sealed coffin, and on 11 June, at four o'clock, was placed in the grave in a well-chosen site in the Jewish cemetery in Prague—Straschnitz, on the outer side of the cemetery, near one of the main gates. When we got back to the house of mourning in Franz's home in the Old Town Square, we saw that the great clock on the Town Hall had stopped at four o'clock, and its hands were still pointing to that hour. Franz's father and mother were later laid to rest in the same grave.

I was able to get the following details of Franz's last hours mainly from Dr. Klopstock's account.

Monday evening, Franz was feeling very well ; he was jolly, showed great pleasure in everything that Klopstock had brought back from the city with him, ate strawberries and cherries, smelled them for a very long time, enjoyed their fragrance, with the double intensity with which he enjoyed everything those last days. He wanted people to take long drinks of water and beer in front of him, because it was impossible for him to do so ; he enjoyed the others' pleasure. In the last few days he talked a lot about drinks and fruit.

On Monday, too, he wrote the last letter which his parents were to get from Kierling, which I quote below—a document of self-control and a child's love of his parents, which can be compared with the letters Heine wrote to his mother from his last bed of illness, in order to prevent any feeling of uneasiness from troubling her. The letter runs :

" DEAREST FATHER AND MOTHER,—Well, these visits you write to me about sometimes. I think it over every day, because for me it's something very important. It would be so lovely, we haven't been together for such a long time, I don't count being together in Prague, that was just upsetting the household, but being together a few days in peace in some beautiful district, only I can't remember when that was really, a few hours once in Franzensbad. And then to drink a ' good glass of beer ' together, as you write, from which I see that Father doesn't think much of this year's wine, in which, as far as the beer is concerned, I agree with him. Apart from that, a thing I often look back on now during the heat, there was a time once when we often used to be beer-drinkers together, many years ago, when Father used to take me with him to the ' civilian ' baths.

"That and much more speaks for your coming, but there's a lot that speaks against it. Now, first of, all, Father would probably not be able to come because of the difficulty with passports. That, of course, robs your visit of a lot of its sense ; but above all Mother, whoever else she may be accompanied by, will be far too much thrown on me, dependent on me, and I am still not very beautiful, not worth looking at. The difficulties I met with in the beginning here in and around Vienna, you know ; they got me down a little ; they kept my temperature from subsiding quickly again, which all helped towards my getting weaker later ; the shock of the larynx business weakened me at first more than it deserved to in reality.

"Now for the first time I am working myself out of all these weaknesses with the help of Dora and Robert, and how great that help is you cannot imagine so far away—where should I be without them ! There are still troubles, as for example a cold on the stomach which I caught in the last few days, and which has not yet quite gone. All that works together, so that in spite of wonderful helpers, in spite of good air and food, and a bath of fresh air almost every day, I am not yet quite better, in fact, on the whole, am not even in such a fit state as I was the last time I was in Prague. On top of that take into account that I may only talk in whispers, and that not too much, and you will be glad to put off your visit. Everything is beginning to go well. Lately a professor found a real improvement in my larynx, and if I can't altogether believe this extremely kind and unselfish man—he comes out once a week in his own car and charges almost nothing for it, so his words were after all a great comfort to me—everything is, as I said beginning to go well. But the best of beginnings are nothing if I can't show visitors—and especially such visitors as you would be—great, undeniable progress, progress that can be recognised even by the lay eye, it's better to leave it. Well, then, shan't we leave it for the moment, dear father and mother ?

"You mustn't think you could do anything to improve or enlarge on the treatment I am getting here. It is true that the owner of the sanatorium is an old and sick man, who can't be bothered with the thing very much, and my dealings with the very unpleasant assistant doctor are more on friendly than on medicinal terms ; but in addition to the occasional visit of a specialist, Robert is there, above all, and instead of thinking about his examinations, thinks of me with all his might, and then there is a young doctor in whom I have every confidence—I have to thank Arch. Ehrmann for him and for the professor I mentioned above —and who comes after all not in a car, but modestly three times a week by train and ' bus '."

On Monday (and apparently also on Tuesday morning, which however I hardly believe) Franz was working on the first proofs which had arrived shortly before of his last book, *The Hunger-artist*. He gave orders for changing the order of the stories, showed some temper with the publisher, who had not paid sufficient care to this or that instruction. Dora once said very rightly, " Really he demanded a great deal of respect towards himself. If one met him with due respect, everything was all right, and he didn't give anything for formalities. But if one didn't, he was very annoyed." At midnight he fell asleep. At four o'clock in the morning Klopstock was called into the room by Dora, because Franz " is breathing badly ". Klopstock recognised the danger, and woke the doctor, who gave him a camphor injection.

Then began the fight for morphia. Franz said to Klopstock : " You have always been promising it me for four years. You are torturing me ; you have always been torturing me. I am not talking to you any more. I shall die like that." He was given two injections. After the second he said, " Don't cheat me, you are giving me an antidote ". Then the words I mentioned before, " Kill me, or else you are a murderer ". They gave him pantopon ; he was very happy about that. " That's good, but more, more, it isn't helping me." Then he went slowly to sleep. His last words were about his sister Elly. Klopstock was holding his head. Kafka, who was always terribly afraid he might infect someone, said—imagining it was his sister he saw instead of his doctor friend—" Go away, Elly, not so near, not so near ", and as Klopstock moved up a little he was satisfied, and said, " Yes, like that—it's all right like that ".

Before this last scene he made a brusque gesture of dismissal to the nurse. " So brusque as he never was ordinarily ", Klopstock told me. Then with all his strength he tore off his icepack and threw it on the floor. " Don't torture me any more, why prolong the agony." As Klopstock got up from the bed to clean some part of the syringe, Franz said, " Don't leave me ". His friend answered, " But I am *not* leaving you ". Franz answered in a deep voice, " But I am leaving you ".

I want to quote from a letter that Klopstock wrote on 4 June from Kierling, without altering his characteristic, odd grammar. " Poor Dora, oh we are all poor, who is so utterly poor in the world as we—she is whispering without stopping ; one can only make out, ' My love, my love, my good one '—I promised her that we should go and see Franz again this afternoon if she would lie down. So she lay down. See him, ' who is so alone, so quite alone, we have nothing to do, and sit here and leave him there [1] alone in the dark, uncovered—O My God ! My love ' . . . and so it goes on. What is happening here with us—I say always so ' us ', we called ourselves, you see, ' Franz's little family ', is indescribable, and should never be described. Who knows Dora, only he can know what love means. So few understand it, and that increases pain and suffering. But you, won't you, you will understand it ! . . . We don't yet know at all what has happened to us, but slowly, slowly it will get clearer and clearer, and more painfully dark at the same time. Particularly *we* don't know it, who have him still with us. Now we are going there again to Franz. So stiff, so severe, so unapproachable is his face, as his soul was pure and severe. Severe—a king's face from the oldest and noblest stock. The gentleness of his human existence has gone, only his incomparable soul still forms his stiff, dear face. So beautiful is it as an old marble bust."

I must add finally that the voices of Hugh Walpole, Huxley, Bennett, André Gide, Hermann Hesse, Buber, Thomas Mann, Heinrich Mann, Werfel, and many others in German, French, Dutch, Czech, Polish, Italian, and Hebrew, in England and America, united in explaining Kafka's importance, and that his works have appeared in all these languages, and awakened admiration.

Postscript—I closed the first (German) edition of this biography in 1937 with the above words. Now, in 1945, one can hardly survey the gigantic essay-literature that is concerned with Kafka. This literature contains, alongside isolated comments which are correct, very many absurdities and contradictions. But Kafka has struck root in some few spirits. In them his pure light continues to burn. Kafka's art has also in other respects been formative of style in many points, without its religious depth and power to convert being clear to everyone who thinks that he is influenced by Kafka or who writes about him. In fact one often has the impression that here and there only the externals of Kafka's methods have been imitated or analysed, but not his essential endeavour, which is perhaps beyond the reach of some who write so much about him and his art. If humanity would only understand better what has been presented to it in the person and work of Kafka it would undoubtedly be in a quite different position ; for which reason the attempt to deal effectively with Kafka's aims cannot be regarded as completed by this book either.

[1] In the mortuary.

APPENDIXES

I

FROM TWO LETTERS OF KAFKA'S ON BRINGING UP CHILDREN

" I HAVE (among many others), a great witness on my side, whom, however, I am quoting here only because he is great, and secondly because I have just been reading him, yesterday, not because I dared to share his opinions. In his description of Gulliver's journey to Lilliput— the arrangements in which country are highly praised—Swift says : ' Their notions relating to the duties of parents and children differ extremely from ours. However, since the conjunction of male and female is founded upon a great law of need, and in order to continue the species, the Lilliputians will needs have it that their tenderness towards their children proceeds from the like natural principle ; for which reason they will never allow that a child is under any obligation to his father and mother, considering the miseries of human life. Upon this, and the like reasonings, their opinion is, that parents are the least of all others to be trusted with the education of their children.' He obviously means here quite in accordance with your distinction between ' Man ' and ' Son ', that the child, if it is to become man, must be withdrawn as soon as possible, as he puts it, from the animal world, the purely animal depend-ence. You yourself admit that selfishness has something to do with your hesitation. But isn't this selfishness, even considered as selfishness, a little topsy-turvy ? For instance, if you are unwilling to give your winter-things to the furrier to be looked after during the summer, because you feel that when you get them back in the autumn your things will be intrinsically strangers to you, and if therefore you keep your things yourself, then they will of course certainly belong completely, intrinsic-ally and extrinsically to you, but they will have been eaten up by moths. This is not a piece of malice, really not, only an example, but one that is very much to the point. . . .

" So I understand your hesitations. There is only one counter argument that I could admit without any reservation, and that you don't mention. Perhaps you think it though. It is this : How can my advice on the bringing up of other people's children be of any value, when I couldn't even give myself any advice on how one gets children of one's own. This argument is unanswerable, and hits me squarely ; but excellent as it is, I still believe that it hits me more than it does this

[167]

advice of mine. Don't let the fact that it comes from me rob my advice of its value.

" It is not what you emphasise—that children need not be grateful to their parents for their existence—that is the main point for Swift. Indeed there is no one really who would go so far as to affirm it as baldly as that. The chief emphasis is on the concluding sentence : ' Parents are the least of all others to be trusted with the education of their children '. It is true that this, as well as the chain of reasoning that leads up to this sentence is much too concisely worded, and I shall therefore try to explain it to you in greater detail ; but I repeat that all this is what Swift thinks (who was, besides, the father of a family) ; what I think is along the same lines, it is true, but I don't dare to be so emphatic.

" Well, then, Swift thinks as follows : every typical family represents in the first place, a solely animal connection, in a sense, a single organism, a single circulation of blood. It cannot, therefore, if left to itself, rise above itself, it cannot create a new man out of itself alone ; if it tries to do so by family education, that is a kind of spiritual incest.

" The family, then, is an organism, but an extremely complicated and unbalanced one, like every organism, it also strives continuously to adjust itself. So long as this struggle to adjust itself takes place between parents and children—the mutual self-adjustment of the parents does not belong here—it is called education. Why it should be so called is ununderstandable, because there is no trace in it of real education, that is to say of the quiet, unselfish, loving development of the capacities of a growing human being, or even of the quiet suffering of an independent development. Rather it is merely the attempt at adjusting itself, which is usually made spasmodically, of an animal organism, condemned for at least several years to the acutest lack of self-adjustment, which we can call the family animal to distinguish it from the individual animal.

" The reason why an immediate fair adjustment is absolutely impossible—and only a fair adjustment is a real adjustment, only such an adjustment has any permanence—within this family animal, is the inequality of birth of its parts, that is the immense superiority in power for many years of the father and mother over against the children. In consequence of this, the parents arrogate to themselves, during the childhood of their children, the position of alone being right, of alone representing the family not only before the outer world, but also in the inner spiritual organisation, so that thereby they rob their children step by step of any right to their own personality and can from this beginning make them incapable of ever asserting their right in a good way, which can later hit the parents no less hard than the children.

" The essential difference between real education and family education is this : the former is a human affair, the latter a family affair. In the human race every human being has his place, or at least the possibility of going to the dogs in his own way ; in the family, however, hedged in by the parents, only certain clearly specified people have their place, people who come up to clearly specified requirements, and, more than this, to terms dictated by the parents. If they don't come up to specification they are not expelled—that would be very fine, but it is impossible, because it is a question of a single organism—but cursed or eaten up, or both. This eating up does not take place physically as in the old parent-image in the Greek mythology, Chronos, who ate his sons—the most honest of fathers—but perhaps Chronos chose his method rather than the usual one out of sheer pity for his children.

" The selfishness of parents—the real parent-feeling—knows no bounds indeed. Even the greatest love of parents is, in the educational sense, more selfish than the faintest love on the part of the salaried educator. It cannot be otherwise. The parents in fact don't stand in a free relationship with their children as any other adult does, for it is their own blood after all—a still further complication, it is the blood of both sides of the parents. When the father—this same thing goes for the mother—' educates ', he finds, for example, in the child things he hated in himself and could never overcome, and which he now hopes he is certain to overcome, for the feeble child seems more in his power than he is himself, and so in a blind temper he sets to work on the growing human being without waiting for it to develop ; or he recognises, for example, with horror that something that he recognises as a distinction of his own and which must therefore—therefore !—not fail in the family —in the family !—does fail in the child, and so he begins to hammer it into him, in doing which he succeeds in fact but at the same time fails, because in doing so he hammers the child to pieces ; or he finds, for example, in the child, things which he loved in his wife but hates in the child—which he continually confuses with himself, all parents do that— as when, for example, one can be very much in love with one's wife's blue eyes but would be disgusted to the core should one suddenly find oneself with eyes like that ; or he finds, for example, in the child things which he loves or longed for in himself and considers necessary for the family, for everything else about the child is a matter of indifference to him ; he sees in the child only the loved one ; he clings to the loved one ; he humbles himself to become his slave ; he eats him up for love of him.

" Those are the two methods of education of parents, both born of selfishness—tyranny and slavery of every shade, whereby the tyranny can express itself very tenderly—' You must believe me, because I am your

mother '—and the slavery very proudly—' You are my son, therefore
shall I make you my saviour '—but they are two frightful means of
education, two anti-educational means, calculated to tread the child back
into the ground from which it came. You see, parents have for their
children only the animal, unreasoning love that is constantly confusing
itself with the child ; the educator has respect for the child, and in the
educational sense, that is incomparably more, even if no love goes with
it. I repeat, in the educational sense ; for when I call parent-love an
animal, unreasoning love, that is in itself no depreciation, it is an unfathomable secret just as the reasoning creative love of the educator is, save that
from the point or view of education, it is true, this depreciation cannot be
great enough. When N. calls herself a hen she is quite right, every
mother is one at bottom, and the mother who isn't is either a goddess or
more probably a sick animal. Now this hen N., after all, wants to have
men as children, not chickens, so she must not educate her children alone.

" I repeat, Swift is not trying to dishonour parent-love, he looks upon
it, even under certain circumstances, as strong enough to protect the
children against this very parent-love. A mother, who in some poem or
other saves her child from under the lion's paws should not be able to
protect this child against her own hands ? And does she do this then
without reward, or, more properly, without hope of a reward ? Another
poem in the school books tells the story of the wanderer who comes back
to his native village after many years, and who nobody recognises any
more except his mother. ' But the eye of a mother knew him.' That is
the real miracle of mother-love, and there is a great truth expressed here,
but only a half one, for the additional point is missing that if the son had
stayed at home she would never have known him, that sitting together
with her son day after day would have made him quite unrecognisable
by her, and that then the opposite of the poem would have happened,
and every one else would have known him better than she. (It is true
that she would then have had no need at all to recognise him, either,
because he would never have come back to her.) You will perhaps say
that the wanderer didn't go out into the world until he was over eleven,
but I know absolutely for certain that he had still a few months to go to
his tenth year [the reference is to the special case of the son of the woman
the letter is addressed to, who was not ten years old], that it was no
mother who wanted greedily to bear the responsibility, who wanted to
share the joys, and, what is perhaps worse, the sorrows of her son—
nothing shall be his entirely ! No mother who would have arranged
things so as to be saved by her son ; a mother, then, who had trust in him—
mistrust is a Prague habit ; besides, trust and mistrust are equally risky as
to consequences, but mistrust is in addition risky in itself—and who could.

just because of that, be saved by her son's homecoming. (At the same time perhaps her danger was not in fact so immeasurably great, because it was not a Jewish woman from Prague, but some strict Catholic woman from Sytytria.)

" Well, what is to be done ? According to Swift, the children should be taken away from their parents, that is to say, the adjusting process which this family animal needs, is first of all to be achieved provisionally through postponing the final adjustment by taking the children away, until the children, independent of their parents, have become equal to them in body and spiritual strength, in short, until the time for the real, for the loving, adjustment has arrived, namely, that which you call ' Salvation ' and what others call ' The gratitude of one's children ', but so seldom find.

" Moreover, Swift understands moderation, and does not consider taking the children of poor people away from them to be absolutely necessary. For in the case of poor people life, workaday life, penetrates to a certain degree into the hovel—as, for example, at the birth of Christ ; in the half-open hovel almost all the world was there, the shepherds, and the wise men from the East—and doesn't permit the thick, poison-laden, child-destroying atmosphere of a beautifully furnished family-room to gather.

" Also, of course, Swift does not deny that parents can, under certain circumstances, form an excellent body of teachers, but only for other people's children.

" Anyhow, that is how I interpret this passage of Swift's."

II

THE AEROPLANES AT BRESCIA

BY FRANZ KAFKA

La Sentinella Bresciana of 9 September 1909, announces with delight " In Brescia we have a throng of people such as we have never had before, not even at the time of the great automobile races ; visitors from Venice, Liguria, Piedmont, Tuscany, Rome, even from as far away as Naples ; indeed, the big men of France, England, and America are crowding our squares, our hotels, every nook and corner of our private houses : all prices are rising splendidly ; the means of transport are insufficient to carry the crowds to the ' *circuito aerio* ' ; the restaurants at the aerodrome can serve two thousand people excellently, confronted with several thousand they could not but break down. The militia was needed to protect the buffets. In the cheap places fifty thousand people are standing the whole day."

As my two friends and I read this news we were filled with courage and fear simultaneously. Courage, because where there are such fearful crowds, things are generally done in a beautifully democratic way, and where there is no room, one needn't look for it. Fear—fear of the way Italians organise such undertakings ; fear of the committee that will take us in hand ; fear of the journey by train of which the *Sentinella* proudly boasts that they are four hours late. All expectations are false, all one's memories of Italy get completely mixed up with each other as soon as we get back home ; they fade, and we cannot rely on them.

As we drive into the black hole of the station at Brescia, where people are screaming as if the ground were on fire under their feet, we are still earnestly warning each other that whatever happens we must stick together. Aren't we going with a kind of hostility ?

We get out ; a carriage that hardly manages to stay on its wheels accepts us ; the driver is in a very good temper ; we drive through almost empty streets up to the palace of the committee, where they overlook our inward wickedness, as if it were not there ; we find out everything we need to know. The inn we are directed to seems to us at first sight to be the dirtiest we have ever seen, but after a while it is not at all so exaggeratedly bad. It is dirt which is just there, that's all, and about which no more is said ; dirt which will never change any more, which has made itself at home, which in a certain sense makes life more tangible, more earthly ; dirt out of which our host hurries forth, proud towards himself, humble towards us, continually stroking his elbows, and casting new and ever new shadows on his face with his hands—every finger is a compliment—bowing from the waist all the time in a way we recognise later at the aerodrome, in Gabriele d'Annunzio, for instance. Who, one must ask, could still have anything on his mind against this dirt ?

The aerodrome is at Montechiari, and can be reached in a bare hour by the local line that goes to Mantua. This local line has reserved itself a length of rail along the general highway, on which it lets its trains travel with all modesty neither higher nor lower than the rest of the traffic, between the cyclists who ride into the dust with their eyes almost closed, between the completely unusable carriages from the whole province—which pick up as many passengers as you like, and are besides so quick, you can't believe it—and between the motor-cars which are often huge, and which, given their head, are deliberately trying to run into each other at any moment, with their manifold hootings which, at the speed, have become one noise. At times one gives up hope altogether of ever coming to the *circuito* with this wretched train. But people are laughing all around you, and to the right and to the left people are laughing into the train. I am standing on a platform, squeezed up against an enormous man who is standing with his legs stretched wide apart over the buffers of two carriages, in a shower of soot and dust that falls from the roofs of the gently shaking carriages. Twice the train stops and waits for a train coming in the opposite direction, as long and as patiently as if it were waiting only for a chance meeting. A few villages pass slowly by, wild posters announcing the last automobile race appear on the walls here and there, all growth on the side of the road is unrecognisable under the olive-leaf colour of the white dust. At last the train stops, because it can't go any farther. A group of cars put their brakes on at the same moment, through the clouds of dust that arise we see not far away a lot of little flags ; a herd of cattle which has got out of all control, swaying on the bumpy ground and deliberately charging the automobiles, holds us up still.

We have arrived. In front of the aerodrome lies a great square with suspicious looking little wooden houses, on which we should have expected to see quite different things written up than, " Garage ", " Grand Buffet International " and so on. Enormous beggars grown fat in their little go-carts stretch their arms out across one's path, one is tempted in one's haste to leap over them. We catch up with a lot of people, a lot of people catch up with us. We look up, at the sky, which is, after all, the thing that matters here. Thank God, nobody is flying ? We refuse to get out of the way and yet we are not run over. Between and behind, and advancing to meet the thousands of vehicles, plunges the Italian cavalry. Order and accidents seem equally impossible.

Once, in Brescia, late in the evening, we wanted to get to a certain street in a hurry and we thought it was rather far. A cab driver wanted three liras, we offered two. The driver wouldn't take us and only out of friendliness, described to us how frightfully far this street really was. We began to be ashamed of our offer. All right, three liras. We got in, the cab made three turns through short streets ; we were there. Otto, more energetic than we two, explained that he had no intention, of course, of paying three liras for a journey that took one minute. One lira was more than enough. There was a lira. It was already night, the little street was empty, the cabby was strong. He flew into a passion immediately, as though the quarrel had been going on for an hour already. What ?— That was swindling. What were we thinking of, then? Three liras was the bargain, three liras we must pay. Out with the three liras, or we should be surprised. . . . OTTO : " The tariff or the police ! " Tariff ?

There wasn't any tariff. How should there be a tariff for things like that ! It was a special price for a night fare, but if we would give him two liras he would let us go. OTTO, enough to scare anybody : " The tariff or the police ! " A little more shouting and searching, then a tariff was produced, on which nothing was to be seen but dirt. So we agreed on one lira fifty, and the cabby went off down the narrow street in which he could not turn, not only raging, but also saddened as I can't help thinking. For our behaviour was, alas, not the right behaviour ; one doesn't behave in that way in Italy. In other countries that may be all right, but not here. Well, who thinks of all that when he is in a hurry ! There is nothing to complain about in that, one can't become an Italian in a short week's holiday tour.

But repentance shall not spoil our pleasure at the aerodrome, that would only give ground for fresh repentance, and we jump into the aerodrome rather than walk, in this enthusiasm affecting each limb in turn, which sometimes suddenly overwhelms us in this country, under this sun.

We pass the hangars, which, with their curtains drawn, look like the closed-up stages of a touring dramatic company. On their pediments are written the names of the aviators, whose machines they house, and over that the colours of their countries. We read the names of Cobianchi, Cagno, Rougier, Curtiss, Moucher (a " Tridentiner " flying Italian colours, he trusts them more than he does ours), Anzani, the Club of Roman Aviators. *And Blériot*?, we ask. Blériot, of whom we have been thinking all the time, where is Blériot ?

In the fenced-in ground in front of his hangar, Rougier, a little man with a conspicuous nose, is dashing about in his shirt-sleeves. He is extremely, if somewhat obscurely, busy, he waves his arms about, with his hands in violent movement, feels himself all over us as he walks, sends his workmen behind the curtain of his hangar, calls them back, goes in himself, thrusting them all on one side, while his wife stands to one side in a tight, white dress, a little black hat pressed firmly into her hair, her legs under a short shirt, gently outstretched, she is gazing into the empty heat, a business woman, with all the cares of business in her little head.

In front of the next hangar Curtiss is sitting all alone. Through the curtains, slightly drawn back, his machine can be seen ; it is bigger than we had heard. As we were passing, Curtiss was holding up the *New York Herald* in front of him, and reading a line on the top of a page. After half an hour we pass him again, he has already got to the middle of this page ; another half an hour and he has finished the page and begun another. Obviously he is not going to fly to-day. We turn and look at the broad field. It is so big that everything on it looks forlorn : the guiding-posts near us, the signalling-mast in the distance, the catapult for starting somewhere to the right, a committee-car, that, with little yellow flags fluttering in the wind, describes a curve over the field, stops in its own dust, and then goes on again. An artificial desert has been created here in an almost tropical land, and the aristocracy of Italy, sparkling ladies from Paris, and all the other thousands of people are here to look at this sunny desert with harrowed eyes for many hours. In this place there are none of the distractions that are otherwise provided on other sports fields. One misses the beautiful hurdles of the racecourse, the white lines of the tennis court, the fresh green meadow of the football ground, the stoney up-and-down of the automobile and cycle tracks. Only two or three times during the afternoon a troop of colourful horsemen rides straight across the plain. The horses' hooves are invisible in the dust, the steady light of the sun doesn't change until about five o'clock in the afternoon. And, that nothing may disturb the view of this plain, there is also no music at all, only the whistling of the crowds in the cheap places tries to meet the demands of the ear and of impatience. From the expensive, tall grandstands which stand behind us, all this crowd, it is true, probably melts into the empty plain without any difference.

On one side of the wooden fence a lot of people are standing together. "How tiny", a group of Frenchmen cries, like a sigh. What's the matter then? We push our way through. But look, here there is indeed, on the field, quite near, with real yellow colouring, a small flying-machine that they are getting ready for flight. Now, too, we see Blériot's hangar, and next it that of his pupil Leblanc ; they have been built on the flying-ground itself. Standing, leaning against one of the two wings of his machine is Blériot, whom we immediately recognise, with his head set firmly on his shoulders, watching the fingers of his mechanics as they work at the engine.

Is he going to go up in the air on this tiny thing? Then people on the water, for instance, have an easier job after all. They can practise in puddles first, then in ponds, and not venture out to sea until much later, for this man there is only the sea.

Blériot is in his seat already, holding some kind of lever in his hand, but he lets his mechanics do their best, as if they were superfluous children. He looks slowly over in our direction, looks away from us and again in another direction, but keeps his look to himself always. He is going to fly now, nothing is more natural. This feeling of naturalness, with the simultaneous, general feeling of the extraordinary that cannot be withheld from him, lends him this attitude.

A workman grasps one of the blades of the screw, in order to turn it, tugs at it, it gives a jerk, too ; one hears something like the gasp of a strong

man in his sleep, but the screw doesn't move any farther. Once again
they try, ten times they try, sometimes the screw stops immediately,
sometimes it lets itself go round for a few turns. It's the fault of the engine.
Work is begun on it afresh, the onlookers get more tired than those who
are taking close part. The engine is oiled on every side, hidden screws are
loosened and tightened up ; one man runs into the hangar and brings
out a spare part ; that doesn't fit again ; he hurries back, and sitting on
his haunches on the floor of the hangar, he holds it between his knees, and
hammers away at it. Blériot changes his seat with a mechanic, the
mechanic with Leblanc. Now this man, now that, tugs away at the
screw. But the engine is intractable, like a schoolboy one always helps,
the whole class prompts him ; no, he doesn't know it, he stops again and
again, he breaks down. For a while Blériot sits quite still in his seat ; his
six assistant workers stand round him without moving, they all seem to
be dreaming.

The onlookers can breathe again, and look around. The young Mrs.
Blériot passes by with a motherly face, two children behind her. If her
husband can't fly, that does not suit her, and if he flies, she is afraid ;
moreover her lovely dress is a little heavy for this temperature.

Once again the screw is given a turn, perhaps a better one than before,
perhaps just the same. The engine comes to life with a roar, as if it were
a different thing ; four men hold the machine from behind and in the
middle of the complete calm all around, the gusts from the swinging
screw go in thrusts through the overalls of these men. One doesn't hear
a word, only the noise of the screw seems to give orders, eight hands
release the machine, which rolls a long way over the waving ground like
a clumsy man on a polished floor.

Four such attempts are made, and all of them end without result.
Each one sends the public rushing up to the bundles of hay on which one
stretches one's arms out partly to keep one's balance, and partly to express
hope, fear, and joy. In the intervals, however, the Italian aristocracy walks
along the grandstands. They say good-day to each other, bow, recognise
each other once again, they embrace each other, they walk up and down
the gangways of the grandstand. People point out to each other
Princess Laetitia Savoia Bonaparte, Princess Borghese, an elderly woman
whose face is the colour of dark yellow grapes, Countess Morosini.
Marcello Borghese is in every lady's company and no lady's company ;
from a distance he seems to have an understanding face, but when you
get close to him, his cheeks overlap the corners of his mouth in the oddest
way. Gabriele d'Annunzio, short and weakly, dances attendance,
apparently shyly, before Count Oldofredi, one of the most important
men on the committee. Over the railings of the stand peers the

strong face of Puccini, with a nose that one might well call a
drinker's nose.

But you see these people only if you look for them. Otherwise one
sees everywhere, devaluating everything, the tall ladies of the present
fashion ! They prefer walking to sitting, in their clothes sitting doesn't
go very easily. All their faces, veiled like Asiatics, are borne in a faint
twilight ; the dress, loose on the bust, gives the whole figure a kind of
faint-hearted appearance ; a kind of mixed, restless feeling overcomes
one when ladies look faint-hearted like this. The bodice is low-cut, one
can hardly reach it ; the waist seems broader than usual because everything else is narrow ; these women want to be embraced lower down.

It was only Leblanc's machine that had been shown so far. But now
comes the machine in which Blériot flew over the Channel ; nobody says
so, everybody knows it. A long pause, and Blériot is in the air. One sees
his straight body over the wings, his legs are stretched down like a part of
the engine. The sun is sinking, and under the baldachin of the grandstands, throws its light on the hovering wings. Devotedly everybody
looks up to him, there is no room in anybody's heart for anyone else.
And everybody looks with outstretched neck at the monoplane, as it
falls, is seized by Blériot, and even climbs. What is happening ? Here,
above us, there is a man twenty metres above the earth, imprisoned in a
wooden box, and pitting his strength against an invisible danger which
he has taken on of his own free will. But we are standing below, thrust
right back out of the way, without existence, and looking at his man.

Everything goes well, the signalling mast at the same time shows that
the wind has got more favourable, and that Curtiss is going to fly for the
Grand Prix of Brescia. Is he really going to, after all ? One has hardly
finished finding out whether he is or not when Curtiss's engine roars,
and one has hardly had time to look at it before he is flying away from
us, flying over the plains that widen in front of him, towards the woods
in the distance that seem to be rising out of the ground for the first time.
His flight extends far over these woods ; he disappears from sight ; we
are gazing at the woods, not at him. From behind some houses, God
knows where, he comes out at the same height as before, and races
towards us ; when he climbs, you can see the under-surfaces of his
biplane dipping darkly ; when he descends, the upper surfaces glisten in
the sun. He makes a turn round the signal mast and, indifferent to the
roars of welcome, turns straight back to where he has come from, only
to become speedily tiny and lonely again. He does five rounds like this,
flies 50 kilometres in 49 minutes 24 seconds, and so wins the Grand Prix
of Brescia—30,000 lire. It is a perfect achievement ; but perfect achievements cannot be appreciated ; everyone, when you come to think of it,

thinks he is capable of a perfect achievement, no courage seems to be
needed for perfect achievements. And while Curtiss is working all on
his own there above the woods, while his wife, whom everybody knows,
is worried about him, the crowd has almost forgotten him. All one hears
on every side is complaining because Calderara is not going to fly—his
machine was smashed ; Rougier has been tinkering about with his
Voisin for two whole days without letting go of it ; and Zodiac, the
Italian navigable balloon, has not yet arrived. The rumours running
around about Calderara's accident are so full of his glory that one is ready
to believe the love of the nation would raise him into the air more
securely than his Wright.

Curtiss had not yet finished his flight before the engines in three
hangars were tuning up, as if out of enthusiasm. Wind and dust are
driven together from opposite directions. One pair of eyes is not enough.
One twists and turns in one's seat, loses one's balance, clutches somebody
or other firmly, apologises ; somebody or other loses his balance, drags
somebody else after him, is thanked. The early evening of the Italian
autumn is beginning ; it is impossible to see everything clearly in the
field any longer.

Just as Curtiss passes over us after his winning flight, and takes his cap
off with a slight smile without looking at us, Blériot begins a little round
trip which everybody is immediately confident will be successful. Now,
one doesn't know whether one is applauding Curtiss or Blériot, whose
big heavy machine is now hurling itself into the air. Rougier sits at his
levers like a great man at a writing-desk which one climbs up to by a
couple of steps behind his back. He climbs in small circles, flies above
Blériot, turns him into a looker-on, and continues to climb without
stopping.

If we want to get a carriage back again, it is high time to get going ;
there are already a lot of people pushing past us. One knows, of course,
that this is only a trial flight ; as it is already getting on for seven, it would
not be counted officially any longer. In the approach to the aerodrome
the chauffeurs and attendants are standing on their seats and pointing to
Rougier ; on Rougier's account three trains crowded to the last buffers
refuse to move. We are lucky enough to get a carriage ; the coachman
squats down in front of us—there is no box—and, having at last become
independent existences once more, we set off. Max very rightly remarks
that one could and should arrange something of this kind in Prague too.
It wouldn't have to be a prize race, he thought, although that would also
be worth while, but to invite an airman would certainly be an easy matter
after all, and none of the promoters would have any grounds for regrets.
The thing would be so simple, in fact ; Wright was now flying in Berlin ;

all you would have to do, then, would be to persuade the people to come a little out of their way. We two others didn't answer a word, first of all because we were tired, and secondly because we had no objections anyway. The road turned, and Rougier appeared, so high in the air that one thought that soon his course would have to be determined only by the stars that were soon about to shine in the sky, which had already grown dark. We couldn't stop turning round ; Rougier was still climbing straight up, but our way led firmly deeper into the Campagna.

III

REMINISCENCES OF FRANZ KAFKA

BY RUDOLF FUCHS

The beginnings of my acquaintance with Kafka I cannot remember. I believe I got to know him in the winter of 1912. At that time we young writers had our reserved table in a café on the corner of Hyberner Street and Pflaster Street. Kafka used to sit with us from time to time.

He gave the impression of a thoroughly healthy person. He seemed to be scrupulously concerned to avoid disease. One hot afternoon I was accompanying him through the old Eisen Street. I stopped at a coffee stall and drank a lemonade, after first wiping the rim of the glass with my hand. Kafka watched me disapprovingly. " That won't help you ", he said.

Once a large party of us were going up to the Weinberge in the night. It was in the winter, and frightfully cold. Kafka was wearing a light over-coat. Werfel began to attack him for wearing such light clothes. Kafka told us he took cold baths in winter too. He took the fun the rest of us made of him with friendly cheerfulness. Werfel in particular laughed at him because he took so much care of his body. I remember we were then standing just above the Weinberg Viaduct. Kafka drew up his trouser-leg and, in the frosty night, showed us his naked calves.

I was living at that time in a very noisy street ; it was the house at the corner of Stephan Street and Gersten Street. I suffered very much from the noise. There was nobody I could discuss this suffering with better than with Kafka. In front of the house was a tram-stop, opposite was an inn with a garden where, in the summer months, a band used to dispense music until far into the night. In an all-night café you could hear a mechanical organ going. The wall of our flat was the partition wall between us and a master-tailor who had galloping consumption ; his wife played the piano. We lived in that flat seven years. I found it difficult to work, and I slept miserably. Kafka, too, slept badly. He told me that in his case, too, it all began with insomnia ; later racking headaches set in as well. He described objectively the kind of headache he suffered from without expecting or asking for the slightest sympathy. They were simply the kind of headache which, so he thought, I had to expect one day.

He protected himself against noise by stuffing cotton-wool in his ears. He most urgently recommended this method to me. I followed his advice and to this day cannot get to sleep without having previously stuffed up my ears. Once I saw him with two miniature pillows tied over his ears. They were, I imagine, a present from some woman.

You could often meet Kafka alone in the Prague parks. He wasn't in the slightest annoyed when one went and joined him. He liked to avoid talking about himself, and if you told him anything, he was all ears. Even when his illness was already torturing him, he retained his smiling expression. There was a kind of Egyptian enigma about his expression.

He was always ready for an argument, that is to say, ready to reach an understanding, whether it were in few, brief, often hasty words, or whether it were with an eloquent silence that could not be misunderstood. He followed the life and career of his friends with great attention. He was the friend of many, although there were very few he allowed to be friends of his. With gratitude I recall the following incident : I met him in the Herren Street. The day before a poem of mine had been published in the *Tagblatt*. It was called " Villa of Gentle Peace ". He praised it. I myself couldn't find it quite so much to my taste any longer. It was rather an old piece. I ventured to express some doubt as to the genuineness of his praise. Whereupon Kafka quoted the whole poem by heart.

When his first book, *Betrachtung*, was published by Wolff, he said to me, " Eleven copies were subscribed by André.[1] Ten I bought myself. I'd only like to know who bought the eleventh." He said it with a smile of satisfaction. Apart from this, one never found out what he was writing and how important or unimportant it was for him.

Once Willy Haas persuaded him to appear at a reading of Prague authors in a small reception room in a hotel on Wenceslas Square. On this occasion Kafka read his short story " The Verdict " which was afterwards published by Wolff. He read with such a quiet magic of despair that, after an interval of what is certainly not less than twenty years, I can still see him before me in the narrow lecture room with the lights turned down. I have forgotten all the rest, it is true.

Kafka was slim, well-built, handsome. About girls he spoke at most only in general terms. In 1917–1918 I was in Vienna. Kafka had sent me a

[1] TRANSLATOR'S NOTE : Famous Prague bookshop.

letter asking me to book him a room in a quiet hotel. He was coming from Budapest. He had already given me hints previously in Prague that whether he would keep on his engagement or break it off would be decided in Budapest. In Vienna he told me he had broken off his engagement with his fiancée. Kafka was perfectly calm about it. He went with me to the Café Central. It was already late, and the place was fairly empty. Kafka was quite satisfied with everything.

A beautiful young girl in Prague told me she had written Kafka a lot of letters. She had fallen in love with him. Kafka answered her at length, and warned her against himself.

Then I saw him towards the end of his life. He had become thin, spoke in a hoarse voice, and had difficulty with his breathing. Even in cold weather he wore a light overcoat. In the street he showed me how wide the coat had grown for him, and how comfortable it was to wear, and how it didn't press on his chest as he breathed. He did regular gymnastic exercises in it.

Another few months went by. He was away from Prague. One heard things were going badly with him. The end was bound to come. I got one more postcard from him which said, " I shall write you more on Monday, if nothing happens in between ".

His funeral. The place of prayer in the Jewish Cemetery in Prague. A large attendance. Hebrew prayers. The grief of his parents and sisters. The dumb despair of his companion, who fell on his grave as if she were dead. The dull weather that cleared up only at odd intervals. God knows, one cannot believe that in that bare wooden coffin is buried Franz Kafka, who was just beginning to be great.

IV

BRIEF MEMORIES OF FRANZ KAFKA [1]

BY DORA GERITT

In rustic retirement, amidst gentle hills and woods, amid winter's snow, Kafka was undergoing a rest-cure, which his failing health imposed on him, lying on the verandah of a little guest-house.

He passed a lot of his time with a lively girl whose age it was hard to guess, who was obviously telling him a lot of interesting things of a general character, but never things about herself. Then one morning as she was coming up to his deck-chair, he greeted her with animation and said, " I have been dreaming about you ! Dressed in a wide, swelling,

[1] Published in *Bohemia*, 27 Feb. 1941. The authoress is unknown to me.

brown silk dress, hemmed with red hearts at the bottom, you were walking with long, swinging, elastic movements along a very broad, long
road—and a tall, slim red-headed man came joyfully to meet you. You
opened your arms and called out in a loud and relieved voice, ' At last ! '
Tell me, have you ever had an experience like that in your life ? " She
gave a quiet smile and said, " Yes, plenty of men have taken an interest
in me, but there was only one where I felt I had met my fate. Between
my falling in love and my engagement lay nine years. In the meantime
that man got married and divorced, and had had two children by the time
he came back to me, the love of his youth. That is the poetic similarity
of your dream with my fate. What you didn't dream and yet had a
presentiment of was that this man soon forgot, and the parting letter
between us was written after three months."

Once, later on, when she asserted that Boz (Dickens), was boring, he
read aloud to her a few funny lines, the first engagement in *David Copperfield* ; he read excellently, she laughed heartily and was converted.

Then he gave her a pile of proofs, asked her to read them and give her
opinion on them, saying a friend had sent them to him. She read his
Country Doctor, his variations on the dreadfulness of this profession ; and
when she gave him the proofs back, she mentioned that a cousin of hers
had had to die in the same pain as the peasant woman in this story. He
had described a quite unusual kind of internal septicaemia. " That is
remarkable ! " exclaimed Kafka. " I never heard of this illness from a
medical point—I only made it up out of my imagination ; I am astounded
to hear it really exists, but it comforts me to think I imagined it all
correctly."

He lay on his deck-chair, wrapped up in lots of blankets, all day in the
fresh winter air, with a cap drawn well down on his forehead. " Oh,
what a lovely flying-cap you are wearing to-day," someone called out to
him. " More of a lying- than a flying-cap," he said with a soft smile,
resignedly glancing from side to side with his steel-blue eyes.

A young girl, burdened with a heavy spiritual inheritance and an
empty life, belonged to his circle, and aroused his sympathetic interest.
He warned her, adjured her, taught her to surrender herself to work in
the future, and to place all hope of improvement in effort and achievement. After he had left, she continued to correspond with him for a
long time, and became an independent farmer.

He defended a child who was being scolded for constant forgetful-
ness : " Perhaps the child has lots of interesting things in his head, and
can keep himself busy with them, while the message he has been given
bores him, and means nothing to him. Let grown-ups speak for
grown-ups ! "

Kafka understood how to find the bright side of everything. It was as if one came up to a lake with the sun shining on it, dancing with a thousand sparkling ripples—and one had, dazzled, to close one's eyes in order to look for a lesser light.

BIBLIOGRAPHY

ORIGINAL GERMAN PUBLICATIONS

Betrachtung (18 short pieces). 1913. ERNST ROWOHLT, Leipzig.
Der Heizer, Ein Fragment. 1913. KURT WOLFF, Leipzig.
Die Verwandlung. 1916. KURT WOLFF, Leipzig.
Das Urteil. 1916. KURT WOLFF, Leipzig.
Ein Landartz (14 short pieces). 1919. KURT WOLFF, Leipzig/Munich.
In Der Strafkolonie. 1919. KURT WOLFF, Munich.
Ein Hungerkünstler (4 short stories). 1924. VERLAG DIE SCHMIEDE, Berlin.
Der Prozess. 1925. VERLAG DIE SCHMIEDE, Berlin.
Das Schloss. 1926. KURT WOLFF, Munich.
Amerika. 1927. KURT WOLFF, Munich.
Beim Bau Der Chinesischen Mauer (21 pieces). 1931. GUSTAV KIEPENHEUER, Berlin.
Vor Dem Gesetz. 1934. SCHOCKEN VERLAG, Berlin.
Gesammelte Schriften. 1935. (Vols. I–IV.) SCHOCKEN VERLAG, Berlin.
1936. (Vol. V.) VERLAG HENRICH MERCY SOHN, Prague.
1937. (Vol. VI.) VERLAG HENRICH MERCY SOHN, Prague.

TRANSLATIONS INTO ENGLISH

The use of italics throughout the foregoing text is reserved for those titles which have appeared in book form in English, with one exception translated by Willa and Edwin Muir. It is proposed to issue a collected edition of all Franz Kafka's known works over the next five years. Dr. Max Brod is at present engaged upon re-editing the German Collected Works, which will then include the final revision of all the novels, short stories, and diaries based on the original MSS. in his possession, and, until the next texts are completed, no start can be made on the projected English Collected Edition in the translation of Willa and Edwin Muir.

The Castle. Trans. Willa and Edwin Muir. London. Secker 1930. Reprinted. Martin Secker & Warburg. 1939, 1942, 1946.
The Great Wall of China and Other Pieces. Trans. Willa and Edwin Muir. London, Secker 1933. Reprinted. Martin Secker & Warburg. 1946.
The Trial. Trans. Willa and Edwin Muir. London. Gollancz. 1937. Reprinted. Martin Secker & Warburg. 1945, 1946.
America. Trans. Willa and Edwin Muir. London. Routledge. 1938.
The Metamorphosis. Trans. A. L. Lloyd. Parton Press. 1937.

6